2

Other titles in the Cognitive Strategy Training Series
Series Editor: Michael Pressley, SUNY–Albany

Cognitive Strategy Instruction that *Really* Improves Children's Academic
    Performance — Second Edition
Michael Pressley, Vera Woloshyn & Associates

Cognitive Strategy Instruction for Middle and High Schools
Eileen Wood, Vera Woloshyn & Teena Willoughby, Editors

Implementing Cognitive Strategy Instruction Across the School:
    The Benchmark Manual for Teachers
Irene Gaskins & Thorne Elliott

Helping Young Writers Master The Craft:
    Strategy and Self-Regulation in the Writing Process — Second Edition
Karen R. Harris & Steve Graham

Teaching Students Ways To Remember:
    Strategies for Learning Mnemonically
Margo Mastropieri & Thomas Scruggs

Teaching Test-Taking Skills:
    Helping Students Show What They Know
Thomas Scruggs & Margo Mastropieri

Textbooks and the Students Who Can't Read Them:
    A Guide for the Teaching of Content
Jean Ciborowski

HELPING STUDENTS BECOME STRATEGIC LEARNERS

Guidelines for Teaching

KAREN SCHEID

Second printing, 1995.

Library of Congress Cataloging-in-Publication Data
Scheid, Karen, 1946–
　　Helping students become strategic learners : guidelines for
teaching and choosing educational materials / Karen Scheid.
　　　　p.　　cm.
　　Includes bibliographical references (p.　　) and index.
　　ISBN 0-914797-85-9
　　1. Thought and thinking--Study and teaching (Elementary)
2. Cognitive learning. 3. Reading (Elementary) 4. English
language--Composition and exercises--Study and teaching
(Elementary) 5. Mathematics--Study and teaching (Elementary)
6. Teaching--Aids and devices.　I. Title.
LB1590.3.S34　1993
372'.01'9--dc20　　　　　　　　　　　　　　　　92-42227
　　　　　　　　　　　　　　　　　　　　　　　　CIP

Published by
Brookline Books
P.O. Box 1047, Cambridge, MA 02238-1047

British Library Cataloguing-in-Publication Data
A CIP record is available from the British Library.

Distributed in the U.K. by:
Drake Educational Associates
St. Fagans Road, Fairwater, Cardiff CF5 3AE

Table of Contents

CHAPTER ONE
Designing Educational Programs for Thoughtful Learning:
The Promise of Cognitive Strategy Instruction 1

CHAPTER TWO
Guiding Students To Develop Strategic Reading Capabilities 21

CHAPTER THREE
Communicating and Learning Through Writing 47

CHAPTER FOUR
Cognitive-based Principles For Teaching Mathematics —
A Problem-Solving Perspective 83

CHAPTER FIVE
Developing Students' Strategic Learning Capabilities Through
The Application Of Collaborative Learning Methods 109

APPENDIX A
Three Examples of Methods Designed to Increase
Students' Strategic Reading Capabilities 141

APPENDIX B
Three Examples of Composition Instruction 153

APPENDIX C
Two Examples of Approaches Designed to
Enhance Students' Problem Solving Capabilities 161

APPENDIX D
Examples Of Collaborative Learning Methods 169

References 181

Index 207

CHAPTER ONE

Designing Educational Programs For Thoughtful Learning: The Promise Of Cognitive Strategy Instruction

INTRODUCTION

The purpose of education is to maximize students' potential for learning during and after formal schooling. Schooling should equip students with the essential knowledge and skills that will enable them to be productive members of the work force, thoughtful and participating citizens in a democratic society, and wise consumers of products and information. If students are to learn to function in these capacities in an ever changing, information-laden society, their schooling must lead them to competency in acquiring, analyzing, and applying new information.

The knowledge and proficiencies that are essential to achieve these outcomes are driven by societal expectations and needs. Thus, the demands of our contemporary, high-tech, world, have served to rewrite and expand the definition of essential skills and knowledge; and while new capabilities are added to the "essential" list, previously cited skills seldom are deemed no longer necessary. One need only turn to this country's evolving standard of literacy for an illustration of this phenomenon. Since the birth of our nation, the definition of what constitutes literacy has expanded from the ability to write one's name; to being able to recite written passages; to the ability to comprehend what is read; to the current definition, which includes the capabilities to examine, explain, and draw inferences from written material (Myers, 1984).

The demands on the modern education system to live up to these expectations require a reexamination of teaching methods and curriculum. Instruction must not only help students achieve their immediate learning goals but must also prepare them to effectively manage learning situations that they will face after their formal schooling has ended. In short, effective instructional methods should help all students, including those with learning problems, to plan and control, to think and inquire, to evaluate and reflect. The desire to determine how to provide such instruction drives much of educational research. And, the wish to bring the best instructional practices into the classroom motivates teachers to seek out those teaching approaches that meet the learning needs of their students. Good teaching is inevitably a process of fine tuning instructional methods that have proven effective in research settings, of discarding techniques that do not work in practice, and of integrating new approaches with those that have been productive in the past.

It is widely acknowledged that teachers are aided in their efforts to provide effective instruction by support from their superiors and their peers. Not as often acknowledged is the help teachers receive from instructional materials. Ready-made materials can serve to introduce teachers to effective teaching methods. When designed to support proven instructional methods, classroom resources help to reinforce lessons presented by the teacher. Since an estimated 80% of students' classroom time is spent with media and materials, it is not difficult to understand how well-designed resources could have a positive impact on student learning. Further, ready-made materials save teachers the time and trouble of having to produce their own resources.

This book, and the others in the Cognitive Strategy Instruction series, aim to assist school professionals in their efforts to better prepare students to become strategic, reflective, self-reliant, flexible, and productive learners by focusing on promising instructional practices that are founded either explicitly or implicitly on cognitive theories of instruction. As discussed in the next section, cognitive instruction emphasizes the development in students of a reflective, self-reliant learning style. The other books in this series provide excellent, detailed descriptions of specific, well-researched strategy instruction techniques. This volume synthesizes and distills findings from researchers at both the university and school levels to pinpoint those instructional components thought necessary to effectively implement strategy instruction in the basic skill areas of reading, writing, and mathematics. In so doing it provides practical guidance to the school professional who desires to design instruction to promote strategic learning but who does not have the opportunity to participate in intensive training programs offered as a part of specific strategy instruction programs.

In addition, this volume assists school professionals in identifying ways classroom resources can be selected and used to help teachers teach and students learn cognitive strategies. Media and materials can save teachers time, reinforce instructional principles, and often provide teachers with a deeper understanding of the methods they are using. Yet seldom are education professionals offered guidelines for how to select or design media and materials supportive of particular teaching methods. Chapters Two through Four of this book provide such guidance. In these chapters, the instructional components thought to be necessary for implementing cognitively based reading, writing, and mathematics instruction are discussed as are the features of media and materials that support these approaches.

Development of strategic learning capabilities often is enhanced by student-to-student interaction. Chapter Five presents a discussion of collaborative learning methods such as peer-tutoring and cooperative learning. Issues related to the use of collaborative learning techniques to foster and support principles of cognitive instruction are addressed, and the ways classroom resources can assist in these efforts identified.

The next section starts this presentation by first providing background information about cognitive theories of learning and indicates why cognitive strategy instruction holds promise in the education of all students, especially for those with learning problems.

COGNITIVE THEORIES OF LEARNING AND HOW THEY INFLUENCE INSTRUCTIONAL DECISION MAKING

The principles that support cognitive theories of learning, which have emerged from the field of cognitive psychology, are best understood when contrasted with the behaviorally-oriented philosophy of learning that underlies many current teaching methods, particularly those used with students who have learning problems. According to the behaviorist point of view, knowledge can be separated into several components and taught through practice and reward. Memorization of facts and rules is the fundamental way learning proceeds. Higher mental functions such as problem solving, reasoning and thinking are not considered **basic** to learning (Resnick & Klopper, 1989). Since students are viewed as the recipients of knowledge, which is usually presented to them by the teacher, their role in the learning process is a passive one.

Cognitively oriented instructional theories, on the other hand, place higher order thinking at the **center** of knowledge acquisition (Resnick & Klopper, 1989). Learning is seen as a process by which students interpret new information, relate it to what they already know, and organize it for later retrieval. Students are viewed as active participants in their learning, responsible for constructing meanings from information and for regulating the learning processes through applying an array of learning strategies. Learning is perceived as a complex process that does not proceed in a neat, linear manner, but rather in recursive phases. What students are capable of learning is influenced by developmental factors, by the amount of expertise they have about a subject or topic, and by what they know and understand about how to approach learning strategically. Instructional programs that are founded on cognitive principles of learning reflect the above beliefs about the learning process. Thus, when designing instruction within given subject areas, teachers consider what is known about how students typically acquire and develop an understanding of that subject and also the behaviors usually exhibited by effective learners within the area. What are the general characteristics of such instruction within the areas of reading, writing and mathematics?

Reading

Reading instruction from a cognitive perspective is strongly influenced by knowledge of how children develop language capabilities and by an understanding of what good readers do as they read. For most children, language development commences early in life in the home environment as they develop the capability to speak (Shook et al., 1989). The rate of language development varies from child to child, but for most children, specific factors facilitate their language growth. These factors include:

- living in a language-rich environment where opportunities exist to learn to speak and to listen;
- having a personal reason for needing to speak; and
- receiving feedback about the adequacy of their communications (Rhodes & Dudley-Marling, 1988).

With time, experience, and the proper environment children become increasingly sophisticated at expressing themselves orally.

It is believed that reading development is influenced by the same factors that govern the formation of oral communication capabilities. That is to say, students are helped to learn to read when they view reading as being of personal value to them and as a way to pursue their interests; when they are actively involved with and immersed in their reading; and when they witness the various uses of and purposes for reading.

To develop into good readers, students need to become proficient in the two separate but interrelated components of reading—decoding or word recognition and comprehension. While many of the cognitively-oriented reading instruction approaches focus on the development of the skills necessary for deriving meaning from text and for regulating the reading process, there is considerable agreement among those advocating such cognitive approaches that students need to be able to decode as a prerequisite for **fully** developing higher order reading skills.

According to Samuels (1988) word recognition is composed of

two elements—accuracy and automaticity. The first obviously deals with students' being able to correctly identify words, while the latter is concerned with the ability to do so quickly. It is theorized that individuals have limited amount of mental processing capability that can be used at one time. When readers struggle with word recognition and devote most of their intellectual energies to it, they have little mental capacity available to apply to higher level skills. Knowing and being able to immediately recall the meaning of words with minimal energy expended on identification allows students to devote most of their attention to deriving the meaning from text. Practice of skills is believed to be the means by which youngsters develop automaticity — a rapid, low energy process for identifying words (Beck, 1989).

While word recognition automaticity is clearly important, it is not sufficient to guarantee successful reading. The process of comprehending and understanding the written word involves the application of an assortment of strategies. Good readers

- assess the demands of a reading task;

- plan their reading approach;

- apply strategies to foster learning, such as clarifying the purpose and identifying parts of the message that are important;

- allocate their attention so they can concentrate and focus on the major content;

- monitor their comprehension by engaging in review and self-questioning; and

- take corrective action when they fail to comprehend (Baker & Brown, 1984; Brown, 1980; Duffy et al., 1987c; Luftig & Johnson, 1980).

As is evident, proficient readers apply a variety of skills and engage in planning, self-regulatory and reflective behavior, sometimes referred to as metacognition (Baker & Brown, 1984).

Reading instruction from a cognitive perspective guides students toward the development of strategic reading capabilities. Youngsters are explicitly taught how to apply strategies such as those to help them activate prior knowledge or call up from memory knowledge that may help them comprehend what they are to read; construct mental images to help them remember text material; ask and answer questions about the text; and summarize what they have read to help them better remember and to evaluate the adequacy of their reading efforts (Pressley et al, 1989b).

Cognitive instruction also concentrates on helping students understand the form and organizational patterns of various literary genre such as narrative, informative, and persuasive writings. A story, for example, usually contains components such as a setting, beginning, reaction, goal, attempt, outcome, and ending. It is believed that knowing that these parts exist helps students to anticipate what they are about to read, and this anticipation aids their comprehension.

From a cognitive perspective the way reading strategies are taught is as important as what is taught. Teachers should not present strategies in a mechanistic way but rather provide lessons that lead children to an understanding of the purposes of strategies and to a flexible thoughtful use. Thus, reading strategies need to be taught as mental processes. To help lead students to this understanding teachers should model not just the application of the strategy but also the thinking that is involved with selecting and applying it (Duffy et al, 1988; Palincsar & Brown, 1989).

It is true that some students as they gain experience with reading will automatically develop strategic reading behavior. For example, a study by Myers and Paris (1978) found that students' knowledge of reading strategies increased with age and school experience. But, we discussed later, many students, particularly those who have difficulties with reading, do not automatically acquire this strategic behavior. These students will not likely adopt strategic approaches to reading comprehension unless they are explicitly taught strategies (Bos & Fillip, 1984; Wong & Jones, 1982).

Writing

As with reading, learning to write for most children commences at home with the development of oral communication and is facilitated by a language-rich, supportive environment. Children learn to write in contexts that have meaning for them, and they learn to induce the rules of written language as they are exposed to a variety of writings (Rhodes & Dudley-Marling, 1988).

Developing the capability to communicate in writing is characterized as a progression from conversation to knowledge telling, to knowledge transforming or goal setting. It is at this most sophisticated level where thoughtful composing occurs. Knowledge transforming is characterized by planning, problem solving, and the reprocessing and reworking of knowledge. Students at this level usually recognize that the process of writing entails three distinct stages: planning, drafting, and revising. These processes are not conducted linearly but rather they are overlapping, interwoven, and recursive (Englert, 1987; Hayes & Flower, 1980).

Developing sophisticated writing capabilities requires that students undergo several behavioral transitions. Students must move from communicating orally to communicating graphically, and from dependence on face-to-face encounters to consideration for the needs of a distant audience (Bereiter & Scardamalia, 1987). Further, students must acquire the ability to gain access to the knowledge that they possess about a subject; to step back and critique their own writing, diagnose problems, and make changes; and to coordinate ideas at increasingly complex levels (Scardamalia, 1981).

Normally, improvement in writing capability occurs in spurts throughout the years of schooling. So it is not surprising that older students exhibit more of the characteristics of good writers than do younger children (Englert et al., 1988c; Englert & Thomas, 1987; Knudson, 1989; McCutcheon, 1986; Shanahan, 1988; Thomas et al., 1987).

While many developmental trends are evident in learning to write, it would be a mistake to conclude that writing behavior is totally or inevitably controlled by developmental factors. Whether or not students effectively communicate in writing depends largely on their understanding and use of writing processes and strategies.

Effective writers, because they view writing as a top down activity (Englert et al., 1988a), set writing goals, which they do not hesitate to adjust as needed (Hayes & Flower, 1980). When faced with the opportunity or need to compose, good writers think before they write (Bereiter & Scardamalia,1987). They explore prospective writing topics by brainstorming mentally, orally, and with others, and they allow for many false starts (Isaacson, 1987; Morocco & Neuman, 1986). When setting their writing goals, good writers are aware of the questions different forms of writing are designed to answer and are aware of the usual structure that characterizes each writing genre (Englert et al., 1988a; Englert et al., 1988b; Morocco, 1990). Effective writers organize related ideas into categories; apply a range of strategies, such as self-questioning, to help them develop their compositions (Morocco, 1990); revise frequently (Hull 1989; Isaacson, 1987); give careful consideration to the assumed needs and questions of their audience (Englert & Raphael 1988); and work toward the goal of satisfying audience informational needs even when the intended readers are not physically present. Thus, good writers not only have command of writing mechanics and the cognitive tools that help them know when and how to apply them properly, but they also employ and monitor an array of strategies as they plan what they are going to write, translate their thoughts into words, and rethink and revise their compositions (Graham & Harris, 1992).

In sum, effective writing entails the application of a variety of skills, processes and knowledge bases. It calls for numerous decisions to be made and much reflection prior to, during, and following the physical act of putting words on paper. Cognitively oriented writing instruction aims to help students to develop the skills so noticeable among good writers. In other words, teachers

- seek to make students knowledgeable about and proficient in the use of writing processes and strategies as opposed to focusing on writing mechanics and grammar learning (Bereiter & Scardamalia, 1987; Bos, 1988; Fitzgerald & Markham, 1987; Graham et al., 1987; Morocco et al., 1987);

- treat writing as a problem-solving act (Bereiter & Scarmadalia, 1987; Hayes & Flower, 1980; Hull, 1989);

- acknowledge that as a form of communication, writing is necessarily a social activity (Graham et al., in press; Hull 1989; Rhodes & Dudley-Marling, 1988);

- emphasize that writers must hold in mind the purpose of the writing to be produced be it informing, explaining, entertaining, persuading or another purpose, since the intent of the writing obviously influences how the piece will be written (Stein, 1986); and

- stress the importance of writing as a means of facilitating learning as well as a means of demonstrating what has been learned (Morocco, 1990; Yates, 1983).

As with reading; some students may on their own develop into thoughtful writers. But many children will not naturally go beyond the knowledge-telling form of communication unless they are explicitly taught the processes and thinking strategies that are used by proficient, effective writers (Scardamalia & Bereiter, 1985).

Mathematics

Cognitively oriented instruction in mathematics also begins with an understanding of how children acquire knowledge of basic mathematical principles. Before they enter school, children have already acquired considerable mathematical knowledge (Allardice & Ginsburg, 1983; Baroody, 1987; Baroody & Ginsburg, 1986; Hiebert, 1984; Romberg & Carpenter, 1986). Preschool-aged children usually can count, and from their knowledge of counting, they begin to understand such mathematical concepts as same, different, and more (Baroody, 1987). Further, these children have reasonably sophisticated skills in solving word problems, can attend to content, are able to model problems, and can invent effective procedures for computing (Carpenter, 1985). Informal mathematics is meaningful to young children because it is developed through their own life experiences (Baroody, 1989a).

Research also indicates some distinct stages in the development of children's mathematical thinking. For example, children progress through four levels of problem solving as they acquire the basic mathematical skills used in adding and subtracting (Carpenter & Moser, 1984). At the first level, children approach simple problems by modeling, i.e., objects are used and manipulated to represent and solve problems. At level two, students use both modeling and counting strategies. Level three marks the point at which children rely primarily on counting strategies, and at level four, children use math facts to answer questions (Carpenter, 1985). Thus, children at the modeling stage will approach a problem such as

> Mike had ten toy cars. He gave three to Kate. How many did he have left?

by taking ten toy cars or other objects representing them and removing three, then counting the remaining cars. Children who have progressed to counting strategies will count from three to the total or ten, while youngsters who have mastered basic math facts will directly produce the answer.

Children's abilities to use the most efficient strategy consistently is related to their developmental level. The gradual transition from one level to another involves significant advances in understanding and procedural skills (Carpenter, 1985; Carpenter & Moser, 1984). These findings point to the need for instruction to be sensitive to how children mature cognitively (Fennema et al., 1989). Baroody (1987) reminds that instruction can be designed to facilitate understanding, but it cannot force it. Rather, advances in children's thinking and learning in mathematics occur gradually as they assimilate and integrate new information with what they already know and understand.

While young children begin to understand many mathematical concepts and principles through their own experiences, they do so at different rates. Therefore, teachers should not assume that all children at a given grade or age possess the same level of understanding. If instruction is provided in a uniform manner, some students will have a difficult if not an impossible time learning and assimilating the new information (Baroody, 1989a; Baroody & Ginsburg, 1986).

From a cognitive perspective, the end goal of mathematics instruction is to enable students to be thoughtful problem-solvers. It is known that good mathematical problem solvers

- have an adequate, well-organized knowledge base (Pressley, 1986; Silver, 1987);

- are able to understand the nature of the problem to be solved (Silver, 1987);

- are capable of generating mental representations of the problem (Derry et al., 1987; Pellegrino & Goldman, 1987; Riley et al., 1983; Silver, 1987); and

- have knowledge of procedures and strategies that can be used to derive answers (Baroody, 1987; Montague, in press; Pressley, 1986).

Moreover, good problem solvers possess metacognitive knowledge, i.e, knowledge that enables them to assess the demands of the problem, select and implement appropriate strategies, monitor the problem-solving process, and make modifications when selected strategies do not seem to work (Baroody, 1987; Garofalo & Lester, 1985; Montague, in press; Pressley, 1986; Silver, 1987)).

To lead students to such a performance level, cognitively oriented instruction places prime importance on the development of students' conceptual knowledge. It is believed that children must acquire an understanding of the concepts that underlie math procedures if they are to be successful problem solvers (Baroody & Ginsburg, 1986). Understanding concepts is accomplished through a construction of meaning rather than an absorption-of-facts process. Students acquire knowledge of concepts through relating or assimilating new information with what they already know about math, by integrating previously isolated facts, or by adjusting existing knowledge to meet the demands of a new learning experience (Baroody, 1987; Baroody, 1989a; Baroody, in press).

Due to the emphasis on conceptual learning, cognitively-based teaching methods contrast sharply with traditional instructional approaches, which emphasize memorization of math facts and procedures. Cognitive theorists believe that memorization is not likely to lead many students, particularly those with learning problems, to a meaningful understanding of mathematics. As is true for reading and writing, acquisition of effective problem solving techniques for many students requires that instruction lead students to an understanding of processes and underlying concepts. Further, it must provide young people with meaningful knowledge of strategies which will help them more thoughtfully approach problem solving situations.

These summaries describe the basic nature of cognitive-oriented education within reading, writing, and mathematics. While the specific activities that are used in cognitive approaches are content embedded and so vary from subject to subject, they equip students with the capabilities to approach learning strategically. In so doing, they place the student at the center of instruction, considering the learning needs of each student.

It is this sensitivity to individual learning needs that has attracted the attention of many special educators. Cognitively-oriented instruction that strongly emphasizes the teaching of learning strategies can be utilized in the educational programs of students with varying abilities including students with disabilities. Indeed, much of the research of strategy teaching has been directed at examining how cognitive strategy instruction can help students with learning difficulties overcome the problems they face learning to read text, write compositions, and solve mathematical problems.

What are some of the learning problems frequently encountered by students with disabilities? The next section addresses that question.

LEARNING DIFFICULTIES OF STUDENTS IN NEED OF SPECIAL EDUCATION

Difficulties with Reading

Students in need of special education experience an array of problems with reading. For example, they do not monitor their reading to determine if they understand what they read, are not aware of the purpose of reading, do not adjust their reading rates to match the demands of the reading task, and have difficulty relating their past experiences to what they have read (Baker & Brown, 1984; Paris & Myers, 1981; Wong & Jones, 1982).

Further, these students show little evidence of skimming, looking back, or employing strategies to remedy problems even when they have detected them. Poorer readers frequently seem to be unaware that they must extend efforts beyond decoding to make sense of what they read (Brown, 1985; Brown & Campione, 1986).

Oka and Paris (1987) point out that besides ineffective use of appropriate strategies and lack of understanding about how to plan, evaluate, and regulate their reading, poor readers also have negative attitudes about reading, negative perceptions of their abilities, and a lack of intrinsic motivation.

Why do students with learning problems experience difficulties reading strategically? Some educators have theorized that deficiencies with word recognition and decoding may be to blame. According to these theories, many learning disabled children's comprehension problems develop because early reading failures with decoding deprive them of opportunities to learn and become skilled as strategy users (Spear & Sternberg, 1987; Samuels, 1987).

Other researchers, while acknowledging that poor decoding skills and poor comprehension are related, do not believe that decoding difficulty is the cause of poor comprehension. Rather, they believe both deficiencies can be traced to poor language abilities, which are evident in these youngsters even at the preschool level (Ceci & Baker, 1987). Whatever the cause of their problems with comprehension, these children need assistance in developing strategic reading behavior.

Troubles Communicating in Writing

The writing behaviors of students with learning problems vary greatly from those of good writers. Students in need of special education experience an array of difficulties with written communication ranging from those with mechanics to those involving implementation and control of writing processes (Graham, 1992; Morocco, 1990).

Mechanical problems include those with grammar and mechanics such as spelling, punctuation, and capitalization (Farley, 1986; Graham et al., in press; Isaacson, 1989; Moran, 1981; Sedlack & Cartwright, 1972; Thomas et al., 1987). While mastery of writing mechanics in and of itself is not the sole or most important factor contributing to successful writing, as with reading, deficiency in these fundamental skill areas can hinder students' learning and use of higher order processes. Flower and Hayes (1981) theorize that when students need to struggle with grammatical rules, spelling, handwriting, and punctuation, they have difficulty concentrating on content or process.

Students with learning problems have difficulties with writing processes as well. These young people

- have trouble generating ideas for written compositions and selecting topics (Morocco & Neuman, 1986; Stires, 1983);

- experience obstacles remembering and gaining access to information that they do have stored in their memory (Englert & Raphael, 1988; Morocco & Neuman, 1986; Thomas et al., 1987);

- do little planning prior to writing;

- tend to engage in knowledge-telling—a writing down of whatever comes to mind (Englert & Raphael, 1988);

- focus on organizing words rather than the idea or overall structure of their writing (Englert & Raphael, 1988); and

- do not engage in much revision, and when they do, it is at a simplistic and superficial level involving the change of an individual word or some punctuation as opposed to substantive modification of organization or ideas (MacArthur & Graham, 1986).

Students in need of special education also lack a working knowledge of or access to the purposes and organization of various forms of writing (Englert & Thomas, 1987; Graham & Harris,1989b; Morocco, 1990). For example, Nodine and her colleagues (1985) found that these students lacked an understanding of story schema, i.e., the components that are usually found in a story. The researchers theorized that this deficiency contributed to the production of fewer and less fluent stories by these students than by their non-learning-disabled peers

(Newcomer et al., 1988a). Indeed, many of the writings of students with learning disabilities did not contain enough story elements to be categorized as stories (Barenbaum et al., 1987). Other researchers have concluded that learning disabled students' stories were chaotic, unorganized, and incomplete (Montague et al. 1990).

Expository writing also has proven to be problematic for students with learning disabilities (Englert & Thomas, 1987; Nodine et al., 1985; Thomas et al., 1987). These students appear to be insensitive to the purposes of expository writing, have difficulty generating ideas for such compositions, fail to monitor their writing and produce compositions that contain more redundancies, irrelevancies, and early terminations than do the writings of normally achieving students (Thomas et al., 1987).

It has been suggested that youngsters with learning problems have difficulty communicating in writing because they

- lack proficiency in writing mechanics, which results in an interference in executing higher order writing skills (Graham & Harris, 1990);

- do not possess knowledge of writing processes or they are unable to access that knowledge (Graham & Harris, 1990);

- exhibit immature or ineffective use of strategies ; and

- do not engage in metacognitive behavior.

Anxiety may also play a role in reducing students' writing capabilities. Research findings show that students with learning problems often can express their ideas orally when they are not able to do so in writing (Morocco & Neuman, 1986). Indeed, MacArthur and Graham (1986) found that dictated stories of students with learning disabilities were three times as long as the stories they wrote.

Difficulties with Mathematical Problem Solving

Research shows that the mathematical deficiencies of students with learning disabilities emerge in the early years of schooling and continue throughout secondary school (Cawley & Miller, 1989). As a group, these youngsters achieve approximately one year of academic growth for each two years of schooling. Although these students do not make as much progress as their non-disabled peers, their mathematical knowledge does continue to grow throughout their years of schooling (Cawley & Miller, 1989).

The difficulties in mathematics faced by students with learning problems range from those with basic mathematical computation to those with more advanced problem-solving. These students tend to lack proficiency in basic number facts; they often must stop and compute answers to math facts rather than directly retrieve answers from memory (Russell & Ginsburg, 1984).

A growing number of researchers are suggesting that the mathematical difficulties of many youngsters with learning disabilities are more characteristic of learning discrepancies or developmental delays than of developmental differences (Cawley, 1984b; Cawley et al., 1988; Goldman et al., 1988). For example, the type of procedural errors made by these students often are akin to those made by younger, regular education students who have not as yet developed an understanding of the meaning of the procedures (Russell & Ginsburg, 1984). These errors obviously contribute to the generation of wrong answers (De Corte & Verschaffel, 1981; Russell & Ginsburg, 1984). Procedural errors can result from a lack of knowledge of appropriate strategies for solving computation problems or from a misapplication of strategies (Pellegrino & Goldman, 1987). When systematically made, procedural errors are referred to as "bugs" (Van Lehn, 1983). Illustrations of some common subtraction "bugs" include the following:

Taking the smaller from the larger number:
```
    304
-   145
    241
```

Putting down a zero instead of borrowing:
```
    304
-   145
    200
```

Taking the smaller from the larger number instead of borrowing from zero:
```
    304
-   145
    161
```

Putting down a zero instead of borrowing from zero:
```
    304
-   145
    160
```

(Romberg & Carpenter, 1986; Van Lehn, 1983). Instruction to remedy "bugs" needs to correct students' conceptual misunderstandings as well as their misapplication of procedures (Van Lehn, 1983).

Not surprisingly, available data indicate that students in need of special education, like their non-handicapped peers, experience difficulties solving word problems. While not the most sophisticated form of mathematical problems, word problems often require the application of more complex skills than do basic computational exercises. Students need to understand the relationships presented in the problem and the actions to be carried out. Further, they need to be able to plan and execute a solution strategy (Riley et al., 1983).

The nature of the deficiencies in word problem solving exhibited by students with learning disabilities has been studied by Montague and Bos (in press). The researchers determined that these youth have difficulties

- predicting operations for solving problems,

- selecting appropriate algorithms to solve multi-step problems, and

- correctly completing problems after deciding how to solve them. Their mistakes were not attributable to computational errors.

Often youngsters with disabilities experience difficulties solving problems containing extraneous information (Cawley et al., 1987), such as:

> There were three boys, five girls, and two dogs in the yard.
> How many children were in the yard?

Students with disabilities often respond to questions such as the above with an answer that represents the total of all numbers mentioned in the problem, e.g., ten instead of eight for the above example (Goodstein et al., 1971; Schenck, 1973). A rote computation habit contributes to some of these errors (Goodstein et al., 1971).

Several explanations have been offered for the problems with mathematics learning experienced by students in need of special education. These youngsters often

- exhibit unstable patterns of development (Allardice & Ginsburg, 1983);

- display short attention spans and are easily distracted (Bley & Thornton, 1981; Cherkes-Julkowski, 1985a; Fitzmaurice-Hayes, 1985a); and

- have deficits in long-term and short-term memory (Bley & Thornton, 1981; Cherkes-Julkowski, 1985a; Fitzmaurice-Hayes, 1985a; Thornton & Toohey, 1986).

Language deficiencies including difficulties with reading and writing mathematical symbols and with comprehending the actions and relationships represented in word problems also can interfere with the mathematical performance of these students (Bley & Thornton, 1981; Fitzmaurice-Hayes, 1985a; Share et al., 1988). As with reading and writing, metacognitive weaknesses inhibit these students' ability to solve problems. Students with learning disabilities have been characterized as less able than their non-learning disabled peers at

- accurately assessing their abilities to solve problems (Slife et al., 1985);

- organizing information to be learned (Cherkes-Julkowski, 1985a; Thornton & Wilmot, 1986);

- identifying and selecting appropriate strategies to apply to a problem (Cherkes-Julkowski, 1985b);

- monitoring their problem-solving capabilities (Goldman, 1989; Slife et al., 1985) and evaluating problems for accuracy (Slife et al., 1985); and

- determining when to appropriately generalize learned strategies to other problem situations (Borkowski et al., 1989; Cherkes-Julkowski, 1985b; Fitzmaurice-Hayes, 1985a).

Motivational problems also can inhibit learning. Students with learning disabilities have been described as passive and lacking in motivation (Schumaker & Hazel, 1984). Often these youngsters' passivity stems from repeated failure in academic work (Cherkes-Julkowski, 1985a), and their lack of success in school in turn contributes to low self-esteem (Borkowski et al., 1989).

THE POTENTIAL OF COGNITIVELY ORIENTED INSTRUCTION

There is no question that students with learning problems face a myriad of problems with learning in school. While these problems range from those with rule learning and memorization to those involving strategic learning and higher order thinking skills, it is the former that receive the most attention in educational programs for these students. Is this because students with disabilities cannot be taught to become more efficient, thoughtful, independent and reflective learners? Research reveals that the answer to that question is "no." For example, in the area of reading, students with learning problems have successfully been taught learning strategies to help them improve their reading comprehension. One approach, **Reciprocal Teaching,** developed by Palincsar and Brown, succeeded in improving students' reading comprehension as measured on the Gates-McGinitie standardized reading comprehension tests (Brown & Palincsar, 1987). In this program, students are taught strategies to help them to summarize the main content of what they have to read, to formulate potential test questions, to clarify ambiguities, and to predict future content (Brown & Palincsar, 1987).

Another approach, the Learning Strategies Curriculum program, developed by Deshler and his colleagues at the Institute for the Study of Learning Disabilities at the University of Kansas, focuses on teaching adolescent learning disabled students an array of strategies aimed at improving their reading as well as listening and writing skills. Strategies are designed to help students improve their capabilities to identify words, produce visual imagery, self-question, paraphrase, and interpret visual aids (Deshler & Schumaker, 1986). This approach reportedly has been successful in raising students' grades in regular classroom settings (Schumaker et al., 1982; Schmidt, 1984).

In the area of writing research, strategy instruction and process writing approaches provide evidence to support the contention that students with learning problems can become more reflective, thoughtful writers. Graham, Harris and their colleagues have successfully taught students with learning problems strategies for

- generating, framing and planning argumentative essays (Graham & Harris, 1988a; 1989c);

- lengthening and improving the qualities of their stories by using a strategy to generate individual words such as action verbs, adverbs, and adjectives (Harris & Graham, 1985); and

- improving clarity and cohesiveness, adding relevant textual material, and correcting errors (Graham & MacArthur, 1988).

Englert and her colleagues (1988a) taught fourth and fifth graders with learning disabilities to sustain their writing, assume an informant's role, and improve the organization of their expository writing. The researchers accomplished these results by teaching students organizational and thinking strategies for use in planning, drafting, editing and revising writing. This strategy instruction took place within a supportive writing environment in which students had an opportunity to write frequently and for sustained periods. This program also stressed peer collaboration and the student's informant role as a writer.

Process approaches to writing instruction also have been successfully implemented with students in need of special education. Process writing is typified by instructional practices such as topic selection by students; teacher-student writing conferences; skill-oriented information presented within the context of, not separate from, composition instruction; and publication of students' writing products (Stires, 1983).

Much of the reported research of process writing interventions has been presented in a case study format describing how students with learning problems have improved their writing as a result of involvement in a process writing program (Atwell, 1988; Graves, 1985; Stires, 1988; Stires, 1989; Wansart, 1988). For example, Nancie Atwell (1988) describes the writing behavior of a student with learning disabilities who was mainstreamed into her eighth grade English class. The student had been identified at the beginning of second grade as having low average ability, short- and long-term memory deficits, low ability to organize and sequence information, and inferior spelling capabilities. Prior to her inclusion in Atwell's class, this student received one-half of her language arts instruction in a resource room setting, where she was introduced to the process writing approach. For the remainder of her school day, the student was a part of a special class of low track students. As a member of Atwell's class, this student took part in the reading and writing program where she wrote daily. During the course of the year, this student completed 21 progressively improving pieces of writing in different genres and read 31 novels. Atwell concludes that a process writing environment, provided over a period of years, can support students in developing sophisticated writing behavior.

Wansart (1988) provides a similar example of a fourth grader with a learning disability who rarely spoke or wrote at the beginning of the school year. As a result of her immersion in a classroom where the teacher used a writing process approach, she began to produce extended writing pieces. In addition, she began to generalize what she had learned about writing without being prompted to do so.

Projects attempting to aid students in improving their mathematics performance often have focused on word problem solving (Case & Harris, 1988; Fleischner et al., 1987; Montague & Bos, 1986). By teaching students problem-solving strategies, Case and Harris (1988) succeeded in improving the abilities of upper-elementary-level students with learning disabilities to solve one-step addition and subtraction word problems, and Fleischner and her colleagues (1987) assisted fifth and sixth grade youth in learning how to solve four types of word problems: addition, subtraction, two-step problems and problems with extraneous information. Montague & Bos (1986) found that most students who received instruction in an eight-step process to solve two-step word problems substantially improved their capabilities to work out the solution of these problems (Montague & Bos, 1986).

Finally, one other study is of interest, although it did not involve students officially designated as learning handicapped. Swing and her colleagues (1988) aimed to teach fourth grade students how to apply thinking skills to their mathematical learning. They taught teachers how to instruct students in the use of several cognitive strategies including defining and describing, thinking of reasons, comparing, and summarizing. A second group of students did not receive this instruction, but rather were taught mathematics for a longer time period (learning time intervention). The classes of students involved in this study were categorized as high ability or low ability according to the average score of the class on an achievement test.

Their results indicate that high ability classes gained more than low ability classes from the thinking strategy intervention. However, when the student data within classes were analyzed, the researchers determined that lower ability students benefited more from the thinking strategy intervention than from the learning time intervention. The researchers theorized that effective thinking skills instruction may depend upon the class as a whole possessing a fairly high level of average mathematical ability. However, lower ability students within a class did benefit from this form of instruction because they were helped to develop strategies they did not previously possess.

Researchers of cognitive instruction approaches would be quick to admit that not all students in all circumstances may benefit from these methods and that some students may not possess the prerequisites necessary for them to profit from strategy teaching. But the research clearly underscores the potential of instruction in cognitive strategies for leading youngsters with learning problems to become more thoughtful readers, writers, and problem solvers.

INSTRUCTIONAL IMPLICATIONS

Reading

It is clear that some students will discover effective learning methods on their own and develop into good readers, writers and problem solvers no matter what the nature of their instructional experience. But many students, particularly those who have learning problems, will not. Even those students who may on their own develop into effective learners may be assisted by being explicitly taught learning strategies. Many educators agree that instruction that is dominated by a skill orientation is unlikely to guide students with learning problems or their non-handicapped peers to becoming more effective, reflective, and thoughtful learners. Instead, they believe that reading should be taught as an active, thoughtful process that is crucial for all learning. Thus, instruction should not be confined to the teaching of decoding and comprehension skills, but rather go beyond these basics to guide students in the use of strategies and processes. Further, youngsters should be taught in an environment where students have ample opportunity to read for a variety of purposes and have access to an array of reading materials (Rhodes & Dudley-Marling, 1988).

Writing

Writing instruction, too, should be presented in a way that helps students see the act of writing as complex, thought-engaging, and social activity. Instruction should

- emphasize the processes involved in writing (Bos, 1988; Hull, 1989; Morocco, 1990);

- encourage children to write in the lower grades before they become proficient readers (Scardamalia & Bereiter, 1985); and

- incorporate writing conferences and peer writing groups into writing instruction (Scardamalia & Bereiter, 1985).

Mathematics

To maximize students' abilities to learn mathematics, instruction should capitalize on, not dismiss, children's existing mathematical knowledge. Students must be helped to understand the meaning behind mathematical concepts; to see the relationship of mathematics to daily living; and to approach problem solving strategically.

The immediate goal of most educational programs is for students to acquire knowledge of subject content. But the usefulness of such content knowledge is limited unless youngsters also understand its meaning and relevance. Similarly if the chief way students have learned such information is through rote memorizing and rule learning, if they have not acquired the capability to plan, control, monitor, and reflect on their own learning, if an emphasis on higher order learning processes has not been at the core of instruction, then it is unlikely that students have been led to their learning potential.

Unfortunately, instruction aimed at helping youngsters become more strategic learners has largely been ignored in educational programs, particularly those designed for students experiencing learning problems, the very students that could benefit most from them.

The goal of cognitive strategy instruction approaches is to remedy that situation and help all students who have not developed their strategic learning potential to do so. The remainder of this book discusses what individual teachers can do to incorporate cognitive learning principles into classroom instruction.

CHAPTER TWO

Guiding Students to Develop Strategic Reading Capabilities

The objective of reading instruction should be to teach students the skills and knowledge that will enable them to comprehend, analyze, and understand what they read. Beginning reading instruction often focuses on teaching children skills for decoding words, for building their vocabulary, and for comprehending what has been read. Thus, traditionally teachers begin reading instruction by teaching children a variety of conventions such as understanding letter/sound relationships, analyzing words, and finding the main idea and supporting details in a written passage. Often such skills are taught in an hierarchial, sequential fashion, in which mastery of one skill is deemed necessary before proceeding to the next.

While such skill learning is important, teachers, even at the primary grade levels, should aim to empower children with a knowledge of processes and strategies. This knowledge is necessary if students are to learn to independently plan, monitor and evaluate their reading efforts, analyze and understand text, and, as appropriate, apply and utilize what they have read.

How can teachers best help students develop such proficiencies? Several programs that aim to help students become more strategic readers have been tried with students of varying ages and abilities. For example,

• *The Strategies Intervention Model* developed by Deshler and his colleagues at the University of Kansas Institute for Research in Learning Disabilities was designed to teach secondary level students with learning disabilities several strategies intended to improve their reading comprehension, writing and listening capabilities. Some of the reading strategies help students learn to self-question, paraphrase, interpret visual aids, and identify words (Deshler & Schumaker, 1986). Students are taught the steps to each strategy and when it should be used (Deshler et al., 1984b). In addition, students are given explicit instruction in how to generalize learned strategies to situations in and out of the classroom (Ellis et al., 1987b).

• *The Direct Explanation Model,* developed by Duffy, Roehler, and their colleagues, is designed for use in teaching reading skills typically found in basal texts in a strategic manner to elementary level children

(Duffy et al, 1986a; 1987b; 1987c). Teachers participating in this program learn to teach those reading skills frequently emphasized in basal texts in a way that is meaningful to children. In other words, they learn to inform students of the rationale for and reasoning behind the use of reading conventions and skills. When presenting a skill to their class, teachers not only model its application but also the thinking and reasoning that accompanies its use. This "thinking aloud" provides insights and understanding that are necessary for students to acquire if they are to correctly apply the skill independently.

• *Reciprocal Teaching* developed by Palincsar and Brown (1988) is a third example of an instructional method that has helped students in the early elementary through post secondary levels to become more strategic readers. This approach relies heavily on the role of social interaction when teaching the key reading strategies of summarizing the main content of what has been read, formulating potential test questions, clarifying ambiguities, and predicting what may come next in the material being read. Through a series of dialogues between the teacher and students focusing on given reading passages, students are introduced to these strategies and informed by the teacher of the purpose and uses for the strategies. Through teacher modeling, students are shown how to go about applying the strategies when reading (Brown & Palincsar, 1987; Palincsar & Brown, 1988).

These three approaches are presented in more detail in Appendix A. They illustrate that there is no one right way to assist students to become more strategic readers. However, several common instructional principles are discernible among these and other cognitive-based approaches for teaching reading. These principles, which affirm the social nature of learning and the need for students to gradually assume responsibility for their own learning, are as applicable to students in regular classrooms as they are to individual students experiencing learning difficulties.

For discussion purposes, these instructional principles are grouped into two categories, the first relating to the content of instruction; the second focusing on teaching techniques and methods that reinforce the principles of strategic learning. Table 2-1 provides an overview of these principles.

WHAT SHOULD BE TAUGHT?

Teach Reading Conventions Meaningfully

Fluency in skills such as decoding and word recognition are essential to good reading. But too often teachers and classroom materials present these skills in a mechanical, isolated manner (Winograd &

Table 2-1
Guidelines for Designing Cognitive-Oriented Reading Instruction

What Should Be Taught?

- Teach reading conventions strategically
- Teach reading processes and strategies
- Relate the teaching of reading and writing

What Teaching Techniques Should Be Used?

- Create an environment conducive to strategy learning
- Incorporate assessment throughout instruction
- Build upon and create prior knowledge
- Inform students about the purpose for learning skills and strategies
- Model the use of strategies and skills
- Promote the flexible use of strategies
- Offer ample opportunity for promoting strategies
- Confer with students
- Utilize group learning
- Encourage students to use learned skills and strategies with other subjects
- Evaluate the effectiveness of strategy instruction

Paris, 1988/89), often fail to link the skill being taught to the process of reading (Duffy & Roehler, 1988), and neglect to let students "in" on the thinking, reasoning, and decision-making that surrounds the use of the skill.

As an example, children generally are taught that when they encounter an unfamiliar word in their reading, they should read ahead to see if later text helps them "figure out" the meaning of the unknown word. But seldom are students explicitly taught what types of clues to look for in the later text. **Teachers should be explicit in their explanations of how to use specific skills such as how to use context clues to find the meaning of an unknown word.** Figure 2-1 contains examples provided by Marzano and his colleagues (1991) of the types of context clues students may look for when they read ahead. Materials also can assist students to learn strategies and processes that will enable them to read ahead when they come to a word they do not know. (Marzano, et al, 1991).

Another illustration of how to present reading skills from a more strategic perspective is offered by Gaskins and her colleagues (1988) who developed fast-paced, game-like lessons to help students think about and apply a skill that has been taught. For example,when teaching students to compare and contrast an unknown word with words that have similar patterns, teachers might have students play a game such as, "What's in My Head." In this game, the teacher offers clues for words on the list of words that students have been studying. For example, if the word to be guessed was "splash," a clue might require students to find a word that would meaningfully complete a

---

Figure 2-1
Using Context Clues to Define Unknown Words

Clue/Description*	Example
Description Clue: A description of the word is provided and often set off by commas.	Taffy, a chewy candy, comes in different flavors.
Compare/contrast Clue: A comparison or a contrast of the unknown word is found later in the text.	He was nervous, not calm, about going to a new school.
Familiar Expression Clue: A familiar expression serves as a clue to the meaning of the unknown word.	The candy was as sour as a lemon.
Synonym Clue: A synonym is used as a clue to the meaning of the word.	The antibiotic was the medicine the doctor gave her for her earache.
Example Clue: An example is given that provides the needed clues for identification.	Joe is a spendthrift. He will spend his money on anything.
Definition Clue: A direct definition of the word is given.	A veterinarian is a doctor that treats animals.

*From Marzano et al., 1991.

sentence, such as, *"A baby likes to — in the bath tub."* Or, students might be directed to find a word that begins with the same initial letter pattern as a clue word, such as, splendid. Or, the teacher might ask students to find the word that rhymes with another word that needs to be guessed, such as, *"Find a word that rhymes with a word that means things you don't want anymore or that is not useful,"* (Gaskins et al. 1988). These types of activities, reinforce skills by requiring students to apply their skill knowledge strategically instead of relying solely on memorization and rote responses.

Teach Students About the Process and Strategies That Will Aid Them to Better Understand and Remember What They Read

Strategies such as those for summarizing what has been read, activating prior knowledge, paraphrasing what they have read, engaging in self-questioning, generating imagery, and understanding story grammar—the components usually included in a story—can assist students to improve their reading capabilities (Pressley, et al., 1989a).

Several suggestions have been offered for activities that could be used to help teach various strategies as we discuss in greater detail later. Before teaching any strategy, teachers need to make clear to students why the strategy is important, how it will help them with their reading task, and how they can flexibly and appropriately apply it to reading situations.

Summarization. Summarization involves identifying the key points of a reading and presenting them either mentally or in writing in a condensed form. It helps students understand what they have read and to determine what part of what they have read is not clear to them. How can teachers help students learn summarization skills? One simple activity is to have students write a one-sentence summary after they have read a paragraph (Jenkins et al, 1986). Another suggestion offered by Anderson and Hidi (1988/89), involves a five step approach, which is reflected in Figure 2-2.

Teachers should use short, well-organized passages containing familiar concepts when beginning summarization instruction. Students should be asked to find topic sentences and main ideas in these passages.

Students should first learn to summarize for themselves since such summaries help them understand what they have read and so serve as study guides. But after students learn to summarize for themselves, they then should be taught to write summaries for others (Anderson & Hidi, 1988/89).

When learning summarization, students should have the opportunity to look at the text they are summarizing and not be expected to

---

Figure 2-2
Recommended Steps For Teaching Summarization

- Choose the right text
- Let students see the text while summarizing
- Stress sensitivity to the points the arthor thinks important
- Teach students to summarize for themselves first
- Extend skills by having students summarize for others

From Anderson & Hidi (1988/89)

---

work from memory. After students have practiced their summarization skills, teachers should introduce them to summarizing text from memory (Anderson & Hidi, 1988/89).

Teachers should routinely provide opportunities for students to practice summarizing. When, for example, a story or book is read in the classroom over a period of days, the teacher could begin each day's reading session by asking one student to summarize what they read the previous day. Periodically during and at the end of the reading session, the teacher should have students summarize what they have read.

A final recommendation offered by Anderson and Hidi (1988/89) is that teachers alert students to be sensitive to the points the author thinks are important. Frequently, these points are found in introductions, topic sentences, and summaries.

Activating and Creating Prior Knowledge. Calling to mind what they already know about the subject of the text they are reading helps students better comprehend the new information that they read. In addition activating prior knowledge provides them with content clues they may use to help figure out the meaning of new words they will encounter. Teachers can encourage students to talk about what they already know about a subject by:

1) having them brainstorm alone or with others about the topics in the upcoming reading assignment; and

2) asking them before reading to compare their experiences and lives with those situations to be discussed in a story or text and to predict what might happen next based upon what they already know (Pressley et al., 1990).

EXAMPLES: For narrative readings, teachers could have students ask themselves if they have had a similar experience to the one described in the story. For expository writing, teachers could have students ask themselves what they have read or seen before about the topic.

Question generation. Students who are actively involved in the reading process are more likely to remember, understand, and connect what they have read than students who are not as involved. Asking questions prior to reading, then reading with the purpose of answering them, is one way for students to be actively involved in their reading (Marzano et al, 1988). Figure 2-3 contains one procedure for guiding students to learn to ask questions, which will guide their reading.

Students also should be taught how to generate questions while they are reading. One technique for doing so is to have students work in pairs or small groups.

EXAMPLES: A pair of students may be assigned to read the same story together. These students would be directed to stop reading at given points and take turns asking questions they believe will be answered later in the reading.

Pressley and his colleagues (1989a) stress that efforts to teach students to generate questions should include a component for helping youngsters examine the quality of their questions. Students should be taught to ask, "Did my questions cover the important material; did they help me relate and integrate new information with what I already knew; did they keep me interested in reading?" If tested on the material that they have been asked to read, students can compare test questions to those they have generated as one means of judging the adequacy of their questions.

Figure 2-3
Asking Questions Before Reading

- Look at the tile and ask

    What is the reading about?

    What do I want to know from the title?

- Look at the subheadings and ask

    What questions are likely to be answered by the author in this section?

- Look at each picture, illustration, figure and map and ask

    Why is this graphic included?

Adapted from Rhodes & Dudley-Marling, 1988.

Question answering. Answering questions during and after reading involves students in the reading process more intensely, and helps youngsters to better remember what they have read. Students can read to answer questions they have generated themselves or use prepared questions, which are frequently contained at the end of text chapters or stories, to guide their reading. Following are guidelines for teaching students about question answering.

- *Teach students that there are four types of questions for which they will be seeking answers in text:*

  1. *questions whose answers are easily found in the text;*

  2. *questions whose answers are in the text but must be put together from different parts of the text;*

  3. *questions whose answers are not in that story but which the reader must derive from thinking about what he or she knows, what the author tells in the text, and how the two fit together; and*

  4. *questions whose answers are not in the text that readers answer from calling upon their own experiences (Raphael, 1986).*

Teachers should explain and illustrate the differences among these types of questions and demonstrate for students how they would proceed to seek answers to them. Students should then be divided into groups and given short passages to read and questions to answer. After they have gained practice answering questions in groups, students should be given longer passages and more questions. Over time, then, students are led from answering questions in groups to doing so individually and independently.

- *Teach students that after reading text and attempting to answer questions that it is alright, indeed smart, to look back at the text to locate information to answer questions they were unable to answer during the first reading (Pressley et al, 1989a).*

- *Teach students to analyze and evaluate their answers. Have them determine if the answers contained correct information and sufficient details.*

As mentioned, group reading situations provide a fertile environment for developing both question answering and question generating skills. Students can take turns asking their peers questions about what they have read, about areas that need clarifying, and about what may come next in the reading.

Story grammar instruction. It is believed that knowledge of the structure and components usually found in various genres help students make sense of and mentally organize what they read. Stories, for example, usually contain elements such as a setting, a beginning, a reaction, a goal, an attempt, an outcome, and an ending (Fitzgerald et al., 1987). Students who are aware of this structure look for these elements as they read stories.

Expository writings also follow various patterns depending upon their purpose. Some expository writing employs a *compare and contrast organization*, some a *problem/solution format*, some a *cause and effect structure*, and so on (Rhodes & Dudley-Marling, 1988). Teachers should help students to recognize and anticipate the various genres and their usual forms. This can be done by

- *selecting pieces of writing from several genres and comparing and contrasting their features. Marzano and his colleagues (1991) suggest making charts on which the teacher and students list the features of each genre;*

- *designing activities to familiarize students with the features of a specific genre.*

EXAMPLES:

- Students could be asked to complete stories and expository pieces with sections missing.

- Students could be given the problem portion of a problem/solution essay and asked to supply a solution.

- Students could be given a problem/solution essay and asked to write down all the problems and all the solutions mentioned;

- taking excerpts from types of writing and having students match them to the genre in which they would most likely be found.

Imagery creation. Students can be helped to remember what they have read by creating mental images. Production of graphic representations of text can also assist students to better understand content and determine what areas of a reading are unclear. To help students learn to form mental images, Marzano and his colleagues (1991) suggest that teachers:

- have students stop periodically when they are reading to close their eyes and create mental pictures of what they have just read;

- describe to their teacher and peers the images they see in their mind's eye;

- practice generating symbolic representations for events or ideas.

Graphic representations may take several forms such as story maps or webs, charts, fish bone maps, matrices, flow charts, or any other form that helps readers understand and recognize patterns and organizations of writings. For example, Marzano and his colleagues suggest that a graphic organizer for a piece of writing that compares and contrasts two items or events may look as follows:

A and B Are Similar
1. They both _____
2. They both _____

A and B Are Dissimilar
1. A _____, but B _____
2. A _____, but B _____

Jones and her colleagues (1988/89) offer the following suggestions for teaching students how to construct graphic organizers.

- *present an example of a completed graphic representation based upon a type of writing;*

- *model how to construct the selected type of graphic;*

- *discuss when and why to use the graphic;*

- *offer students guidance and feedback as they work as a whole class or in small groups to construct their own graphic;*

- *have students practice producing graphics on their own.*

This discussion highlights some of the key strategies that help students better understand what they have read. Teachers are urged to explore and introduce to students other strategies that they observe to be effective. Pressley and his colleagues (1989a) recommend that teachers familiarize themselves with various strategies, select those they think will serve the interest of their students, and develop lessons to teach about them. The first step in following these recommendations is to read books and articles about cognitive and metacognitive strategies in order to become familiar with strategies that are available. The other publications in this series are good examples of books that provide additional information about strategies and their teaching. In addition, recent publications by the Association for Supervision and Curriculum Development such as *Dimensions of Thinking: A Framework for Curriculum and Instruction* by Robert Marzano and others (1988) and *Strategic Teaching and Learning: Cognitive Instruction in the Content Areas* edited by Beau Fly Jones and others (1987) also are valuable resources for professionals desiring more information about strategy instruction.

When teaching reading strategies it is important for teachers to stay within their means and not try to accomplish too much too soon. Pressley and his colleagues (1989a), suggest beginning with a few across-domain strategies that address deficiencies observed in students, accomplish educationally important goals, and have been proved through research to be effective.

Teach an Integrated Reading and Writing Curriculum

Teaching reading and writing together enhances instruction in both areas. This integration should begin at the earliest grade levels (Rhodes & Dudley-Marling, 1988). Early intertwining of the subjects provides an opportunity to simultaneously reinforce reading skills while introducing children in the primary grades to writing. For example, when students are introduced to words to help them increase their reading vocabulary, they could also be asked to write the word in a meaningful sentence. Or when teaching about identifying main ideas in passages, teachers could have students write their own paragraphs with main points and supporting details instead of just having children identify these items on worksheets (Shanahan, 1988).

These suggestions form the content core of strategy-oriented instruction. From a cognitive perspective, how instruction is presented is as important as the content that is taught. The next section provides guidelines for teachers to follow when designing instruction and teaching students to become more strategic readers.

WHAT TEACHING TECHNIQUES HELP STUDENTS LEARN TO READ STRATEGICALLY?

Create an Environment Conducive to Learning to Read

Reading instruction, from a cognitive perspective, should take place in an environment that motivates students to want to read and that reinforces the importance and multiple purposes of reading (Rhodes & Dudley-Marling, 1988). Most educators acknowledge the pivotal role that motivational states play in learning. Attention to motivation is particularly crucial when instructing students who have demonstrated past problems comprehending and utilizing what they have read. Because these youngsters often have doubts about their ability to learn, teachers need to be particularly sensitive to providing instruction in a way that bolsters these students' beliefs about their ability to learn (Borkowski et al., 1984; Brown et al., 1983; Ellis et al., 1987a; Graham et al., 1987). Motivational tactics include

- *teaching skills and strategies that are challenging but not so difficult as to frustrate and discourage students (Pressley et al., 1989a);*

- *instilling in students a sense of control over their own learning and thinking (Oka & Paris, 1987);*

- *supplying appropriate feedback and encouragement (Brown, 1985; Brown & Palincsar, 1987; Deshler et al., 1981; Deshler et al., 1984a);*

- *assuring that ample amount of time is set aside daily for reading activities (Rhodes & Dudley-Marling, 1988).*

- *giving students ample opportunities to explore their reading processes and to express to others their ideas and feelings about what they have read.*

A classroom environment that fosters interaction can also prove to be a motivating factor. A "lecture only" format works against the development of self-directed learning that is the intent of teaching students processes and procedures that will empower them to improve their reading comprehension (Dowd, 1988; Harris, 1988; Meichenbaum, 1985; Palincsar, 1988).

The way the classroom is physically arranged also can contribute to the motivation of students. Classrooms should be filled with books that students can easily access; be decorated with posters, poems and other written material; contain a reading center where students can go to read by themselves, with a partner, or the teacher. Furniture should be movable so it can be clustered for small group work.

Materials can provide teachers with suggestions for making the classroom more attractive and reinforcing students' motivation to read by including ideas for bulletin board displays, offering floor plans to physically arrange their room to foster reading activities, and suggesting what books could be available in the classroom reading center. In particular, teachers should look in the teacher's manuals for hints and advice about how they could motivate poor readers who are frustrated, or apply techniques suggested in this chapter.

Incorporate Assessment Through Instruction

When teaching students to become more strategic readers, assessment is crucial prior to, during, and following instruction. Before teaching students strategies, teachers need to determine if their students are ready to learn them since prerequisite skills and knowledge are often needed for them to reap the most benefit from reading strategy instruction (Brown et al., 1983; Deshler et al., 1984b; Graham et al., 1987;

Palincsar, 1986b).

Most developed reading strategy instruction approaches require that students be capable of functioning at a specified skill level. For example, adolescents involved in the Learning Strategies Curriculum are expected to be reading at the fourth grade level or above (Deshler et al., 1984b;), and Palincsar has indicated that students involved in Reciprocal Teaching should be able to read 80 words per minute with no more than two errors (Palincsar, 1986b). Obviously these criteria are adjusted when the approaches are to be used for different purposes or with different students. In other words, first graders being instructed in Reciprocal Teaching to enhance their listening skills would not be expected to meet the same criteria as seventh graders being instructed in reading comprehension.

Students will also differ in the extent to which they currently use strategies (Deshler & Schumaker, 1986). Observing students reading and having them verbalize the processes they undergo when reading may help teachers better understand the extent of students' strategy knowledge.

In the area of reading, assessment of word knowledge, phonological awareness, and simple comprehension is fairly straight forward. Determining students' understanding and use of strategic information can be more difficult. Teachers who are successful at conducting such assessments, according to Valencia and Pearson (1988), focus on the major goals of reading instead of the smaller, enabling goals; interact with students daily and observe them reading; use a variety of real-world and school-like reading material during assessment; engage students in tasks requiring the application of reading skills and strategies to new situations; and may have students conduct self-evaluations of their progress in developing strategic reading behavior.

Valencia and Pearson (1988) offer suggestions for constructing more thoughtful assessments. For example, a teacher assessing summarization skills, might provide each student with two or three different summaries of a written passage. The teacher would direct students to determine which summary would be most effective in helping them study for a test; which best captures the point the author is making; which would help a reader obtain a quick picture of the selection; which best supports the main conclusion; and which is filled with too many unimportant details. Other assessment suggestions offered by Valencia & Pearson appear in Figure 2-4.

Teachers should look in materials for guidelines for conducting informal assessments of students' knowledge of the content area and their understanding and use of reading skills and strategies.

Figure 2-4
Suggestions For Constructing
Reading Assessments

- modify multiple choice test questions so that there are more than one right answer;

- require students to justify their answers to multiple choice questions;

- have students select or write questions that they think would help them to understand and remember the important information in the text;

- require students, after reading, to identify the most important points and the main theme;

- have students evaluate prepared summaries from the standpoint of which would be most helpful to them as readers, which best presents the author's point of view, which would help readers quickly determine the subject of the writing, which best provides support for the conclusion of the passage, and which has too many details.

From Valencia & Pearson, 1988

Build Upon and Create Prior Knowledge

It is most important for teachers to teach students how to activate their prior knowledge of the content they are about to learn. When students lack previous experiences to make such a strategy workable, teachers should help them gain familiarity with the topics. The teacher should routinely preview the new content/topics, talking about them and so providing an introduction to familiarize students with the book's subject, setting, etc. When appropriate, teachers could

- *provide hands-on experiences related to the book's subject;*
- *show students films, filmstrips or videos (Rhodes & Dudley-Marling, 1988);*

- *take students on a field-trip to a location related to the subject they will be reading about; and*

- *have students interview individuals who possess some relevant expertise.*

Teachers should look for and/or create examples for how they might engage students in brainstorming sessions so they can have them explore what they already know about the subject they are about to study. They should look for lists of books, films, videos, and other resources they could use to create or tap students' knowledge about the readings contained in the text.

Inform Students of the Purpose for Learning the Skill or Strategy

Teachers should not assume that students automatically understand why they are learning a skill or strategy. Instead, students need to be given explicit explanations of reasons for learning the strategy, why the strategy is important, and how and when the strategy could be applied in and out of school. For example, students should be told that use of a question asking strategy when reading will help actively involve them in the reading process and thereby help them recall more of the text following reading. This knowledge has been shown to be very important in determining whether or not students appropriately use strategies after instruction (Borkowski et al., 1986; Brainin, 1985; Brown et al.,1983; Brown & Palincsar, 1982; Brown & Palincsar, 1987; Duffy & Roehler, 1987; Ghatala, 1986; Graham et al., 1987; Graham, 1988; Meichenbaum, 1985; Palincsar, 1986b; Paris & Oka, 1986a; Pressley, 1986).

Materials should help explain the reasoning behind the use of a reading skill or strategy use. As Fine (1988) has indicated, classroom resources frequently contain directions on student materials such as, "Read the passage and check the statement that best states the main idea," but seldom do they contain explanations for "how" to find the main idea or to summarize what has been read. Materials should expand these suggestions, helping the student discern the reasoning behind the "how to" of skill and strategy use and include examples of uses of the skills and strategies that would be meaningful to students. Teachers need to remember that what is obvious to adults and good readers may not be obvious to children learning to read or to those students experiencing difficulty with the reading process.

Model the Use of Skills and Strategies

Teachers need to *show*, not just tell, students how to use the reading strategies, They may do so by modeling (Brown & Palincsar, 1982; Brown & Palincsar, 1986; Deshler & Schumaker, 1986; Ellis, 1986; Ellis et al., 1987a; Englert & Raphael, 1988; Graham et al., 1987; Graham, 1988; Harris, 1988; Paris & Oka, 1986a; Pressley & Levin, 1987). But modeling should include more than just a demonstration of how to apply a strategy. The reasoning and thinking behind the use of the skills and strategy must also be made known to students (Duffy & Roehler, 1987; Herrmann, 1988b).

While teacher modeling is thought to be one of the best ways to explain reading skills, processes, and strategies to students, teachers often have difficulty with modeling, particularly mental modeling in which the thinking that underlies the use of the skill, process or strategy is revealed. Enhancing the teacher's understanding of his or her own way of thinking and teaching may be the first step in helping teachers become effective modelers, since teachers need to take time to think about their thinking if they are to make their thought processes explicit to students (Sheinker, 1988).

Videotapes that provide examples of teachers modeling the application and thinking of various strategies can be very helpful to teachers and students. These can be made by teachers when they and their colleagues are learning to model (Fine, 1988). Videotaping teachers during training and after they have tried to apply what they have learned in the classroom allows teachers to see themselves in action. They then have a better idea how to modify their teaching.

Short of videos, written examples of how teachers may present skill and strategies assist teachers. Appropriate examples could be presented as dialogues between the teacher and students, lesson outlines, or sample scripts. Such illustrations may be particularly helpful to the teacher new to the strategy instruction approach. They could be developed in brainstorming discussions among the teachers using the text or materials in their classrooms.

Figure 2-5 contains an example of how a teacher might think aloud when demonstrating to students how to activate prior knowledge. Modeling, particularly mental modeling, is considered by many to be one of the most important elements in teaching students to be more strategic readers.

Make Clear to Students That Skills and Strategies Should Be Used Flexibly

While reading instruction should teach students the procedures for becoming more strategic in their reading, it must also make clear to students that strategies should be used flexibly and appropriately

(Palincsar, 1988; Roehler et al., 1986; Sheinker, 1988). Instruction should not lead the student to conclude that a strategy's use must be rigorously adhered to in all situations (Allington, 1988). For example, while creating mental images when reading can aid memory, students should not feel compelled to engage in this strategy every time they read. Summarization or question asking and answering may be more appropriate strategies to use. For some reading, particularly "pleasure" reading, students may not wish to use any strategies, and should be encouraged not to do so unless they wish. Reading, to be an easy recourse for students, must have a pleasurable aura or associations.

Offer Students Ample Opportunities for Practice

Reading instruction must incorporate ample opportunities for practice. As with the learning of anything, practice is necessary to develop

---

FIGURE 2-5

Example of Teacher Thinking Aloud to Explain the Activation of Prior Knowledge Strategy

Teacher: I found an article in a magazine that looks interesting, and I am going to read it. Its about the attack on Pearl Harbor. Before I start to read the article I want to stop and think for a moment about what I already know about Pearl Harbor. If I call to mind what I already know, I think it will help me to better understand any new information that I read in this article. Well, let's see, I know that Pearl Harbor, which was a naval base in Hawaii, was attacked by the Japanese on a Sunday morning, December 7, 1941. Because of the attack, the United States declared war on Japan, and our country entered World War II. I remember seeing films of President Roosevelt giving a speech about the attack and how solemn he looked. I remember seeing pictures in books of a lot of ships burning after they had been bombed. I also remember seeing a movie several years ago about the Sunday of the bombing and the days right before it. I recall that it showed how really surprised people were when the attack occurred. That is something that I never understood, how the attack could have been such a surprise. Maybe this article will provide me with some insights about that. Well, I've now called to mind some important facts that I remember. I am sure as I start to read, other memories might come to mind.

proficiency (Brown & Palincsar, 1982; Duffy & Roehler, 1987; Ellis et al., 1987a; Graham et al., 1987; Graham, 1988; Paris & Oka, 1986a; Pressley, 1986). But it is important that practice occur with a variety of materials (Feldman, 1988) and that it involve meaningful tasks (Harris, 1988).

Materials provide teachers with opportunities for activities that could be used to practice skill and strategy use. These activities should be varied and easily accommodated to the diverse learning needs and competencies of children. For example, suggestions for practicing summarization might include having the student make audio tapes to record her oral summaries, using a graphic organizer to record the main points of a reading, or for a story, drawing a comic strip representation. Practice activities should be diverse and go beyond the usual type of activity frequently suggested.

Guide Students in Their Efforts Through Teacher-Student Conferences

Teacher-student interactions play a crucial role during reading instruction. Teachers need to be sensitive to the learning needs of individual students and through appropriate interaction lead students to a greater understanding and use of the skills and strategies being taught (Duffy et al.,1987c; Palincsar & Brown, 1988). Conferencing also gives students an opportunity to talk to the teacher about what they have read and to tell about any areas of difficulty. From the teacher's perspective, conferences affords them an opportunity to assess student progress and provide help and additional teaching when needed (Rhodes & Dudley-Marling, 1988).

Teacher-student conferences can take several forms such as: *pre-arranged meetings* when students are scheduled in advance to meet individually with the teacher during a particular class period; *roving conferences,* which the teacher conducts informally as he or she moves from desk to desk; *group conferences,* that occur when the teacher meets with several students who are reading the same book or materials; and *whole-class conferences* which essentially involves a general discussion (Rhodes & Dudley-Marling, 1988).

Conferencing with students does not necessarily come naturally to teachers, particularly those whose past teaching has been dominated by whole group instruction. Students also may have difficulties adjusting to conference situations, particularly individual conferences, if most of their previous educational experiences have been in traditional classroom settings.

What guidelines should teachers follow when having individual conferences with students? Some suggestions:

- *begin a conference by creating a rapport with the students (Marzano, et al., 1991). The teacher may ask a general question to prompt students to talk about their reading. Teachers should be prepared for students who may be reluctant to talk. This may happen in particular with roving or informal conferences that teachers may conduct as they move from desk to desk.*

- *pose questions to help students to share and extend their comprehension (Rhodes & Dudley-Marling, 1988). For example, teachers could ask what students liked best about what they read, what their reactions were to what they read, why they reacted the way they did, what problems or confusions they experienced when reading, and so on (Marzano et al., 1991).*

- *ask questions that lead students to apply their knowledge of skills and strategies. Questions such as what did you know about this topic before you read this material, where would you look for more information, what questions did you ask yourself when you were reading, are examples of such questions.*

- *listen closely to students' responses to questions, respond appropriately, and encourage and guide them in their efforts to acquire greater strategic reading abilities (Marzano, et al., 1991).*

Teacher's guides could be used to help teachers generate questions when interacting with students. Rhodes & Dudley-Marling (1988) stress the need for teachers to formulate questions to go beyond the content of what is read to include questions about the processes the student used during reading, such as, "How did you choose this book to read?" and "What difficulties are you encountering as you read?." Again, video tapes would be helpful in demonstrating for teachers how to conduct conferences. (See Rhodes & Dudley-Marling, 1988; Marzano, et al., 1991 for more suggestions on conferencing).

Help Students Gain Control Over Their Use of Strategies

If students are to develop into purposeful and independent learners instruction should be designed in a way that will lead them to take responsibility for their own learning (Palincsar, 1990).

Over the course of instruction, control of strategies must be transferred from the teacher to the student. In other words, students need to move from being regulated by teachers or other adults to being self-regulated if they are to apply these strategies in appropriate situations on their own without external prompting (Brown & Campione, 1986; Brown & Palincsar, 1982; Brown & Palincsar, 1987; Duffy & Roehler,

1987; Graham et al., 1987; Harris, 1988; Meichenbaum, 1985; Palincsar, 1988).

This fading of teacher control obviously must occur gradually, and it often requires that the teacher play many roles along the way. For example, in *Reciprocal Teaching*, teachers function first as informants, then as mediators and facilitators, and then, after control has been transferred, as reflectors and coaches (Palincsar, 1988).

This transfer may be facilitated by materials such as end of chapter or unit questions that would guide students to assess their own understanding of strategies and how they use strategies to think about the decisions they make about their learning processes.

Utilize Group Learning Situations

Collaborative or group learning can be an effective instructional method to help establish a supportive environment for students learning to read strategically. Some researchers believe that participation by students in collaborative learning activities is a key component in the development of students' strategic reading capabilities (Palincsar, 1990).

Group learning situations can be used to fulfill a variety of instructional needs: more able students can tutor or model for their less able peers, introduce students to strategies to help them improve their comprehension, engage groups of students in implementing strategies such as activating prior knowledge or producing a graphic representation (Graham & Johnson, 1989; Jones et al., 1988/89; Palincsar & Brown, 1988). Materials provide teachers with ideas for activities that can be performed in small groups. Chapter Five provides an overview of factors to consider when designing collaborative learning situations.

Reinforce the Use of Skills and Strategies in Areas Beyond Reading Instruction

It is unwise to assume that when students learn reading strategies they will automatically, without being reminded, apply them outside the instructional setting. Therefore, effective strategy instruction needs to stress generalization opportunities (Deshler et al., 1981; Deshler et al., 1984a; Ellis et al., 1987b; Graham, 1988; Graham & Harris, 1987; Harris, 1988; Meichenbaum, 1985; Palincsar, 1986b; Pressley & Levin, 1987; Ryan et al., 1986). A simple way teachers at the intermediate or higher grade level can do this is by embedding strategy instruction within a content area, such as social studies, or at the very least, reminding students to use the strategies when reading material in those areas

(Dowd, 1988; Feldman, 1988).

When students with special learning needs receive reading instruction in a resource room, close cooperation between the resource and regular classroom teachers will help ensure that these students apply their knowledge of reading strategies to their regular classroom assignments. Resource room teachers need to communicate with their students' regular classroom teachers so they can prompt, cue, and reinforce these students' reading strategy use in the content areas (Ellis et al., 1987a; Ellis et al., 1987b; Schmidt, 1984). It is important that reading skills and strategies taught to students be reinforced outside the reading instruction setting. Teachers who work with a group of students in such content area subjects as social studies and science should be conferring regularly so they are all working to reinforce the students' use of appropriate strategies while learning the different content materials. It is these coordinated activities that encourage students to generalize and appropriaretly use the strategies they have been taught.

Undertake Regular Evaluation

Provision should be made for incorporating an evaluation component to assess periodically the effectiveness of reading strategy instruction (Harris, 1988; Palincsar, 1988). Student progress should be reviewed to determine if the expectations for the instruction are being met, if students use learned skills and strategies routinely when reading, and if strategies are being taught using the recommended techniques discussed above. If results are less than expected, appropriate adjustments should be made in efforts to teach reading strategies. Adjustments might include spending more time teaching strategies; modifying the way in which the strategies are taught; or focusing on different skills and strategies.

HOW CAN CLASSROOM MEDIA AND MATERIALS HELP?

As we have indicated, classroom resources can help teachers help students become more strategic readers depending on how teachers use them. Traditionally, teachers have been guided in their reading instruction by the content and methods reflected in basal readers. Basals in the past focused on skill development and devoted little time to improving students' comprehension capabilities. They included little information about strategies that would enhance youngsters' reading (Durkin, 1981). In recent years, increasing numbers of classroom materials, including basal readers, are being developed with the expressed goal of supporting the teaching of reading strategies as well as skills. This increased availability of media and materials supportive of teachers' efforts to improve the strategic reading capabilities of all students, including those with learning difficulties, is a positive development. Readily available classroom resources can provide considerable assistance to teachers who are learning to teach strategies and to experienced instructors as discussed above.

Resources Can Support Content-Related Suggestions

How do classroom resources provide the most assistance to teachers who wish to implement the suggestions presented above? We have suggested ways in the previous discussion. Other examples:

- When teaching students how to acquire the meaning of an unknown word from context, it is better for materials to present students with an extended reading passage and have each student, not the publisher or teacher, identify the words the student does not know (Palincsar, 1990). Teachers can support these materials by reminding students to read ahead to identify unknown words from context.

- Some strategy teaching can be aided by specially designed worksheets. Worksheets that contain blank boxes, each labeled for a different element such as problem, action, outcome and other elements usually found in a story, can help students to learn about story grammar. Use of such sheets has been shown to improve students' reading comprehension (Idol, 1987b).

- Other worksheets could accompany reading materials representing other types of writing. For example, charts containing spaces for students to supply information about important events, main ideas, other viewpoints and opinions, the reader's conclusions, could be designed for use by students when reading history texts (Idol 1987a).

- Rhodes & Dudley-Marling (1988) suggest using what they refer to as open-ended frames, which students would complete as they read expository writing. Figure 2-6 contains an example of such a frame. Materials can also stimulate activities that give students practice in developing their own graphic organizers.

Materials can offer students varied and realistic opportunities for applying newly acquired skills and strategies. For example, materials that are intended to teach students how to find the main idea and to summarize can be structured to offer students varied and realistic activities for practicing these strategies (Fine, 1988). Summarization skills can be facilitated by materials that present end of passage

Figure 2-6
Example: Reading Frame for Expository Writing

In this passage, the problem is defined as

_____.

The various solutions that have been suggested include

_____

_____, and _____.

The author believes that _____
is the best solution because _____.2

From Rhodes & Dudley-Marling, 1988

questions that prompt students to mentally recall what they have read. Supplementary materials or text selections can help students learn to write summaries to present short, well-organized passages from what they are learning. Increasingly longer and more difficult passages should be used as students perfect their summarization skills.

Not only could materials introduce students to reading strategies, but they also may be designed to prompt students to use strategies. Questions could be inserted:

- at the beginning of a unit or section to help students activate their prior knowledge or generate questions;
- throughout the reading to help remind students to read to answer questions; and
- at the end of the chapter to cue students to answer, respond to major issue, summarize the passage, and reflect on what they have read.

Worksheets could contain questions that would ask students to identify the strategies they used, which strategies seemed to work best, and what other techniques and strategies they have devised on their own.

Materials can also assist by providing teachers with background information about the effectiveness of the strategies. Directions to teachers could be contained throughout materials to remind them to prompt students to use strategies as appropriate. Materials could serve to remind educators that information about strategies and their effectiveness changes over time (Graham, 1988; Harris, 1988). As more

Figure 2-7
Checklist For Evaluating Adequacy Of Media and Materials To Support The Teaching Of Strategic Reading

                                                                Yes   No

- Is advice provided on how to teach reading skills strategically?

- Does the material provide information about the following reading comprehension strategies:

  summarizing

  identifying story grammar

  creating visual images

  activating prior knowledge

  generating questions

  answering questions?

- Are the purposes and uses of the strategies explicitly stated?

- Does the material provide multiple examples in print or video of the uses of skills and strategies?

- Do these examples provide insights to the thinking, reasoning and decision making that underlie skill and strategy use?

research is conducted, more will be learned as to which strategies should be taught to whom.

There are general books which can help teachers determine which reading strategies are most likely to help students learn, why, and how to teach them (Harris, 1992; Palincsar, 1986b). These books focus on strategies that have been proven effective in improving students' reading capabilities such as summarizing, activating prior knowledge, employing imagery, understanding story grammar, and generating and asking questions (Pressley et al., 1990). Gaskins (1991) focuses on how teachers implement strategies in their classrooms, ranging from first through eighth grade.

Remember: Students are more likely to understand and execute reading conventions when they learn them in meaningful contexts. Skills should be taught in a way that allows students to connect their use to real reading situations.

Figure 2-7 (cont.)

Yes   No

- Are guidelines provided to help students and teachers determine when skill and strategy use may be appropriate?

- Does the material provide ample and varied exercises that enable students to practice using reading skills and strategies?

- Are students encouraged to use skills and strategies throughout the material by the inclusion of appropriate questions or prompts?

- Are reading and writing activities integrated?

- Is background information presenting a summary of the theories about and research on strategy instruction included for teacher use?

- Are teachers provided with guidelines for how to teach specific strategies?

- Are teachers prompted to reflect upon their own use of strategies?

- Are ample suggestions offered to teachers for how to assess students' knowledge and use of strategies?

- Are ideas included for evaluating students' progress in mastering strategy use?

Also, that strategy use is best promoted when the teaching of reading and writing is integrated, and includes activities that give students ample opportunities to write about what they have read and to read about what they are to write. More about writing strategies in the next chapter.

The important features to look for in identifying media and materials supportive of methods to help students become strategic readers are contained in Figure 2-7. Increasing numbers of reading textbooks and supplemental materials publishers are introducing reading processes and strategies in their instructional materials. Some present extensive, useful information and guidance for teaching, reading thoughtfully and strategically; others address strategy teaching superficially. The checklist in Figure 2-7 can help school district professionals to determine if materials being considered for adoption and purchase provide the desired level of support for teachers.

CHAPTER THREE

Communicating and Learning Through Writing

The production of written language—the committing of word to paper—requires that the writer apply an array of abilities from the fine motor to the metacognitive. Unlike other forms of communication, such as speaking and listening, writing frequently is produced in the absence of direct human interaction or feedback (Bereiter & Scardamalia, 1982). Yet writers must be mindful of the motivations and informational needs of their audiences and must periodically evaluate their products in light of these perceived needs.

Within the context of schooling, written expression constitutes not only an area of study, but also a major vehicle by which students demonstrate what they have learned in numerous subject areas (Christenson et al., 1989; Graham,1982; Harris & Graham, 1985). It is not surprising that improving students' writing is an oft-cited educational goal (Englert et al., 1988a).

But teaching students to learn to use writing to communicate ideas and information and to express feelings, thoughts, and imagination is a difficult, complex, and necessarily time-consuming undertaking. Too often, little time is set aside during the school day for sustained writing. Typically the writing instruction that is provided emphasizes mechanics and grammar, not writing processes and strategies.

Writing instruction is further hampered because many teachers are not properly prepared to teach composition, do not frequently engage in writing themselves, and have little knowledge of effective methods for teaching writing (Englert et al., 1988a; Graham, 1982). And, some teachers believe that students need to be proficient readers (Isaacson, 1987) or to have mastered skills such as grammar, spelling, vocabulary, and handwriting before being introduced to more complex processes (Graves, 1978; Roit & McKenzie, 1985).

Writing instruction that is dominated by a skill orientation is unlikely to guide students, including those experiencing difficulties with writing, to becoming more effective, reflective, and thoughtful writers (Rhodes & Dudley-Marling, 1985). In recent years more notice has been paid to instructional approaches that treat the learning of writing as the complex, thought-engaging, social activity that it is. More attention is being given to instruction that emphasizes the processes involved in writing (Bos, 1988; Hull, 1989; Morocco, 1990), encourages children in the lower grades to write before they become proficient readers, and incorporates writing conferences and peer writing groups into writing instruction (Scardamalia & Bereiter, 1985). Examples of approaches that incorporate most or all of these principles include

• *Self-Instructional Strategy Development.* This approach, developed by Steve Graham, Karen Harris, and their colleagues at the University of Maryland, is intended to help students with learning disabilities to learn processes and techniques employed by good writers through the use of strategies (Harris & Pressley, 1991; Harris & Graham, 1992). Strategies have been developed that help students brainstorm ideas or words (Graham et al., in press; Harris & Graham, 1985); generate and organize ideas (Graham & Harris, 1989c); and plan the construction of stories (Graham & Harris, 1989a). Students are taught to use these strategies through a seven-stage process beginning with the development of skills that students will need to use the strategy and ending with an emphasis on independent application of the strategy by the student (Graham et al., 1987).

• *Cognitive Strategy Instruction in Writing.* Developed by Carol Sue Englert and her colleagues at Michigan State University, this program emphasizes the social nature of writing and the importance of the knowledge of text structure in planning, organizing, drafting and revising compositions. Teachers introduce students to both poorly and well-written compositions within various genres. As the teacher reads these compositions to students, he or she asks key questions that good writers would ask as they write and revise. The program also uses "Think Sheets," which contain a series of prompts intended to help youngsters develop a sensitivity to both audience needs and text structure (Englert & Raphael, 1988; Englert et al., 1988a).

• *The Process Writing Approach.* Process writing emanated from the work of Donald Graves and his associates at the University of New Hampshire. This approach stresses student-teacher conferencing, the need for sustained writing, skill teaching within the context of writing, student selection of writing topics and peer interaction (Graves, 1982; Graves, 1985). Process writing is usually implemented through a workshop approach where students discover and act upon their own intentions and where the teaching of reading, writing, and other language arts is word integrated (Atwell, 1988).

All of the above approaches, which are described in greater detail in Appendix B, aim to help students become more capable, reflective, thoughtful, and independent writers. They differ in the emphasis they place on specific instructional procedures. Most fundamental differences revolve around the means by which information about strategies, procedures, and processes should be presented to students in need of special education. Those who advocate a formal, structured approach to strategy teaching have been criticized by some educators who contend that strategy instruction casts students in a passive learning role and discounts the active role children must assume to become capable, proficient learners. Strategy instruction advocates strongly dispute this claim (Harris & Pressley, 1991). Harris and Pressley (1991) insist that good strategy instruction does not involve having students memorize strategy steps or procedures in a meaningless way. They concede, however, that strategy instruction, as any method of instruction, can be poorly implemented by professionals who ignore essential principles such as placing students in an active learning mode, connecting new learning with what students already know, and scaffolding instruction, i.e., providing support to a student at the beginning of a learning task and then gradually removing it as students gain proficiency in the task.

Process writing approaches, on the other hand, have been criticized by some educators who, while acknowledging that process writing can be beneficial in improving the quality of writing of students with learning problems, question the total reliance on this form of instruction particularly for students experiencing learning difficulties (Englert et al., 1988a; Graham et al., in press). Graham and his colleagues (in press) observe that while process approaches may build students' confidence in their abilities to write and may help students improve their writing over time, these approaches usually do not lead to rapid gains in performance. Further, it is not clear that the process approach will lead to proficiency in all the types of writing tasks students face in school, or that it is suitable for use with students who are learning handicapped.

Englert and her colleagues (1988a) remark that while daily writing, sustained writing, student assumption of an informant status, and peer collaboration should be fundamental and necessary components of writing programs, they are not sufficient to develop the expository writing skills of students with learning problems. These students need to learn to monitor and control specific organizational and thinking strategies for planning, drafting, peer editing and revising.

The best form of writing instruction for all students may involve the infusion of strategy teaching into programs that are based primarily on process writing principles.

Recommendations for components of such an instructional program are listed in Table 3-1 and are discussed in the following sections of this chapter. These recommendations cluster into two categories: those that address what is believed to be appropriate content for instruction, and those that discuss how instruction should be presented. This chapter concludes with a discussion of how media and materials could

---

Table 3-1
Guidelines for Designing Cognitive-Oriented Writing Instruction

What Should Be Taught?

- Teach mechanics, grammar, spelling, and handwriting, but teach them meaningfully
- Teach the purposes, processes, procedures, and strategies involved with writing
- Teach about the different forms of writing and their goals

How Should Writing Be Taught?

- Create a supportive environment
- Allow enough time for writing
- Make writing an authentic activity
- Establish ownership
- Create an audience for writing
- Arrange the classroom to support writing
- Do not overemphasize student errors
- Interweave assessment throughout writing instruction
- Establish writing groups and peer collaboration
- Collaborate with students in the learning process
- Model desired writing behavior
- Connect the teaching of writing with other teaching

---

be designed to assist teachers in implementing these recommendations.

WHAT SHOULD BE TAUGHT?

Teach Mechanics, Grammer, Spelling, and Handwriting, But Teach Them Meaningfully

While it is generally agreed that an undue emphasis on grammar does not improve composition (Brennan, 1988; Hillocks, 1987; Morocco et al., 1987; Rhodes & Dudley-Marling, 1988), totally ignoring mechanics and grammar is not wise either (Graham et al.,in press; Isaacson, 1987; Isaacson, 1989; Isaacson, 1990), since failure to develop proficiency and fluency in such skills may impede students' writing in several ways (MacArthur & Graham 1987).

Ideally, grammar and mechanics should be taught indirectly, as an integral, purposeful part of real writing activity (Graham & Harris, 1988b; Graham et al., in press; Hillocks, 1987; Isaacson, 1987; Morocco et al., 1987; Stires, 1990). When doing so, teachers can stress the importance of standard forms of communication in aiding readers to understand what they have written (Rhodes & Dudley-Marling, 1988). Occasionally, teachers may choose to provide a lesson directly focusing on a specific skill such as capitalization or use of commas. Examples and rules should be explained and an opportunity given for students to practice the skill. One activity that may help link direct instruction in use of writing skills to real writing is having students edit one of the compositions they wrote several weeks or months earlier and to discuss why they made the changes that they did (Marzano et al., 1991).

It is appropriate for teachers to directly note or comment on errors in writing conventions in students' compositions. But teachers need to be judicious when doing so, since the main focus of the teacher's attention during composition instruction should be on helping students develop their abilities to organize and express their thoughts and feelings. Graves (1983) suggests that when dealing with student errors

- *avoid marking spelling errors on first drafts;*

- *do provide help that is in the context of improving the writing work;*

- *do place primary focus on the content of the writing or audiences needs; and*

- *do offer as many opportunities to write as possible.*

Providing students with many opportunities to read is an important element in the indirect approach to teaching writing conventions. Reading can also be a powerful tool in helping students acquire an appreciation for appropriate use of writing conventions. Seeing grammar and writing mechanics properly used in the material they read is believed to be one of the best ways for students to learn the importance of proper usage of words and punctuation (Rhodes & Dudley-Marling, 1988).

Although indirect teaching of writing conventions is ideal, in some instances more direct and intense instruction in skills such as **spelling, punctuation,** and **handwriting** is needed especially for students experiencing learning problems (Graham, 1982; Isaacson,

1987). But instruction should be presented in a thoughtful, strategic way.

Teachers should abandon the practice of giving students spelling lists containing words that often appear to be selected at random. Instead, teachers should adopt more meaningful word selection techniques such as identifying words that contain common features (Graham, et. al., in press).

Students can be helped when actually studying spelling words by working with another student. One student in the pair can ask how to spell a word; the partner responds. When not sure of the spelling of the word, encourage the student to spell the word in two or three different ways and then selecting the spelling that he or she believes to be correct. The first student then determines whether the spelling is correct. Students then switch roles (Marzano et al., 1991).

Or, teachers could have students work in pairs to identify from their text or other sources words that follow specified spelling rules. For example, students could be asked to work with a peer to find as many words as they can that followed the *ie/ei* spelling rule—*i* before *e* except after *c* or when sounded ay as in neighbor (Marzano et al., 1991).

How should students be guided to study spelling words on their own? Graham and his colleagues (in press) urge teachers to have students form visual images as well as trace and sound out words; incorporate games and other practice activities; and make use of peer tutoring and cooperative learning for practice and testing.

Traditionally, common practices for teaching handwriting have included

- *teacher modeling of the formation of letters;*
- *comparing and contrasting features of the target letter with other letters that share common formational characteristics;*
- *using prompts and cues, either visual or physical, to help guide students in the making of letters;*
- *practicing letter formation by tracing, copying and then writing without these aids;*
- *providing feedback and praise;*
- *correcting wrongly formed letters through the help of the teacher;*
- *encouraging students to self-evaluate their handwriting; and*
- *creating charts for graphing progress by students (Graham & Miller, 1980).*

Graham and his colleagues (in press) suggest that these methods could be enhanced if specific problem areas received most attention. For example, concentrating on correcting common errors such as the malformation of letters a, e, r, and t, may result in considerable improvement with minimal effort. Teachers must remember when teaching handwriting that student capabilities develop gradually and, according to Graves (1983), students' handwriting improves with increased opportunities to write about topics of interest to them.

In sum, when teaching mechanics and grammar, teachers need to stress to students the role both good spelling and clear handwriting play in communicating to others.

Teach the Purposes, Processes, Procedures, and Strategies Involved with Writing

Teachers need to make the purposes of writing explicit to students (Graham & Harris, 1988b; Thomas et al., 1987). Students must come to understand that writing involves setting goals, formulating problems, searching memory for relevant information, and evaluating decisions (Bereiter & Scardamalia, 1987; Graham et al., in press; Scardamalia & Bereiter, 1985). Young people must come to understand that good writing is not a mindless activity, but rather an active, constructive process which requires thinking about and organizing thoughts (Roit & Mckenzie, 1985). The good writer thinks about the processes involved in writing (Englert & Raphael, 1988); contemplates what he or she is going to write (Isaacson, 1988); devises methods for solving problems that occur throughout the composing process (Shanahan, 1988); and uses writing as a means of clarifying thoughts (Langer & Applebee, 1986).

Concern for readers and their needs also must be a key feature of the writing curriculum. Teachers must instill in students a desire to produce clear, meaningful communications that will be understood by the intended audience (Isaacson, 1987; Roit & McKenzie, 1985).

Appreciation for writing processes and audience needs comes in part from opportunities to frequently and regularly engage in composing and from implementation by the teacher of principles of process writing such as

- *selecting of topics by students;*

- *planning what is to be written;*

- *producing a draft;*

- *revising the draft;*

- *editing the composition;*

- *sharing the final product with others.*

However, many, if not most, students, particularly students with learning problems, benefit from being directly taught **how to apply** writing processes. Thus, writing instruction must also include attempts to enlighten students about the procedures and strategies that can assist them to manage the complex demands of writing (Englert & Raphael, 1988; Isaacson, 1987; Morocco et al., 1987). An array of strategies can be taught to young people to help them to become more effective writers (Isaacson, 1990). Writing strategies have been developed to help students plan, draft, and revise compositions (Graham & Harris, 1989a; Graham & MacArthur, 1988; Graham et al., in press; Harris & Graham, 1987; Harris & Graham, 1992).

Selecting The Topic

Students often have difficulties coming up with ideas and topics about which to write. Teachers can teach students to use magazine photographs or other illustrations to help think of story topics. Once a topic has been selected, students may be helped to generate supporting ideas by learning to use a procedure such as mapping. Mapping or webbing is a way to visually represent the relationships among main and supporting ideas. Such a technique can help students think through their topic for writing and generate ideas.

The example below illustrates a web or map a child may construct as he or she thinks about what information to include in a composition about sights and sounds encountered on a walk in the woods. (Figure 3-1)

Another strategy to help students produce story parts employs a visual prompt such as a photograph or drawing selected by the teacher (Graham & Harris, 1989a). In this approach, students are asked to look at the prompt and do the following:

- *Look at the picture;*
- *Let your mind be free;*
- *Write down story part reminders such as*
  - *who is the main character and who else is in the story, — when does the story take place,*
  - *where does the story take place,*
  - *what does the main character do,*
  - *what happens when he or she tries to do it,*
  - *how does the story end, and*
  - *how does the main character feel;*
- *Write down story part ideas for each part; and*
- *Write the story.*

Figure 3-1
Story Map

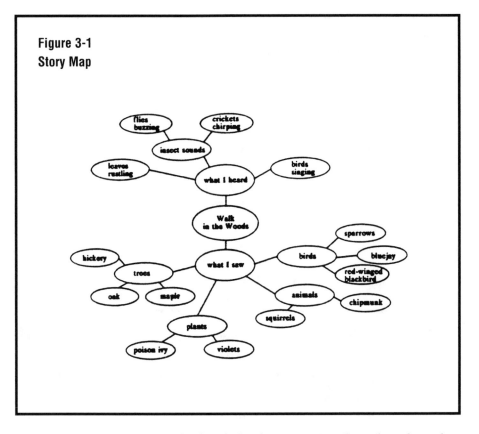

Students may be further helped to organize their thoughts when planning or drafting stories or expository writings by use of outlines or other visual patterns. More will be said about this in the next section, which addresses the teaching about different writing genre.

Producing the Draft

Too often, students view the production of a draft as the final step in the writing process. Teachers therefore must impress upon students the need to rethink and revise their compositions. In Figure 3-2, Graham & MacArthur (1988) provide an example of one strategy that may be taught to students to help them learn to revise their essays.

Atwell (1984) recommends self-conferencing as a drafting and revision strategy. She suggests that students be taught to ask themselves questions about what they are doing as they are writing. For example, students should ask themselves questions about whether they have included enough or too little information, the effectiveness of the beginning and ending of their composition, and the suitability

Figure 3-2
Revision Strategy

- read your essay;
- find the sentence that tells what you believe and ask, "Is it clear?";
- add two reasons why you believe it;
- scan each sentence to determine if it makes sense and is connected to your beliefs, to determine if more information can be added, and to note errors;
- make changes; and
- reread the essay and make final changes.

From Graham & MacArthur, 1988

of the title and the style of writing used. Some examples of the questions suggested by Atwell are

- *Have I told where, when and with whom this is happening;*
- *What parts are not needed;*
- *Does the beginning of the story bring the reader into the action;*
- *Does the ending leave the readers with the feeling intended;*
- *Does the title fit the story; and,*
- *Are any sentences too long, too short, or chopped up?*

Teach About the Different Forms of Writing and Their Goals

Each type of writing has its own signature and pattern. Knowing what elements are commonly included in various forms of writing can help students with their reading comprehension. This topic is discussed in the last chapter. But knowledge of genre types and purposes and the different components often found in these genre helps students to plan, organize and write their compositions (Englert et al., 1988a; Hillocks, 1987; Stein, 1986).

Teachers should provide students with ample opportunities to produce various types of writing (Shanahan, 1988) and to instruct them in techniques used to produce various genres. For example, activities suggested by Fitzgerald and her colleagues (1987) for teaching students the parts that compose a story (i.e., setting, beginning, reaction, goal, attempt, outcome, and ending) appear in Figure 3-3.

Expository writing takes several forms such as problem and solution, comparison and contrast and so on. When learning the patterns often seen in expository writing, students may be helped by seeing patterns graphically represented. Figure 3-4 provides a graphic

---

Figure 3-3
Teaching Students About Story Parts

- have students produce cumulative stories, where one child writes one part of a story, another student writes the next part, and so on;

- use a template on which appears a setting written across the top and headings for the story parts to be written by students;

- present to students for their elaboration simple, well-formed stories with only one or two sentences written for each part; and

- have students supply missing parts to stories.

From Fitzgerald et al., 1987

Figure 3-4
Graphic Representation of Writing
Following a Definition Pattern

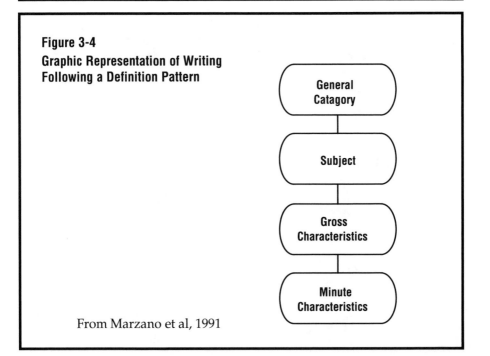

From Marzano et al, 1991

representation of writing that follows a definition pattern, i.e., describes a particular concept in detail and then gives an example of it.

Figure 3-5 offers another example, this of writings that follow an argumentative pattern intended to persuade the reader to adopt a particular point of view.

Create a Supportive Environment

A supportive environment contributes to learning within any subject area. Because writing is such a complex undertaking, it is particularly important that teachers create a classroom atmosphere conducive to the exploration, risk taking, and creativity that accompanies learning to write. Attention to creating a non-threatening environment that allows students to develop their potential at their own pace and supports and motivates them while doing so is especially important for students who are experiencing any type of learning difficulties and who may have a negative attitude toward writing (Graves, 1985; Isaacson, 1987; Roit & McKenzie, 1985). Similarly, the instructional

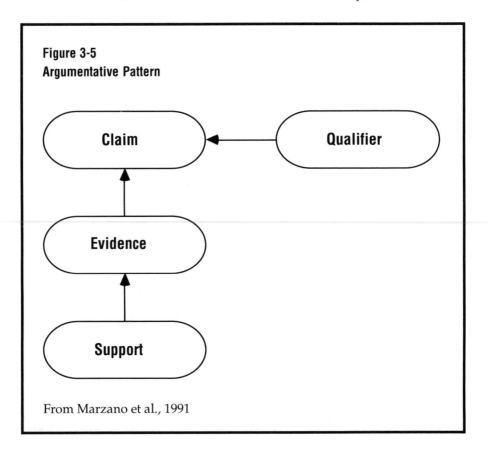

Figure 3-5
Argumentative Pattern

From Marzano et al., 1991

techniques selected to teach writing must be compatible with and reflect the intended goals of instruction. Discussed below are suggestions thought to be important elements of such a secure, predictable writing environment which supports the teaching of needed content.

Take enough time for writing. Children learn to write by writing, so it is widely believed that an opportunity for frequent composing is a necessary component of any writing program (Bos, 1988; Brennan, 1988; Englert et al., 1988a; Graham & Harris, 1988b; Graves, 1985; Isaacson, 1990; Shook et al., 1989; Sunstein, 1990; Thomas et al., 1987; Wansart, 1988).

How much time should be set aside for writing? Many believe that students should be required to write at least four days a week (Graham et al., in press; Graves, 1985; Isaacson, 1988; Rhodes &Dudley-Marling, 1988). The major portion of writing instruction time should be devoted to the sustained writing assignments that allow students the opportunity to develop their ideas and to explore and reflect on what they know, not just on short writing activities or worksheet tasks (Englert, et al., 1988a; Thomas et al., 1987).

Journal writing, particularly when it is done daily, is an example of a sustained writing activity that helps students learn to commit their thoughts to print and to become more fluent in their written expression (Graves, 1985). Teachers desiring to incorporate journal writing into their instructional program may need to provide students with guidance in how to express thoughts and ideas. Initially, topic selection may be problematic for students who have done little writing. When this is so, teachers should introduce students to techniques such as **brainstorming** to help identify topics about which to write. Providing a specific time that should be devoted to the activity (e.g., fifteen minutes) and for the length of journal entries (one-half to one page) also helps journal writing proceed more smoothly (Rhodes & Dudley-Marling, 1988).

Make writing an authentic activity. Too often, writing is taught as an end in itself—undertaken only to fulfill a school assignment or to demonstrate learning. Students need to be led to see how writing can fulfill a range of purposes, formal and informal, from expressing ideas, opinions, and feelings to providing information and direction—writing for "real" purposes (Fear & Fox, 1990; Graham, 1982). Writing letters to public or school officials or to friends; producing reviews of movies, audio recordings or television programs for publication in a class or school-wide newsletter; or generating in-depth reports focusing on school, local, or national issues of importance to students are a few examples of such writing activities. Teachers should note that writing activities need not be confined to language arts instruction, but rather could and should be incorporated into instruction in a variety of subject areas, as will be discussed in more detail later (Yates, 1983).

Establish ownership. Motivation to write increases when students have a sense of ownership or personal involvement in and control over their efforts (Calkins, 1983; Kirby et al., 1988; Langer & Applebee, 1986; Wansart, 1988). Having students select topics for writing in which they have an interest and perhaps some knowledge is one method to motivate students to become involved in their creations (Bos, 1988; Graham et al., in press; Stires, 1983; Sunstein, 1990).

Create an audience for writing. Writing is a communicative, social act (Graham et al., in press; Graves, 1985; Morocco, 1990).Too often, instruction fixates on the private nature of the writing act and ignores the contribution of social interaction in aiding students to develop fluency and understanding. Students who write in isolation often remain ignorant of the social nature of writing and of its ultimate purpose: to communicate. They seldom develop the sense of audience that is essential for the production of a variety of written communications.

Children need to learn to see themselves as informants, as individuals who have something to say or report that is unknown to others (Raphael et al., 1986). Unfortunately, students seldom see themselves in this light. School writing instruction frequently identifies the teacher as the chief, and in many cases, the only audience for written products. Students tend to believe that the teacher represents a knowledgeable audience, someone who knows as much or more about the subject of their writings as they do. Students who write only for the teacher often produce compositions that are superficial and devoid of details needed for a less knowledgeable audience (Englert et al., 1988a). Writing for a variety of audiences helps students to develop a sense of audience, learn to see themselves as informants, and understand the purposes of various writing forms (Bos, 1988; Graves, 1985; Morocco, 1990; Rhodes & Dudley-Marling, 1988; Shanahan, 1988; Thomas, et al., 1987; Yates, 1983).

To foster this attitude within a class, compositions should be shared informally with classmates in a large group or as a part of a writing group. Bos (1988) offers the following suggestion for a sharing activity to be tried in a group setting:

EXAMPLE: Have one student read his or her composition out loud; next, have another group member retell what he or she has "heard."

This simple activity provides the author with an idea of how other students perceive his or her work, and by so doing, help the writer develop an understanding of audience perceptions.

More formal approaches to sharing writing include publishing student writings in newsletters, class magazines, books or yearbooks

(Graham et al., in press; Isaacson, 1990; Stires, 1983). Graves (1983) points out that besides contributing to a sense of audience, publishing helps writers acquire a perception of time. When students start to write, they do not have a sense of the past or future, only the present. Knowing that their work will be published helps young people develop a sense of the future, while their previously published works serve as a reminder of their past efforts.

Graves (1983) points out that publishing should always be a part of a total writing program, not an end in itself, nor should it be used as a substitute for a writing program. He stresses that publication is important for all students and should not be used as a way of singling out the work of a few outstanding writers.

These authentic writing activities not only make writing meaningful but also gives students opportunities to write for various audiences, which helps them to understand better the many purposes of writing (Rhodes & Dudley-Marling, 1988).

Arrange the classroom to support writing. The physical arrangement of the classroom contributes to maintaining and supporting a writing environment. Opportunities for mobility and flexibility are a must if some features of the writing program such as group work and conferencing are to be implemented (Graham et al., in press). For example, Stires (1988) describes seating students at round tables situated around the periphery of the room. With this arrangement, the center of the classroom is used to house a library, writing materials, and resources. Classroom walls may be covered by the art and writings of students as well as published authors.

Do not overemphasize student errors. Many young people, particularly those with learning problems, frequently have negative self-images about their abilities to write. Special care must be given not to overemphasize students' errors. Instead, an effort must be made to provide feedback that is supportive and encourages improvement (Graham, 1982). Students should be praised generously and only provided feedback on aspects of their compositions for which they have received instruction (Isaacson, 1987). Graham and Harris (1988b) suggest that teachers concentrate on errors that occur often and obstruct the understanding of the text.

Interweave Assessment Throughout the Writing Instruction

Assessment should be used to determine a student's weakness, to individualize instruction, to monitor performance and to evaluate the effectiveness of the writing program (Graham, 1982; Graham, 1987; Isaacson, 1988). Clearly, assessment is critical at the beginning of a writing program, since the results are needed to design instruction to meet the learning needs of students (Davis et al., 1987; Graham & Harris, 1987; Stein, 1986).

The issue of how best to assess students' writing has received increasing attention in recent years. While in the past the product of the writing effort was the subject for evaluation, increasing attention is now being given to examining students' knowledge of the writing process as well (Graham, 1982). Figure 3-6 contains suggested questions a teacher could ask of students to determine their knowledge and use of writing processes.

Teacher observation of students when they are writing also is an important means of assessment (Isaacson, 1990). Rhodes and Dudley-Marling (1988) offer guidelines for conducting such observations. They suggest that teachers

- *conduct their observation of students' writing over time;*
- *consider the setting in which the observation occurs;*
- *when possible, supplement observations with audio and video tapes; and*
- *when necessary, ask students to provide clarification of some of their writing behaviors.*

Teachers should consider several factors in the actual evaluations of student writing products, according to Rhodes and Dudley-Marling (1988). Teachers should establish a clear objective for their writing

---

Figure 3-6
Questions to Assess Students Knowledge of Writing Processes

Questions prior to writing could include

- What are you going to write about?
- How are you going to put that down on paper?
- How did you choose the topic?

After writing, students could be asked

- How did you go about writing the composition?
- What are you going to do next with the composition?
- What is your assessment of your writing product?

From Graves & Giacobbe, 1988

instruction and these objectives should guide teachers' actions, comments and assessment. Teachers should evaluate only the area of writing on which they have focused instructions. For example, if writing fluency is the goal of instruction, teacher assessment and feedback should be concerned with how the student is progressing in his fluency. Including

- *who initiated the writing, since students are more likely to produce their best writing when they initiate it;*
- *who chose the topic;*
- *how much was written;*
- *how much time was spent by students producing their products;*
- *whether students talked during writing or revealed their feeling through body language;*
- *whether students revised their writing;*
- *the audience for whom the writing was intended;*
- *the purpose of the writing;*
- *the coherency of the writing product;*
- *whether students appropriately used language structure;*
- *how effectively students used words;*
- *how written language compares to oral lcnguage;*
- *if the student's writing performance proved consistent; and*
- *what the writer knows about writing mechanics.*

Portfolio assessment, where a student's works are collected over time in a folder, allows the student and teacher to judge what progress the student has made (Sunstein,1990). It also demonstrates students' progress to their parents and school administrators (Graves, 1983).

Establishing Writing Groups and Peer Collaboration

Small group work is frequently used in writing instruction as a way to help students acquire the many skills and processes involved in composition (Bos, 1988; DuCharme, 1989; Englert et al., 1988a; Gere & Abbott, 1985; Graham et al., in press; Graves, 1983). Groups assist students to

- *become more conscious of themselves as writers (Gere &Abbott, 1985);*
- *see writing as a problem-solving activity (Calkins, 1983; Graham et al., in press; Isaacson, 1988; Isaacson, 1990);*

- *strengthen their knowledge of writing processes and strategies (DiPardo & Freedman, 1988; Englert & Raphael, 1988; Graves, 1985);*

- *acquire necessary skills (Graham et al., in press);*

- *develop a sense of audience (Englert et al., 1988a; Wansart, 1988);*

- *understand that writing is difficult for everyone sometimes and almost everyone needs help and suggestions (Wansart, 1988);*

- *see writing as a social, communicative process (Graham et al., in press).*

For peer conferencing to achieve these ends, it needs to become an integral and frequently used part of the writing instruction program (DiPardo & Freedman, 1988).

Teachers may find that students need guidance in how to be a part of a writing group. Graves (1983) suggests that when groups are first formed, teachers model how to listen to another student and how to ask the type of questions that will help the student improve his or her writing. Following the first meeting, students should be brought together to discuss the experience and identify which types of responses were helpful and which were not (Brady & Jacobs, 1988). As young people gain more experience working in groups, they may require less monitoring. However, the teacher should be aware that problems may arise occasionally which, according to Brady & Jacobs (1988), are best solved by the group itself. More information about peer tutoring and cooperative learning methods is contained in Chapter Five.

Collaborate With Students in the Learning Process

The role the teacher adopts in writing instruction can be instrumental in assisting students to learn to approach writing as a problem-solving activity (Isaacson, 1990). The teacher's role should be an active, directive, facilitative and supportive one (Newcomer et al., 1988b), thus the evaluative, judgmental aspects of teaching need to be deemphasized (Graves, 1985; Hull, 1989; Langer & Applebee, 1986; Scardamalia & Bereiter, 1986).

Teachers should guide students' planning and revision, help them understand the nature of writing, and teach them appropriate processes and strategies. Conferences with students keeps teachers functioning interactively with students (Calkins, 1983; Graves 1977; Graves, 1985; Rhodes & Dudley-Marling, 1988; Wansart, 1988).

Scaffolding is an important concept which can be used by the teacher to guide the student in acquiring knowledge and skills and then gradually withdrawing the support as students take increasing responsibility for their own learning (Calkins, 1983; Harris & Pressley, 1991; Hull, 1989; Langer & Applebee, 1986; Morocco, 1990). Graves (1983), indicates six scaffolding components should govern teachers' conferencing with students. These appear in Figure 3-7.

A teacher should spend considerable time during conferences listening to students evaluate their own writing, discuss the processes they applied when producing the writing, and explain the subject matter (Murray, 1982). Teachers also must be adept at questioning students. Graves (1983) discusses six types of questions typically asked by teachers during conferences:

- **opening** *questions are used to begin a conference and may be as simple as, "What are you writing about now?";*

- **follow up** *questions are intended to help the student keep talking and explain further his or her writing and any problems being encountered;*

- **process** *questions help students become more conscious of how they write and of the thinking that goes into writing: "How did you write this? Did you make any changes? What are you going to do next?" Questions that reveal students' development tend to be process-oriented questions. Students' answers to such questions, when compared over time, can provide evidence of their growth as writers;*

Figure 3-7
Conferencing Principles

- students should be able to predict most of what will happen in the conference;

- during any one conference, only one or two areas should be the focus of attention;

- teachers need to demonstrate solutions to writing problems;

- students should have the option of asking questions and demonstrating their solutions to problems;

- teachers and students should develop a growing language to discuss the process and content of subjects; and

- conferences should be characterized by a sense of experimentation, discovery and humor.

From Graves, 1983

- **basic structure** *questions are those that help the student focus, reconsider major relationships in information, and look at fundamental issues in a writing piece. One such question is asking students what is the main idea;*

- **temporary loss of control** *questions are those that pose challenges for students to rethink some aspect of their writing and to do so on their own, outside the confines of the conference. In a subsequent conference, the student can be asked to share how he or she went about solving the problem.*

Teachers who have little or no experience in working directly with students in conferencing often are unsure about how to begin a session, how to encourage students to talk, and how to lead them to see the problems in their writing even when they think no problems exist.

Graves (1983) offers some advice about these areas of common concern to the teacher.

1. *The best way to start a conference is to concentrate on whatever the information is that the student has thus far provided and ask a question or questions that lead the child to provide additional information.*

2. *Students can be encouraged to talk by allowing them time to think about what they are going to say. Teachers should not feel the need to rush students into talking or to fill a lull in the conversation by talking themselves.*

3. *When the teacher disagrees with the student regarding the quality of the writing, the teacher should ask the child why he or she believes the piece is good. The student's response may provide a new perspective or even change the teacher's mind about the quality of the writing. If not, the teacher should then zero in on one problem area and ask questions that will lead the student to recognize and hopefully address the problem.*

Besides concerns related to the conduct of conferences, teachers may also worry about finding time for conferring with students, what to do with other students in the classroom while conferences are being conducted, and how to keep records of what transpires during the meetings. Graves (1983) once again offers advice. He provides a suggested schedule for making conferencing with students a part of a thirty-seven minute class period. The first ten minutes of the period is devoted to helping students who need immediate help; the next fifteen minutes is set aside for regularly scheduled conferences—each child would be assigned a day during the week for a regular meeting with the teacher. The last twelve minutes would be spent with children who are at a crucial point in their composing and require special attention.

The conferences are necessarily brief, but several educators have pointed out that brief, frequently conducted conferences are more effective than long, less frequent ones (Murray, 1982; Rhodes & Dudley-Marling, 1988).

Conferencing occurs in a one-on-one, teacher-with-student situation. The conference setting should be structured as a collaborative, interaction. Teachers should sit beside rather than across from students (Graves, 1983).

While a teacher is involved in conferencing, the other students should be writing. Interruptions can be minimized if students have been provided instruction in how to address problems on their own, such as what to do when they cannot spell a word, think of the next thing to write, figure out the one thing the writing is about, or think of the next topic (Graves, 1983).

An easy way to keep records of conferences is to use a loose-leaf notebook with a section for each child. For each conference the teacher notes the date, the title of the composition on which the student is working, the skill discussed, the rating of the overall quality of the conference and any other pertinent information (Graves, 1983).

Other conferencing options are possible. The teacher may conduct a "roving conference" as he or she moves among students to question them as they start or end their writing.

Group conferences involving a few students or the whole class also are possible (Rhodes & Dudley-Marling, 1988). Fitzgerald (1989) provides guidance for teachers who wish to provide group conferences. After the teacher makes the writing assignment, a group consisting of four to eight students is formed. The students share their written pieces. After a student has read his or her composition, the teacher initiates discussion by asking three broad questions:

- *What was the piece about?;*
- *What did you like about it?;*
- *Do you have comments, questions or suggestions?*

After the discussion, students are then given a chance to revise their works.

Conferencing in some form is seen as an important component of writing instruction because it brings the student and teacher into an interactive relationship which is essential for helping students develop their writing potential.

Teachers Should Model Desired Writing Behavior

Teachers should serve as a writing model in at least two ways. First, strategies and processes should be overtly and explicitly modeled to illustrate to students the procedures, thinking, and inner dialogue that accompany them (Bereiter & Scardamalia, 1987; Bos, 1988; Englert & Raphael, 1988; Graham et al., 1987; Graham et al., in press; Hull, 1989; Isaacson, 1987; Isaacson, 1990). Wansart (1988) points out that teacher modeling of writing as a problem-solving behavior is particularly important because students see that writing is not a simple task, but instead, an array of "problems" that need to be encountered and worked through. An example of teacher modeling of a process for selecting a topic for a writing appears in Figure 3-8.

Teacher modeling also is important for another reason. Through their actions, teachers convey to students their true beliefs about the value of writing. By writing and being observed doing so, teachers clearly communicate that they value this form of communication (Boynton, 1988; Brennan, 1988; Fear & Fox, 1990; Graves, 1983; Graves, 1985; Shook et al., 1989).

Figure 3-8
Teacher Modeling of Topic Selection

Teacher: I've been asked to write an article about some issue related to education for the neighborhood newspaper. There are so many things that I could write about. But, I want to choose a topic that will be of interest to many of the people who are likely to read the newspaper. Too, I want to choose a topic, which will be of interest to me to write about because I know that I write better when I'm really interested in my topic. Well, let's see, I think what I should do first is to list a few issues that would be of interest to me and also to the people who might read the piece. Now let me think. . . (Teacher thinks for a half a minute or so). O.K here's one idea—drug education, why it is needed and what our schools are doing about it.(Teacher writes "Drug Education," on the board, then pauses for a few seconds.) Here's another idea, business involvement in schools. Businesses can help schools sponsor special activities and programs and also they can do a lot to introduce students to various types of jobs and careers. (Teacher writes "Business involvement with schools," on the board). Now let me think of one more topic. Oh I know, the importance of parents being involved in the schools and in their children's education. (Teacher writes on the board, "Parents support of schools and schooling."). Well there I have three, good ideas. Which should

---

Connect the Teaching of Writing and Other Teaching

Writing should be integrated with other language arts instruction (DuCharme, 1989; Rhodes & Dudley-Marling, 1988). Shanahan (1988) believes that reading and writing should be integrated from the earliest grades. **Particularly, writing instruction should not be delayed until children can read.**

Other researchers stress the role of writing in learning and studying subjects throughout the curriculum (Atwell, 1990; Hittleman, 1978). Writing is a powerful learning tool since it can be used to help students think through and make sense of issues (Kirby et al., 1988). For example, Morocco (1990) in Table 3-2 illustrates how writing activities can facilitate and encourage problem solving in science.

Hittleman (1978) advocates the use of thematic units as a way to mesh language instruction with instruction in other areas. These units

---

Figure 3-8 cont.

I choose? I think each of these topics would be of interest to many of the newspaper's readers. Now drug education would be a good topic because our school district will be starting a new drug education program next fall, and the community should know about it. But maybe it would be better to have an article about that program published closer to the time when the program actually starts. Maybe I'll talk to the newspaper staff and see if I may write an article about drug education next summer or fall. So that leaves the business and parent topics. You know if I remember right I think an article appeared in the newspaper a few months ago about a school in a nearby district that had been adopted by a local business. Businesses have adopted schools in our district too, and readers should know about these school-business relationships. What about the issue of the involvement in schools of parents? You know I really feel strongly about this topic from two perspectives, as a teacher and as a parent myself. I think I have some good ideas about how schools and home can work more closely together, and I know I could describe some interesting programs and activities we do in our school to encourage parents to become more involved in our school. Both the school-business relationship issue and parental involvement in schools are good topics, but because I am most interested in the parent involvement issue, I think I'll choose that as my topic.

Table 3-2
Writing as a Problem Solving Strategy in Science

Problem Solving in Science	Functions of Writing	Suggested Strategies
Surfacing preconceptions	• Stimulates recall • Makes conceptions and misconceptions explicit	• Writing stories • Producing lists and diagnostic questions • Making analogies • Recording option statements in notes • Conducting peer interview
Organizing	• Highlights task features • Points up areas of new information • Develops sequence of action steps • Facilitates asking for help	• Developing graphic organizers of major parts of task • Producing checklists and schedules • Maintaining daily running record • Writing memos to teacher
Observing	• Focuses attention on relevant information	• Recording observations • Taking notes • Producing attribute lists • Developing questions to guide reading, listening, and observation

Table 3-2 (cont.)

Problem Solving in Science	Functions of Writing	Suggested Strategies
Comparing/measuring	• Stimulates comparisons	• Producing attribute lists • Recording results of peer interviews
Relating information	• Categories, chunks information • Relates new and old information	• Producing attribute lists • Writing monologues and dialogues
Making inferences/predictions	• Facilitates leap from facts to inferences • Links evidence with hypothesis • Facilitates idea sharing with peers	• Dialoguing with peers • Answering "what next" questions • Writing hypotheses/predictions • Writing memos to teacher • Writing explanations
Drawing conclusions	• Focuses child's attention on his or her own learning process • Promotes conscious planning	• Producing research reports • Keeping running log • Reviewing log entries • Listing writing strategies

Adapted from Morocco, C., Education Development Center, Inc. (1990). *The Role of Media and Materials in Teaching of Writing to Special Education Students.* Presentation at the ICSEMM Third Annual Instructional Methods Forum, Washington, D.C.

are organized around specific themes in which students have an interest. A series of lessons is built around each theme. Thematic units may increase students' opportunities for reading and writing by having them read and write to explore a topic of interest to them. This may be particularly beneficial for students with special learning needs. The continuity to their instruction adds purpose to their writing activities.

Learning logs also have been suggested as a means to help students utilize writing as a part of the learning process in other subjects. Learning logs are notebooks that young people use throughout the school year to record a variety of information, thoughts, and observations in response to teacher prompts and questions (Atwell, 1990).

Students can maintain logs in such subjects as social studies and science. The logs are particularly useful when used by students as they research topics for reports and compositions. Students can be directed to use their logs at several points during their research efforts. When students are attempting to identify a topic for study in science, for example, they can be directed to write in their logs answers to such questions as, "What do I already know about this topic?"; "What do I want to learn?"; and "How can I go about learning about the topic?" Students also use their logs to take notes as they gather information, make visual representations of ideas, to organize and integrate their collected information, to write brief summaries, to brainstorm, to help remember and retrieve information, and to generate predictions, such as guessing what might happen on an upcoming field trip (Thompson, 1990).

Activities such as mapping, described earlier, can be used to help students access their prior knowledge about the topics. For example, when starting a unit on weather, the teacher may have students brainstorm a list of weather-related words. The teacher could write the word "weather" in the middle of a large sheet of paper. The other words that students suggest can be written around it. Lines are drawn to illustrate relationships among the words. In subsequent lessons, words are added to the map and new relationships identified. This simple activity helps students understand and organize ideas (Farnsworth, 1990).

HOW CAN CLASSROOM MEDIA AND MATERIALS SUPPORT STUDENT WRITING?

How can media and materials help students become more thoughtful writers? As in other subject areas, media and materials can be designed to support both the content-related and teaching method suggestions.

Content Related Suggestions

Instruction in writing conventions— including grammar, spelling, and handwriting—should not be ignored when teaching students about writing. These skills need to be taught in a way that allows students to understand them and their importance in the communication process. Their introduction needs to be accompanied by examples or exercises that reinforce them.

Isaacson (1990) points out that texts frequently include too few or no examples of the concepts and offer confusing definitions. For example, a text might define a *sentence* as "a group of words that expresses a complete thought," and then ask students why the phrase "*his old hat*" is not a complete thought. Isaacson cites the following example from a recently published text of an exercise intended to teach the difference between imperative and exclamatory sentences:

Add words to each group of words below:
Write imperative or exclamatory sentences.
    —Please keep your_____.
    —Look at _____.
    —What an exciting _____!

The exercise requires only that a word be supplied. The decision about whether a sentence is imperative or exclamatory has already been made by the publisher.

When directly teaching skills, materials must provide meaningful explanation of what is being taught and give students multiple opportunities to learn each skill. Materials should offer learning games that make learning the skills more motivating for students. Teachers can use these materials also to establish peer-assisted learning situations.

Many teachers need assistance in teaching writing conventions indirectly. Materials can guide teachers to refrain from correcting all grammatical, spelling, and mechanical errors they find in students' compositions, but rather to selectively correct errors in writing conventions, to concentrate on assessment of the quality of writing represented in the composition, and to focus on conventions for which students commonly need assistance. One suggestion offered is to include in materials mini-lessons for teaching an array of mechanical, spelling, or grammatical problems commonly encountered by students with learning problems (Isaacson, 1990; Schwartz & Shoemaker, 1990). Materials could also advise teachers on ways to minimize the impact of poor knowledge of conventions by using alternatives to paper and pencil communication such as computers.

Computers have the capacity to ease some of the difficulties students with learning difficulties experience with writing mechanics such as handwriting and spelling. Students with handwriting problems can be trained in keyboarding to produce text that is more readable than their handwritten compositions. Word processing packages commonly contain spell checkers and other revision features that can be helpful. Word processing has been shown to stimulate students' spelling and mechanical revisions (Morocco et al., 1987). Thus by removing or minimizing physical and mechanical barriers to writing, students may be freed to concentrate more on processes that underlie the content of their writing (Dalton, 1989).

Besides easing the mechanical difficulties of writing, computers offer the possibility for incorporating prompts and procedures through on-line formats. Computer graphics, cartooning, and drawing capabilities can help students generate ideas (Morocco, 1990). Thus computers have the potential to facilitate students' application of writing strategies.

Many teachers are unaware of the processes and strategies that are involved in effective writing activity. Texts and other materials can provide them with information about the processes of writing and suggestions for how to lead students through those processes. Supportive materials might include:

- *excerpts from articles or books that concisely present the key ideas from research and state-of-the-art practice (Schwartz & Shoemaker, 1990)*

- *a variety of suggested strategies and procedures that could be tried by teachers to assist students with specific writing difficulties*

- *sample lessons providing illustrations for how procedures and strategies could be taught and used in a variety of real writing experiences (Hittleman & Moran, 1990; Isaacson, 1990; Morocco, 1990; Schwartz & Shoemaker, 1990)*

- *reminders to teachers that strategy teaching is not an end in itself but rather needs to be integrated within the total writing instruction experience*

- *examples for various ways to introduce, adapt and teach strategies to accommodate the learning needs of students who experience difficulty with writing (Hittleman & Moran, 1990; Morocco, 1990; Schwartz & Shoemaker, 1990)*

- *videotapes showing teachers presenting strategy instruction and student reactions to the instruction (Schwartz & Shoemaker, 1990)*

While materials can assist professionals to present instruction in strategies and procedures, resources can contain features to help students learn to plan, write and reflect upon their writing. Prompts, questions, or self-evaluation checklists have all been recommended as tools that could be incorporated into student materials. Activities and worksheets, such as those described above for mapping or webbing, would also be of assistance in reinforcing the teaching of processes to students.

Materials should introduce students to various types of writings. Examples should be provided of different writing genre, and activities that will lead students to understanding the purposes and components of various forms of writing. Through the inclusion of checklists or other prompts, materials can guide students to evaluate whether or not they have included the components of the genre in which they are working in their compositions. Models of exemplary and/or deficient genre pieces can be incorporated into materials for students to evaluate and analyze (Schwartz & Shoemaker, 1990). Teacher guides can assist teachers to be more knowledgeable about various writing genre and their features by incorporating background information, teaching suggestions, and recommendations of writings that illustrate different genres.

Support for Instructional Techniques

Often texts and other materials present writing as a dull, dry, lifeless, even torturous undertaking. Media and materials have the opportunity to enliven writing instruction, to help motivate and excite young writers and to guide teachers as they establish a classroom environment conducive to nurturing the development of young people's written communication capabilities. The multiple purposes and reasons for writing can be illustrated throughout materials with samples from published authors. Videotapes of interviews with authors, particularly student writers, may be particularly effective in portraying writing as a fundamental human activity. Teacher guides can assist teachers to provide authentic and sustained writing activities by

- reminding teachers to engage students daily in sustained writing and to link writing assignments to current social or personal issues of concern to students;

- suggesting activities such as writing a letter to the editor of the school or local newspaper, to a congressman or to a school administrator; preparing an article for publication in the school or classroom newspaper; and writing pro and con positions on an issue (Schwartz & Shoemaker, 1990);

- including questions for the teacher to use to lead students to a consideration of the attitudes, beliefs, and information needs of the intended readers;

- containing suggestions for publishing student materials and ideas for how publication of student products could be facilitated by use of word processing (Graves, 1983); and

- incorporating sample lessons into teacher materials to illustrate how these activities could be integrated into lessons.

Teacher manuals can be helpful by providing guidance to teachers in how to smoothly manage their classroom writing program. Tips such as how to coordinate divergent activities as whole-class and group instruction, teacher-student conferences, independent seat work, and how to chart student progress can be very helpful. The guides could also include floor plans that illustrate options for arranging classroom furniture to support instructional activities (Schwartz & Shoemaker, 1990).

Textbooks have also been accused of ignoring research findings about effective writing instructional methods (Giacobbe, 1988). Brennan (1988) has commented that publishers, by what they do and do not emphasize in their materials, seem to be saying that: students learn best in whole-group instruction; students must be taught skills over and over again; children learn through topic assignments with little choice; students need to know parts of speech to write and speak effectively; teachers should talk about writing but not write themselves; and evaluation should be based on workbook exercises and tests that stress form over content.

Shaw (1985) believes that some commercial resources are beginning to reflect recent research findings about writing, but not all do; indeed, many new materials here simply repackaged approaches found in earlier texts that placed a major emphasis on writing mechanics.

Appropriate manuals and teacher's guides hold the potential for helping teachers to learn effective teaching methods by including background information and recommended activities for implementing the methods (Schwartz & Shoemaker, 1990). There are several specific areas in which materials could be particularly helpful to teachers.

Assessment

Traditionally, emphasis in writing assessment has focused on testing grammar and mechanics. This emphasis in part may be traced to the uncertainty that teachers feel about making qualitative evaluations of their students' writing. Materials could assist teachers to make such judgments by including

- *checklists of questions that teachers could use in judging compositions (Schwartz & Shoemaker, 1990)*

- *reminders to teachers to limit their evaluations to those areas that have been taught and are in line with writing objectives (Isaacson, 1990)*

- *charts that teachers could reproduce and use to monitor students' progress (Schwartz & Shoemaker, 1990)*

Writing Groups

Materials could support peer conferencing and writing groups by providing:

- *guidelines for how teachers should form and manage groups (Schwartz & Shoemaker, 1990)*

- *activities that could serve as the focus for group writing activities such as the mapping exercise mentioned earlier (Morocco, 1990)*

More information about writing groups and collaboration may be found in Chapter Five.

Teacher Conferencing

Functioning as a collaborator in the learning process is a role that many teachers do not naturally assume. Materials should provide:

- *suggestions for how to help children with special problems (Hittleman & Moran, 1990; Morocco, 1990)*

- *examples of questions that are appropriate in specific situations (as discussed earlier in this chapter); and*

- *a demonstration of conferencing techniques through videotapes showing teachers engaged in conferences with groups or individual students (Fear & Fox, 1990; Schwartz & Shoemaker, 1990)*

Modeling. Teacher modeling of the actions and thinking that occur during the various processes of writing is believed to be a particularly important teaching method for helping students to understand how to appropriately use writing strategies and procedures (Hittleman &

Moran, 1990; Morocco, 1990). Materials should assist teachers in the following ways:

- *provide guidelines for modeling and examples of questions to ask students to gauge their understanding of the strategy and procedure being modeled;*

- *caution teachers against modeling in a rigid, mechanical, lock-step manner;*

- *illustrate effective modeling through video tapes (Hittleman & Moran, 1990; Schwartz & Shoemaker, 1990); and*

- *remind teachers to write along with their students (Boynton 1988).*

Integrating Writing Into Other Subject Areas

Materials can play a major role in helping the teacher integrate writing in learning in all subject areas. Suggestions for doing so include:

- *integrating reading, writing and oral communication into a single subject (Boynton, 1988)*

- *incorporating numerous writing activities and thought-provoking questions within subject area materials as a means to encourage student thinking, discussion and learning (Morocco, 1990; Schwartz & Shoemaker, 1990)*

- *prompting teachers to use writing activities such as mapping to introduce units in science or social studies (Morocco, 1990)*

- *producing writing "tool kits" that would contain guidelines such as those for use to write school reports. These guides could provide tips to students in areas such as how to select a topic, locate information, take notes, organize information, produce visuals to accompany the report and so on (Schwartz & Shoemaker, 1990)*

Numerous suggestions have been offered for how computers can contribute to the use of these instructional techniques. The open, public screen and large print on a computer monitor promote teacher-student collaboration by making student writing accessible to the teacher. Teachers are able to view students' writing as soon as or shortly after the student produces it, and this feature encourages interaction between students and teachers. In a similar manner, computers can provide a vehicle for collaborative writing activities among students. Computers may also be used by teachers to model writing processes and for various other activities. In Table 3-3, Morocco (1990) provides a listing of suggested ways in which computer applications may assist in reinforcing writing instruction principles.

Figure 3-9

Checklist for Evaluating the Adequacy of Media and Materials to Support the Teaching of Composition

	Yes	No

- Are activities included that would help students learn to strategically apply writing conventions?
- Is advice provided on how to teach writing skills strategically?
- Does the material provide information about writing processes such as planning, drafting, editing, and revising?
- Are teachers provided with suggestions for how to explicitly teach students to apply these processes?
- Does the material provide examples either in print or video of students using strategies as they apply writing processes?
- Do the materials provide the teacher with several suggestions for a variety of student writing activities?
- Are activities included that help in developing an appreciation of audience needs?
- Are students introduced to a variety of writing genres and their common structures?
- Does the material include activities that help students to acquire an appreciation for different writing types and their purposes?
- Does the material contain prompts to help students remember to use learned processes and strategies?
- Is the teacher provided with background information about the theory of writing, processes, strategies, and genres?
- Are teachers provided with guidelines for how to establish an environment conducive to composition instruction?
- Does the material contain guidelines for holding teacher-student conferences?
- Are guidelines and examples for assessing student's writing development included?
- Does the material suggest or demonstrate how writing activities should be incorporated throughout the curriculum?
- Are teachers prompted to reflect upon their own writing behavior?

Table 3-3
Computer Support for Effective Writing

Instructional Design Principles	Computer Support
1. Create a writing environment in which students continually interact with each other and with the teacher around meaningful composing.	Public screen encourages sharing and reading aloud. Network software links writers electronically.
2. Embed writing strategies and writing elements in specific genre (letters, adventure stories, autobiographies, folk tales) as students are composing those genre.	Students easily revise writing, focusing on one revision element at a time.
3. Model writing strategies in the whole class to promote students' gradual acquisition and independence in using the strategy.	Teachers can use a large screen to model writing processes.
4. Provide repeated opportunities for students to engage in writing strategies with other students.	Collaborative writing on the computer provides practice.
5. Provide students with specific procedures for collaborating in composing processes/strategies with other students.	On-line formats can provide procedures and prompt students.

Table 3-3 (cont.)

Instructional Design Principles	Computer Support
6. Provide students with visual and visualizing strategies for planning and organizing their thinking and writing.	Graphic and story studio software can stimulate ideas for visual learners.
7. Take into account students' developmental abilities in teaching them writing strategies.	Graphic, cartooning, and drawing tools help with generating.
8. Use media to promote student interaction and enhance the teachers' writing needs and process.	Open screen makes writing accessible to teacher for early intervention.
9. Assess students' writing needs and strengths throughout their composing process.	Networking tools provide teacher ongoing access to students' writing.
10. Provide students with procedures for reflecting on their writing and their use of composing strategies in their own writing (metacognition).	Readable print makes writing more accessible for rereading. Saving multiple drafts allows students to revise.

From Morocco, C., Education Development Center, Inc. (1990). *The Role of Media and Materials in Teaching Writing to Special Education Students.* Presentation at the ICSEMM Third Annual Instructional Methods Forum, Washington, DC.

All of these components are important elements of effective writing. Ideally, all should be incorporated into a writing program, but in practice, the learning needs of specific students and constraints such as lack of time or other curricular demands may influence a teacher to emphasize some elements over others.

Most of the media and material design suggestions offered focus on ways materials can guide the teacher to implement procedures and processes thought to contribute to successful composition instruction as opposed to recommendations for how student-oriented materials could be designed. These suggestions reflect two predominant beliefs: that writing instruction will improve only to the extent that teachers become aware of and implement effective methods for teaching writing, and that a greater emphasis in instruction needs to be placed on sustained writing activities for students, as opposed to worksheet-type exercises. Thus as Morocco (1990) states, classroom resources can be most effective by helping teachers understand the following:

- *the writing problems of their students;*
- *the components of composing activities;*
- *the need for writing to occur in a supportive environment that includes interaction with other students as well as the teacher;*
- *the need for thoughtful assessment of writing processes as well as products; and*
- *the procedures and strategies that can be targeted to students to help them to become more effective writers.*

The checklist appearing in Figure 3-9 will help school personnel evaluate the suitability of media and materials to support sound writing instruction.

CHAPTER FOUR

Cognitive-Based Principles for Teaching Mathematics — A Problem-Solving Perspective

Schooling seeks to develop young people's understanding of basic mathematical concepts and procedures. *All* students need to acquire the knowledge and skills that will enable them to "figure out" math-related problems they encounter daily at home and in future work situations.

Yet according to results of several studies, applying mathematical principles in problem solving situations poses considerable difficulty for American students (Brown et al., 1988a., Brown et al., 1988b., Kouba et al., 1988a). American education, while good at teaching students mathematical skills, falls short in helping youngsters understand the concepts that underlie those skills (Baroody, 1987). Without such understanding, it is unlikely that young people can make appropriate use of the skills and procedural knowledge that they do possess (Baroody, 1989a; Baroody, in press).

Traditional mathematics instruction stresses computation skills and "getting the right answer quickly." Little attention is paid to developing students' abilities to think mathematically, to judge the reasonableness of answers, and to justify selected procedures (Burns, 1985).

Current mathematics instruction also has been criticized for being too abstract, presenting concepts and skills before many children are able to learn them meaningfully (Allardice & Ginsburg, 1983; Ginsburg, 1989). When children do not understand what they are being taught, they often resort to rote memorization (Baroody, 1989a; Baroody, in press). When this happens, youngsters fail to transfer procedures they have learned to novel situations, or they apply the procedures in an unthinking manner (Schoenfeld, 1982). Further, these students often come to conclude that school or formal mathematics involves nothing more than the memorizing and mastering procedures that have little relevance and meaning for real life problem solving (Schoenfeld, 1987).

Cognitive-based methods for teaching mathematics have the potential to lead both regular and special education students to a greater understanding of mathematical concepts and procedures so they can be more strategic problem solvers. These approaches are founded on the beliefs that meaningful math learning requires the student to acquire conceptual and procedural knowledge and that students' independent problem-solving capabilities need to be nurtured.

Two examples of instructional approaches that have been developed to help students learn mathematical skills and apply them in a meaningful way are the following:

• *Cognitively Guided Instruction* (CGI) developed by Thomas Carpenter and Elizabeth Fennema of University of Wisconsin and Penelope Peterson of Michigan State University (Peterson et al., 1988/89) provides teachers with knowledge about how children think about and learn mathematics. Teachers who possess this knowledge are believed to be more adept at listening to students and assessing their mathematical understanding and at designing instruction based upon what children already know. (Fennema et al., 1989). When providing instruction, CGI teachers select math problems from everyday situations, build upon students' responses, prompt students to use and apply their knowledge solving the problems, challenge students to test their conclusions, and lead students to explore new concepts and strategies. Often teachers will place students in small groups where they will be assigned problems to solve as a group. The approach has also been used in whole-class settings.

• *The Verbal Problem Solving for Mildly Handicapped Student Project* (John Cawley of the State University of New York at Buffalo) was designed specifically to develop instruction for use with students experiencing learning problems. The project relied heavily on the use of specially-designed materials that contained an array of problem solving activities (Cawley, 1989). Materials were developed for use with junior and senior high students as well as those in the elementary grades. The materials for younger students help teach fundamental skills and concepts within a problem solving framework, while materials for older students include activities such as graphic information that must be "read," analyzed, and interpreted. Use of the Verbal Problem Solving Project materials was intended to provide students with an opportunity to apply a variety of mathematical skills, process information, analyze data, and develop metacognitive capabilities (Baker, 1989).

The two approaches above, which are described in greater detail in Appendix C, differ in their procedures, but both aim to help students become more strategic mathematical problem solvers. Their programs contrast with traditional math instruction by their placing problem solving situations at the center of mathematics instruction. From these and other research efforts have emerged principles for developing instruction to promote meaningful mathematical learning which are discussed in the following sections of these chapter. These principles are listed in Table 4-1. As with reading and writing, they are divided into two general categories, those related to content and teaching methods. This chapter concludes with a discussion of features of media and materials that assist teachers in implementing these recommendations.

WHAT SHOULD BE TAUGHT?

The curriculum believed to lead students to a deeper understanding of mathematics is one that blends an emphasis on skills, concepts, and procedures.

Table 4-1
Principles for Designing and Teaching Mathematics from a Cognitive Perspective

Content-Related Suggestions

- Teach students concepts and mathematical relationships as well as skills
- Present students with strategies to approach mathematical problem solving
- Do not ignore the need to improve students' attitudes and beliefs about mathematics
- Go beyond the teaching of basic skills and present students with a comprehensive mathematics curriculum

Methods-Related Suggestions

- Be sensitive to the developmental level of students
- Build upon students' prior knowledge of mathematics
- Cast instruction within a problem solving framework
- Question and listen to students
- Utilize small group learning situations
- Model problem solving
- Use manipulatives and calculators when appropriate
- Regularly assess students' problem solving capabilities

Teach Students Concepts and Mathematical Relationships As Well As Skills

Students need to be taught fundamental mathematical skills and procedures. But they must be led to conceptual understanding as well (Cherkes-Julkowski, 1985b; Fennema et al., 1989; Fitzmaurice-Hayes, 1984). What is conceptual understanding? Or more precisely, what are concepts? The National Council of Teachers of Mathematics (1989) describes concepts as the substance of mathematical knowledge. They are, according to Holmes (1985), ideas that represent a class of objects or events that have certain characteristics in common. Place value, one-half, square, rational number—are examples of broad concepts. Concepts help students make sense of math procedures. As they grasp the meaning of concepts, students begin to think mathematically.

Conceptual knowledge not only is necessary to understand the meaning behind mathematical procedures, but also for determining **when** the various procedures are appropriate to apply in new situations. Emphasis on instruction of concepts may help prevent the development of misunderstandings or "bugs" that result in arithmetical errors.(See Chapter One; Resnick & Omanson, 1986).

In traditional mathematics instruction teaching concepts often takes a back seat to rule and procedural instruction. Often the latter does not include explanations of why the procedure is important, when it is appropriate to use, and how it relates to other procedures and concepts. It is difficult for students to meaningfully apply math procedures in novel problem-solving situations if they do not have a clear understanding of the purpose of the procedure and the concepts that underlie it.

How should teachers lead students to conceptual understanding? Fridriksson and Stewart (1988) recommend a three-step process

1. introduce students to concepts through manipulatives,

2. move to a semi-abstract level of instruction where the knowledge that children have gained through manipulation is connected to symbolism, and

3. present concepts at the symbolic or abstract level.

Instruction should provide students with opportunities to see how the concepts apply in a variety of situations. Ample opportunities to generalize learned concepts should be provided to students, particularly youngsters with learning problems, since these students have difficulties utilizing their knowledge in novel situations (Baroody, in press; Bley & Thornton, 1981; Deshler et al., 1981; Fitzmaurice-Hayes, 1985b).

Concept development is fostered when teachers, as they present concepts, provide numerous examples and non-examples of the concept (Baroody, in press; NCTM, 1989). The example below illustrates this principle.

Instruction also should be designed to help students to see patterns and relationships among concepts (Baroody, 1989a; Baroody, in press; Fennema et al., 1989; Holmes, 1985; Peterson et al., 1988/1989); between concepts and mathematical procedures (Baroody, in press; Hiebert, 1984); and between real world applications and school mathematics. As Fitzmaurice-Hayes (1985b) stresses, it is through the recognition of patterns and relationships that ideas about concepts and rules are initially formed. Figure 4-1 contains an example, based upon an activity suggested by Fitzmaurice-Hayes (1985b), illustrating how students can be helped to draw conclusion about relationships:

Figure 4-1
Helping Students See Patterns and Relationships

Look at the shapes, then follow the directions below.

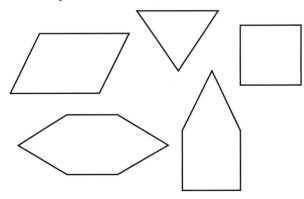

1. For each shape
    • Find the sum of the angles.
    • Divide the sum by 180.
    • Compare your answer to the number of sides in the shape.

2. Compare your answers for each of the figures.
    Do you see a pattern?

Adapted from Fitzmaurice-Hayes, 1985b,

Further, students should be shown how procedures can be represented symbolically and given the opportunity to make these connections, for example, by constructing number sentences to represent the problem posed in a verbal problem (Fennema et al., 1989) or by substituting numbers for symbols as is illustrated below.

```
#####      +  ###    =
5          +  3      =
```

Throughout instruction, teachers should take care to explicitly illustrate the connection between procedures with which children are familiar and the symbols that represent the procedures (Baroody, 1987; Cawley, 1989).

Present Students With Strategies To Appoach Mathematical Problem Solving

One of the goals of cognitive-based mathematics instruction is to help students to become more strategic learners (Baroody, in press; Goldman, 1989; Mayer, 1985; Thornton & Smith, 1988; Thornton & Wilmot, 1986). Students, including many who have learning problems, are thought capable of learning cognitive and metacognitive strategies to assist them in becoming more efficient, effective, and independent learners. Strategies that have been identified as contributing to effective problem solving are visualization and mental imagery, pictorial representation or diagram production, estimation, and checking one's progress (Montague, in press; Montague & Bos, in press).

Numerous strategies have been generated to assist students in performing specific procedures. For example, Thornton and Toohey (1985) have produced and tested strategies that help students master basic number facts. Montague and Bos (1986) developed and tested a process for use by students when solving two-stage word problems, which appears in Figure 4-2.

Strategies can assist students to think and work through math problems. But care must be given to teaching strategy instruction in a meaningful manner and within the context of conceptual learning. Strategies should not contribute to superficial understandings of mathematical procedures (Carnine, in progress). The "key word" approach is an oft-cited example of a strategy gone wrong (Baroody, in press; Cawley & Miller, 1986; Schoenfeld, 1982; Schoenfeld, 1988). Students are taught that "key" words in word problems signal certain operations, for example, "more" signals the need for addition, as is the case in the illustration below.

Figure 4-2
Steps for Working a Two-stage Word Problem

- Read the problem aloud
- Paraphrase the problem aloud
- Visualize the problem
- State the problem, what is known and what is unknown
- Hypothesize
- Estimate
- Calculate

From Montague & Bos, 1986.

> Joe had four marbles. Kyle gave him three more. How many marbles does Joe now have?

However, the following problem also uses the word "more," but solving it requires subtraction, not addition:

> Kate has eight marbles. She has two more marbles than Jennifer. How many marbles does Jennifer have?

A student blindly applying the "key word" strategy would often produce an erroneous answer.

Students must have an understanding of the purpose of the strategy and why and when it should be used if they are to apply it appropriately. Thus, students should be informed of the reason for learning and using a strategy and instructed about when it should and should not be used (Palincsar, 1986; Pressley, et al 1990). Students should be led to see how multiple strategies may be applied to solve problems (Peterson et al., 1988/1989).

Whether or not students thoughtfully and appropriately apply strategies when the need arises also depends upon youngsters' metacognitive capabilities—their ability to assess the demand of a problem, and plan, implement, monitor, and evaluate their selected course of action to solve it (Garofalo & Lester, 1985; Kilpatrick, 1985; Lester, 1985). All students benefit from instruction that fosters the development of metacognitive capabilities, but students with learning problems are in particular need of such instruction (Cawley & Miller, 1986; Cherkes-Julkowski, 1985b; Fitzmaurice-Hayes, 1985b; Rivera & Smith, 1987; Thornton & Wilmot, 1986). Figure 4-3 contains ideas for designing activities that would so assist youngsters.

Figure 4-3
Activities to Help Students Develop Metacognitive Capabilities

- give students a problem and asked them to plan the steps to its solution;
- give students answers to problems, then have them determine the steps that were taken to solve the problems; and
- have students talk out loud as they attempt to solve a problem.

From Cherkes-Julkowski, 1985b

Do Not Ignore the Need to Improve Students' Attitudes and Beliefs about Mathematics

Instruction should not ignore the need to develop positive beliefs and attitudes toward mathematics. Many students, especially those with learning problems, often have negative self-concepts relating to their ability to learn in general and mathematics in particular. These perceptions may be accentuated by instruction that places too much emphasis on memorizing facts and procedures. Such instruction contributes to the belief that mathematics is composed of a set of facts and procedures that are not related to real-world problems and situations (Baroody, 1989a; Schoenfeld, 1987). An undue emphasis on speedy problem solving may lead students who are slower in mathematics performance to conclude they are incapable of grasping mathematical ideas (Baroody, in press).

Therefore, teachers must clearly communicate in word and by action that it is smart for students to ask questions when they do not understand; that errors are a natural part of learning; and that mathematical knowledge gleaned from daily living experiences is relevant to understanding the formal mathematics taught in school (Baroody, in press). To enhance students' motivation, teachers should provide a supportive learning environment, help students establish attainable learning goals, incorporate challenging and interesting problems in mathematics instruction, and stress that effort affects achievement. (Holmes, 1985).

Go Beyond the Teaching of Basic Skills and Present Students With a Comprehensive Mathematics Curriculum

Students in regular education settings generally follow a math curriculum that exposes them to an array of math subjects and topics. The same cannot be said for students who have identified problems with math learning. Because these youngsters experience difficulty with tasks such as memorizing math facts it often is assumed they cannot possibly benefit from instruction in more advanced areas. This assumption has been challenged by some educators who believe that students with learning difficulties can achieve beyond current levels.

John Cawley and his colleagues (1988) have proposed a "priority" curriculum for students with learning problems that includes topics such as space, relations, and figures; basic operations with whole numbers; fractions; measurement; and problem solving. Other professionals have suggested that specific content strands be embedded in and integrated throughout the mathematics curriculum for students with learning problems. Estimation, functions, probability, statistics, algebraic reasoning, translation of symbols, logic, spatial reasoning, geometric figures and properties, and use of calculators have been suggested as strand topics (Bulgren & Montague, 1989). Not all students with learning problems will be able to master all the concepts involved in these areas (Cawley et al., 1988), and, some may not be able to progress beyond the most basic procedures and concepts.

Additional guidance for designing math curriculum and instruction for students with math learning problems within some of the curricular areas referred to above is available in sources such as *Cognitive Strategies and Mathematics for the Learning Disabled* (1985), *Developmental Teaching of Mathematics for the Learning Disabled* (1984), and *Secondary School Mathematics for the Learning Disabled* (1985), all edited by John Cawley; *Mathematics for the Mildly Handicapped—A Guide to Curriculum and Instruction* (1988) by John Cawley, Anne Marie Fitzmaurice-Hayes, and Robert Shaw; *A Guide to Teaching Mathematics in the Primary Grades* (1989) and *Children's Mathematical Thinking* (1987) by Arthur J. Baroody; *Teaching Mathematics to Children with Special Needs* (1983) by Carol Thornton, Benny Tucker, John Dossey, and Edna Bazik; and *Teaching Mathematics to the Learning Disabled* (1981) by Nancy Bley and Carol Thornton. *The National Council of Teachers of Mathematics' Curriculum and Evaluation Standards for School Mathematics* (1989) also provides examples of teaching ideas and activities.

HOW SHOULD MATHEMATIC INSTRUCTION BE PRESENTED?

Be Sensitive to the Developmental Level of the Students

In the primary grades, in particular, developmental factors affect what students understand about math. Teachers should be sensitive to how children mature cognitively, and design instruction to facilitate the acquisition of concepts that lead to greater understanding (Baroody, in press; Fuson & Secada, 1986; Secada et al., 1983; Thornton et al., 1983;

Thornton, 1989b). Math learning proceeds from the concrete, incomplete, and unsystematic to the abstract, complete, and systematic. Students progress through these stages at different rates, and these variations in student learning patterns must be taken into account by teachers as they sequence topics for instruction (Peterson et al., 1988/89). While teachers need to be sensitive to developmental levels of students and not expect too much, too soon, they need also understand that students can be assisted in concept and skill development by appropriate instruction (Fennema et al., 1989).

Build Upon Students' Prior Knowledge About Mathematics

Too often, teachers do not take advantage of students' prior mathematical knowledge. Lesson content should be framed to draw connections between what a youngster already knows and understands and what is to be learned (Allardice & Ginsburg, 1983; Baroody, in press; Fennema et al., 1989; Fridriksson & Stewart, 1988; Silver, 1987; Trafton, 1984). This instructional connecting needs to commence when formal mathematics instruction is first presented, since most students, including those with learning problems, start school with a store of informal mathematical knowledge upon which formal school instruction can be built (Baroody, 1987; Baroody, 1989a; Romberg & Carpenter, 1986).

Cast Instruction Within A Problem-Solving Framework

Mathematics instruction should be presented within a problem-solving context. Doing so helps introduce youngsters to mathematical operations and the reasoning behind them (Baroody, 1987; Carnine & Vandegrift, 1989; Cawley, 1989; Peterson et al., 1988/1989). To the extent possible, teachers should seek problem solving opportunities in everyday situations. For example, on the first day of the baseball world series, a teacher could ask students who want the National League team to win to stand on one side of the room, students who want the American League team to stand on the other side of the room, and students who do not care who wins to remain seated. After students determine the number of their peers in each category, the teacher could lead them to use these data to explore concepts such as more or less, percentages, majority and plurality. This simple exercise could serve as the basis for exploring such concepts as more and less, categories, and percentages.

The following activity is another example of how students are led into a math lesson through a problem solving activity.

- *Place students in small groups. Give one child in each group several tokens and ask the child to give two tokens to every student in his or her group.*

- *Next, give one student in each group several tokens and ask the child to distribute them so that each group member has the same number of tokens.*

- *Then give a student in each group some tokens and direct the child to divide the tokens in such a way that all the children in the group receive an equal number (Adapted from Carnine & Vandegrift, 1989).*

The preceding activity introduces students informally to the concept of division in the context of sharing, an issue that is important to children. Such types of problems allow students to work from their knowledge base and to become comfortable with the concept of dividing before the word "division" and its formal, symbolic representation are introduced (Cawley, 1989).

Word problems either written or posed orally, can also serve to engage students in a problem-solving activity and help them to improve their problem-solving capabilities (Fennema et al., 1989). Teachers need be aware, however, that not all word problems are of equal difficulty or require the same strategies to be solved. Several factors contribute to word problem difficulty including the action required to solve the problem and the information provided and not provided. Numerous taxonomies of word problems have been constructed by researchers (for example, see Carpenter, 1985; Peterson et al., 1988/1989; Riley, 1981; Riley et al., 1983) to help illustrate differences among problem types and to provide guidance for teachers and instructional designers when developing and constructing problems. Table 4-2 presents frequently referred-to categories of word problems. These examples illustrate how the complexity of problems change with the major action required (i.e, change, combine, compare, and equalize); the information that is provided; and the information that needs to be determined.

Studies have been conducted to determine how difficult these various types of problems are for young children to solve. Research has focused on problems categorized as change, combine, or compare items (Carpenter, 1985; Carpenter & Moser, 1982; Carpenter & Moser, 1984). The results of these studies indicate that generally most types of compare problems pose more difficulties for younger children (kindergartners and first graders) than do most type of problems in the change and combine categories. But it should be noted that considerable differences in difficulty are evident among items within categories. For example, combine problems that involve subtraction are more difficult for young children to solve than those involving addi-

Table 4-2
Taxonomy of Word Problem Types*

CHANGE	RESULT UNKNOWN	CHANGE UNKNOWN	START UNKNOWN
by adding	Maria has 3 crayons. Kyle gave her 4 more. How many crayons does Maria have now?	Maria has 3 crayons. How many more does she need to have 7?	Maria has some crayons. Kyle gave her 3 more. Now she has 7. How many crayons did Maria have to start with?
by subtracting	Maria had 7 crayons. She gave 4 to Kyle. How many crayons does Maria have left?	Maria has 7 crayons. She gave some to Kyle. Maria has 3 crayons left. How many crayons did she give to Kyle?	Maria had some crayons. She gave 4 to Kyle. She has 3 left. How many crayons did Maria have to start with?

COMBINE	TOTAL MISSING	PART MISSING
by adding	Abby has 10 orange balloons and 2 green ones. How many balloons does she have altogether?	
by subtracting		Abby has 12 balloons. Two are green and the rest are orange. How many orange balloons does Abby have?

Table 4-2 (cont.)

	DIFFERENCE UNKNOWN	COMPARED QUALITY UNKNOWN	REFERENT UNKNOWN
COMPARE			
by adding	Joey has 12 pencils. David has 7 pencils. How many more pencils does Joey have than David?	David has 7 pencils. Joey has 5 more pencils than David. How many pencils does Joey have?	Joey has 12 pencils. He has 5 more pencils than David. how many pencils does David have?
by subtracting	Joey has 12 pencils. David has 7 pencils. How many fewer pencils does David have than Joey?	Joey has 12 pencils. David has 5 fewer pencils than Joey. How many pencils does David have?	David has 7 pencils. He has 5 fewer pencils than Joey. How many pencils does Joey have?
EQUALIZE			
by adding	Jesse has 6 stickers. Tina has 4 stickers. How many more stickers does Jesse have than Tina?	Tina has 4 stickers. If she collects 2 more, she will have the same number of stickers as Jesse. How many stickers does Jesse have?	Jesse has 6 stickers. If Tina collects 2 more stickers she will have as many stickers as Jesse. How many stickers does Tina have?
by subtracting	Jesse has 6 stickers. Tina has 4 stickers. How many stickers does Jesse need to lose to have the same number of stickers as Tina?	Tina has 4 stickers. If Jesse loses 2 stickers he will have the same number of stickers as Tina. How many stickers does Jesse have?	Jesse has 6 stickers. If he loses 2 he will have the same number of stickers as Tina. How many stickers does Tina have?

* This taxonomy was constructed based on information appearing in Baroody, A., and Standifer, D. (in progress); Carpenter (1985); Peterson, P., Fennema, E., and Carpenter, T. (1988/89); Riley, M. (1981); and Riley, M., Greene, J., and Heller, J. (1983).

tion, and change problems when the starting amount is unknown are more difficult than the other types of change problems (Riley, 1981).

As a rule, children gain proficiency in word problem solving within all categories as they progress through the primary grades, i.e., as they acquire more advanced concepts and skills (Carpenter, 1985; Carpenter & Moser, 1982; Carpenter & Moser, 1984; Riley, 1981; Riley et al., 1983). Children can be assisted in their concept and skill development if their instruction incorporates an array of word problems that vary in their complexity (Fennema et al., 1989).

Thus, when selecting word problems, teachers should choose those that are challenging enough to lead students to more sophisticated problem-solving behavior. Guidelines for constructing or selecting word problems appear in Figure 4-4.

Problem-based approaches to teaching mathematics, then, should serve to extend students' conceptual knowledge (Holmes, 1985), provide youngsters with the opportunity to apply the procedures and skills they have acquired (Zhu & Simon, 1987), foster the development of metacognitive capabilities (Cawley et al., 1987), and illustrate why and how mathematics is important in daily living.

Question and Listen to Students

Teachers need to rely heavily on questioning and listening to students explain the thinking and reasoning they use to solve problems (Garofalo & Standifer, 1989). Teachers can use information obtained from such conversations to assess and analyze the student's degree of understanding (Fennema et al., 1989; Garofalo, 1987; Good et al., 1983). To engage in questioning and listening, particularly of individual students, requires that instruction be organized to allow teachers the opportunity to interact with students. It also requires that teachers be aware of how to effectively construct questions best in conferences with students. Guidelines for constructing questions are found in Figure 4-5.

Utilize Small Group Learning Situations

Research indicates that small group work can enhance students' conceptual development and computational capabilities (Slavin et al., 1984; Slavin & Karweit,1985). Small group work also is believed to facilitate problem solving (Garofalo & Standifer, 1989; Holmes, 1985; Schoenfeld, 1987; Silver, 1985). Group work requires that students communicate and discuss the problem to be solved. Talking about problems can help students to integrate new knowledge with what they already know (Fitzmaurice-Hayes, 1985b, Thornton, 1989a), and

Figure 4-4
Guidelines for selecting or constructing word problems

- Use nonroutine problems. These include items that have too much, too little, or incorrect information; can be solved in more than one way; have multi-steps; have more than one possible answer; and/or require an analysis of the unknown (Baroody, 1987). Examples of some categories of these types of problems include

Analysis of the unknown: Max and Steve want to buy a Frisbee that costs $4.00. Max has $1.00 and Steve has $2.00. Do Max and Steve have enough money to buy the Frisbee?

Too much, too little, or incorrect information: Ann ate two brownies for dessert. Her brother Peter ate one. There are six brownies left. How many brownies did both Ann and Peter eat?

Leslie gave two baseball cards to Jill, four to Keith, and three to Brian. How many baseball cards does Leslie have left?

Problems solved in more than one way: Anna had 50 cents when she went to the grocery store. She wanted to buy a candy bar that cost 40 cents and a jawbreaker that cost 5 cents. Did she have money enough to buy both? (This problem can be solved by adding the cost of the items and subtracting that from 50 cents or by subtracting 40 cents from 50 cents then subtracting 5 cents from 10 cents).

Multi-step problem: Tim has painted five pictures to give away as presents. He wants to give one each to his mother, his father, his grandmother, his grandfather, his uncle, his sister, and his brother. Has he painted enough pictures?

Problems with more than one answer: Julie is at her school festival. She has 90 cents. Balloons cost 25 cents, candied apples cost 35 cents, hot dogs cost 50 cents and ride tickets cost 25 cents each. What can Julie buy?

- Modify problems as necessary to accommodate the learning problems of students. For example, if a student has difficulty reading a problem, rewrite it (Cawley et al., 1987).

- Consider using a few interesting and challenging problems as opposed to many trivial ones (Baroody, in press; Bley & Thornton, 1981; Cawley, 1989).

- Allow students to construct their own word problems (Bulgren & Montague, 1989; Cawley et al., 1987).

justify their selection of solution approaches. Listening to what their peers have to say do can lead students to more mature problem-solving strategies (Fennema et al., 1989). More information about small group learning and its use with mathematics and other instruction may be found in Chapter 5.

Model Problem Solving

Teacher modeling of problem-solving activities and strategy applications is a technique frequently used in teaching to demonstrate procedures or cognitive strategies for solving problems, to explain the reasoning behind the actions and to demonstrate metacognitive behavior. Modeling has the potential for being an effective instructional technique when it does not lead students to the false conclusion that mathematical problem solving is a neat, clear cut process (Schoenfeld, 1987). Cherkes-Julkowski (1985b) warns that many students are adept at memorizing and performing steps to a process modeled by the teacher without having grasped the meaning behind it. As with other techniques, teachers need to use modeling judiciously and in combination with other methods such as questioning and listening. An example of how a teacher may model problem solving appears in Figure 4-6.

Use Manipulatives and Calculators When Appropriate

Use of manipulatives is frequently recommended as a good method for providing a concrete visualization of abstract concepts and of

---

Figure 4-5
Guidelines for Constructing Questions for Use in Conferences

A teacher should ask questions that help students to

- recall knowledge they may already possess from their past experiences or former lessons;
- think through the processes they should follow to solve the problem;
- explain the steps that they followed to solve the problem and articulate why they chose them;
- identify alternative ways to solve the problem;
- identify other problem-solving situations in which the chosen process could be correctly applied.

Figure 4-6
An Example of Teacher Modeling of Problem Solving

Teacher: When I am faced with a problem that I know has several steps I try to take the problem apart and work it through that way. For example, let's look at the following problem

Sara is trying to decide whether or not to join a book club that will send her, every month, three new paperback books from her favorite reading series. She thinks this will be an easy way to receive books she likes to read every month. Every time these books are sent, Sara will receive a bill of $12.95 for the books and $2.95 for the cost of mailing of them. Sara knows that she often can find these books in a bookstore, and when she does they cost about $4.95 each plus about 25 cents in tax. And, the library also has some of the books. But because these books are popular among girls Sara's age, they often are checked out when Sara wants to read them.

Every week Sara receives three dollars for an allowance and another three to four dollars for baby sitting for her little brother.

Sara wants to know first if she can afford to join the book club and if it would save her money if she did.

Now, a lot of information is presented in this problem. I need to sort it all out. First, I need to find out what I know or can easily figure out. Lets see, I know that if Sara joins the club she will have to pay $12.95 plus $2.95 a month. So I'll add those numbers together (Teacher goes to board and adds the two numbers.) The cost to Sara would be $15.90 per month. (Teacher writes on the board, "Cost to be a club member is $15.90 a month.")

Next, I think I'll try to figure out the cost to Sara if she bought three books at the bookstore. The problem says that these books usually cost about $4.95 a piece plus about 25 cents taxes. First I'll determine the cost of a book at the bookstore by adding together $4.95 and 25 cents (Teacher adds on the board.) I get $5.20. (Teacher writes on the board, "Bookstore cost for a book is about $5.20.) Now to get the cost of three of these books a month I need to multiply by three, which I will do. (Teacher multiplies $5.20 by three.) I get an answer of $15.60. (Teacher writes, "Cost for three books bought at bookstore is $15.60.)

Now I think I have enough information to determine whether or not Sara would save money by joining the book club. It costs $15.90 for the three books bought through the book club and $15.60 at the bookstore. So, it is more expensive by 30 cents a month to be a member of the book club.

Next, I need to determine if Sara can afford to join the club if she wants to. Let's see she gets $3 a week allowance and another $3-$4 for baby sitting so that is about $6-$7 dollar per week she has to spend. There are about four weeks in a month so to get an estimate of how much income Sara receives I'll multiply that number by 4. (Teacher, on the board, multiplies 6 by 4 then 7 by 4). O.K. I determined that Sara receives from $24 to $28 dollars per month (Teacher writes, "Sara's monthly income is between $24 and $28 dollars.) Well I can now answer the other part of the question. Sara with an income of $24 to $28 per month can afford to join the book club costing $15.90 a month if she wishes to do so. I also know that it is cheaper for Sara to just buy the books at a bookstore.

actively involving students in the learning process (Cawley, 1989; Fleischner et al., 1982; Good et al., 1983; Hendricks, 1983;Holmes, 1985; Kennedy, 1986; Thornton & Wilmot, 1986). Although manipulatives can accomplish these ends, they do not automatically provide support for abstract thinking (Callahan & MacMillan, 1981; Garofalo & Standifer, 1989). That is to say, students can mindlessly manipulate items without reflecting on the why of their activity or without understanding the reasoning behind it (Baroody, 1989c).

Successful use of manipulatives requires thoughtful planning and organization (Martin & Carnahan, 1989). Thornton and Toohey (1986) offer guidelines for using manipulatives with students with learning problems. They suggest:

- *The teacher should question students about their actions as they work with manipulatives.*
- *Have students verbalize their thinking.*
- *Require students to write out the problems that they have solved with manipulatives.*
- *Have students use manipulatives to check answers.*

Many educators believe that greater use of calculators would free students from burdensome calculations and give them more time to engage in problem-solving activities (Bulgren & Montague, 1989; Callahan & MacMillan, 1981; Cawley & Miller, 1986; Fitzmaurice-Hayes, 1985c). However, calculators should not be used as a substitute for procedural understanding. Fitzmaurice-Hayes (1985c) cautions that knowledge of basic number concepts, understanding of place value, knowing the four operations, and some knowledge of mathematical facts should be prerequisites for calculator use. Too, introduction of calculators into instruction underscores the need to teach students to estimate and judge the reasonableness of their answers (NCTM, 1989).

It is important to remember that calculator use does not come naturally to many students and that some students will need to be explicitly instructed and given practice in the appropriate and effective application of calculators (Bulgren & Montague, 1989).

Regularly Assess Students' Problem-Solving Capabilites

Teachers need to determine the progress students are making in developing their mathematical thinking and learning applicable skills and strategies. Through conferencing, teachers can informally determine what students understand and why. While this ongoing informal assessment is an integral part of cognitive-based instruction, more formal assessments also are needed. These may include formal observations of students' problem solving as well as paper and pencil tests.

HOW MEDIA AND MATERIALS CAN SUPPORT TEACHING PROBLEM SOLVING

Media and materials can be invaluable in assisting teachers to reinforce math instruction intended to help students become more strategic problem solvers. They can support both the content and teaching methods recommended in the preceding discussion. This chapter ends with a checklist of media and material characteristics to assist school district personnel in selecting materials for classroom use.

Support for Content Related Recommendations

Materials can emphasize conceptual learning and mathematical relationships by providing ample illustrations and representations of concepts (Fitzmaurice-Hayes, 1985b).

Materials should support activities that actively involve children in making connections between mathematical ideas or concepts. For example, the learning of the concept of place value could be facilitated by use of worksheets containing multiple images of items, such as sticks, cars, and stars, which children would be asked to group. Doing so helps students to see the connection between individual units and groups of units, for example, that seven individual items or units can be placed into a group containing seven items (Baroody, 1989b).

Such a method for teaching place value contrasts with the usual presentations found in texts and other materials. Typically, students are shown pre-bundled items—ten sticks, for example—that are intended to represent a group of ten. Representations of pre-bundled items do not help children to actively construct the unit and group concepts (Baroody, 1989b).

Illustrations in classroom materials help students see the relationships between symbolic representations and the procedures for which they stand (Baroody, 1987).

Explanations of concepts should precede or accompany procedural instruction. Materials should never use explanations that are conceptually incorrect for the sake of expediency. For example, directions for completing long division problems sometimes instruct students to begin solving an item such as $5 \div 127$ by asking, "Does 5 go into 1?", and if the answer is no, to then ask, "Does 5 go into 12?" This type of direction can lead to confusion since the 1 referred to is actually 100, and the 12 is 120. While children may be easily taught this procedure, it will do little to expand their understanding of what they actually are doing when they divide (Carnine & Vandegrift, 1989).

Appropriate materials can assist students to learn and apply an array of cognitive and metacognitive strategies by providing demonstrations of the use of strategies, explanations of the purpose for and reasoning behind the application of the strategies, and illustrations of how strategies can be applied in a variety of subjects and different kinds of content. Materials also could inclue exercises such as those requiring students to identify when the application of a specific strategy facilitates or works against the solving of certain problems. Videotapes may be particularly helpful in illustrating these behaviors to students.

Appropriate materials should provide teachers with numerous ideas for how to approach the teaching of mathematical concepts, strategies, and procedures (Bulgren & Montague, 1989). These suggestions can help teachers to introduce a lesson, listen to and question students, prompt students' prior knowledge, and present the lesson. Videotape sample scripts, illustrating the application of various techniques would be of assistance to many teachers.

Materials can assist students to develop a positive attitude toward math by providing suggestions for adapting instruction to meet the learning needs of particular students. Especially important when teaching students with learning problems, are providing examples of how activities could be adapted to make them more accessible, making problems less complex, suggesting alternative algorithms, and allowing for the flexible presentation of content (Carnine & Vandegrift, 1989). Considerable variation in learning potential exists among students with learning problems. These youngsters may tend to learn at a slower rate than nonhandicapped students and they may not be able to cover as much content as students without learning problems.

Materials, particularly textbooks, could assist teachers by providing an integrated presentation of topics across units and chapters. For example, a topic introduced in an earlier unit could be explicitly related to newly introduced topics. Activities throughout the text would help further develop skills and reinforce the texts or instructor's guide introduced earlier (Bulgren & Montague, 1989). The text or instructor's guide could provide suggestions for activities which can be presented before the topic is formally taught.

Teachers are helped when materials

- *identify those areas and activities that are most important to emphasize and those which could be de-emphasized (Carnine & Vandegrift, 1989);*

- *present content in small steps (Bley & Thornton, 1981) and in a format that is clear and understandable (Callahan & MacMillan, 1981);*

- *provide meaningful reinforcement and further development of skills introduced earlier (Bulgren & Montague, 1989); and*

- *provide ample practice activities at the concrete and conceptual as well as the symbolic level (Bley & Thornton, 1981; Cawley, 1984c).*

Support for Teaching Methods

Media and materials can assist teachers by providing support for techniques that facilitate meaningful mathematics learning.

Be sensitive to children's mathematical development. Cognitive approaches stress the need for teachers to be sensitive to children's mathematical development. Many teachers are not aware of the research that describes the normal course of growth in children's mathematical thinking and how instruction can facilitate or hinder students' mathematics learning. Clear summaries of this research and its implications for instruction of specific concepts and procedures should be made available as part of materials used in service activities and in teacher guides (Bulgren & Montague, 1989; Garofalo & Standifer, 1989).

Build upon prior knowledge. Teachers need ample illustrations and suggestions for how to connect what students are likely to know about a given math topic to new information. In other words, they need guidance in tapping into the math knowledge that children already possess. Frequently this knowledge will not have originated from math classes, but rather from the students' own life experiences and problems they personally have confronted.

Cast instruction within a problem-solving framework. Supplementary materials can feature word problems as vehicles for introducing mathematical procedures as opposed to using them solely as end-of-lesson practice exercises (Baroody, 1989b; Cawley, 1989; Peterson et al., 1988/1989). A variety of word problems are needed for use in instruction (Baroody, 1987; Carnine, in progress; Cawley et al., 1987; Marten, 1989).

Textbooks have been criticized for having too many simple word problems included as exercises. One analysis of an elementary math textbook series revealed that over 90% of the word problems could be solved by applying the "key word" strategy referred to earlier (Cawley, 1985b; Cawley et al., 1988).

Textbooks need

1. *challenging word problems (Baroody, 1987);*

2. *problems that depend on what the student has learned earlier;*

3. *integrate mathematics with other subjects;*

4. *require the application of a variety of math procedures;*

5. *require the collection and analysis of data, and drawing of conclusions;*

6. *provide suggestions to teachers for altering the complexity of problems to match the math functioning level of the individual students.*

Figure 4-7

Checklist For Determining if Elementary-level Classroom Resources Incorporate Principles of Cognitive Instruction

Yes　　No

- Does the material contain ample illustrations examples and non examples of concepts such as the one immediately following for one-half?

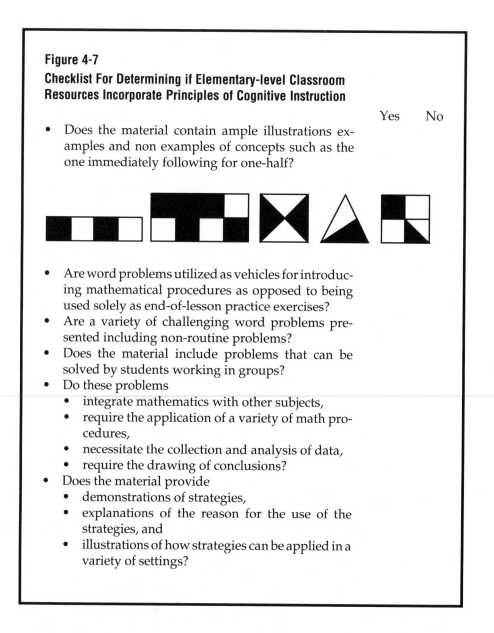

- Are word problems utilized as vehicles for introducing mathematical procedures as opposed to being used solely as end-of-lesson practice exercises?
- Are a variety of challenging word problems presented including non-routine problems?
- Does the material include problems that can be solved by students working in groups?
- Do these problems
  - integrate mathematics with other subjects,
  - require the application of a variety of math procedures,
  - necessitate the collection and analysis of data,
  - require the drawing of conclusions?
- Does the material provide
  - demonstrations of strategies,
  - explanations of the reason for the use of the strategies, and
  - illustrations of how strategies can be applied in a variety of settings?

7. *whenever possible, include problems based on situations and topics that are of interest to students and/or relate to their world (Bley & Thornton, 1981; Bulgren & Montague, 1989; Callahan & MacMillan, 1981; Cawley et al., 1987; Cawley et al., 1988).*

8. *problems based in familiar contexts that allow students to utilize their prior knowledge in interpreting the demands of the problem.*

Figure 4-7 (cont.)

                                                   Yes   No

- Are recommendations included for ways teacher can utilize manipulatives to help illustrate concepts and procedures?
- Is guidance provided to the teacher for how to plan for and monitor students' use of the manipulatives to ensure that youngsters understand the *why* of their activity?
- Is the material designed to be used flexibly to meet the varying learning needs of children with disabilities by
    - identifying those areas and activities that are most important to emphasize and those which could be de-emphasized;
    - presenting content in small steps;
    - providing meaningful reinforcement and further development of skills introduced earlier; and
    - incorporating ample practice activities at the concrete and conceptual as well as symbolic level?
- Does the teacher guide for the material provide
    - background information about children's mathematical thinking and development;
    - numerous ideas for how to approach the teaching of concepts, strategies and procedures provided;
    - examples for how activities could be adapted to make them more accessible to students experiencing learning problems; and
    - ideas for how teachers could assess students to determine their level of understanding?

Questioning and listening to students. Classroom materials can provide teachers with ideas for questions to ask to students and guidelines as to what to listen for in student responses. Videotapes can be exceptionally helpful in providing illustrations of teachers questioning students and responding to student questions.

Small group learning. Materials, particularly textbooks, should provide more activities specifically designed for group problem solving. Such group problem-solving activities offer opportunities to embed mathematically-related problems within the context of other subject areas such as science, social studies and health. Good and his colleagues (1989/1990) point out that the lack of curriculum materials designed for small group work has served to impede implementation of this method of instruction in mathematics. These authors also point out that when materials are lacking and teachers must create their own classroom resources for group work, lack of continuity of content within classes and across grades often results. Well-designed classroom materials could help provide such continuity. More information about these materials which can facilitate small group learning appears in Chapter Five.

Manipulatives and calculators. Textbooks and supplementery materials could provide directions and recommendations for when-manipulatives could be used to illustrate a concept or procedure or to learn concepts. Explicit instruction and guidelines would help teachers know when problem solving and the type of exercises and problems that can guide students to greater proficiency. Activities that provide students with practice in estimating and judging the reasonableness of their answers should be interwoven throughout materials (Bulgren & Montague, 1989).

Modeling. Teachers may benefit from inservice experiences of teachers' modeling strategies. Videotapes would be particularly helpful to teachers.

Assessing students. Teachers need to be provided with techniques and ideas for designing assessment procedures that will help them determine the degree to which youngsters understand and apply math concepts.

Teachers also could benefit from guidelines for analyzing common computational errors made by students (Carnine & Vandegrift, 1989; Maurer, 1987). Children frequently develop "buggy" algorithms due to misunderstandings of concepts. Teachers need to know how to identify these bugs and how to help students to a more accurate understanding of the concepts and correct procedures.

Figure 4-7 contains a checklist of features of media and material suggested to support the teaching of mathematics from a cognitive, strategic perspective. This checklist can assist school personnel to make judgements about the adequacy of classroom materials.

CHAPTER FIVE

Developing Students' Strategic Learning Capabilities Through the Application of Collaborative Learning Methods

Actively involving students with other students in the learning process is a common theme in discussions of how to best lead students to becoming more effective and efficient learners and problem solvers. Teaching methods too often have underplayed the social aspects of learning. Through designing and utilizing collaborative learning methods such as peer tutoring and cooperative learning, teachers can capitalize on the social nature of learning and promote cognitive growth. Teachers should be aware that these grouping methods, which usually involve students with varying abilities and skills, contrast with homogenous grouping methods that have been used frequently to better manage the delivery of instruction, particularly in the teaching of basic skills. Reading groups, where students of like-abilities are brought together for reading instruction, are a common example of homogeneous grouping. Teachers who form homogeneous groups reason that children learn basic skills best when they are taught withchildren of similar abilities.

While homogeneously grouping students may be beneficial in helping some students achieve learning objectives on some occasions, this practice has negative consequences especially for students with learning problems. Research shows that students with learning problems perform worse in homogeneous groups than they do when instructed along with students of differing abilities (Cohen & Benton, 1988). The continued use of like-ability grouping for instruction may stem more from tradition than from proof of its effectiveness.

To explore whether or not grouping methods that involve students of differing abilities foster the improvement of peer socialization and the enhancement of students' problem solving and reasoning skills, researchers have designed and conducted studies to investigate questions such as: How can group learning techniques be used to assist students in acquiring higher order learning skills? Are social benefits derived from group instruction and, if so, under what conditions? Can grouping facilitate mainstreaming of students with disabilities? How do group structure, composition, and goals affect academic achievement?

Findings of these studies point to the potential of group learning to meet a multitude of educational objectives, at various grade levels, and with a variety of students.

WHAT RESEARCH REVEALS ABOUT COLLABORATIVE LEARNING

Collaborative learning methods have been well researched compared to many other educational interventions (Bailey & Dyck, 1990; Sharan, 1990; Slavin, 1991b). In general, research findings substantiate the two major claims made by advocates of collaborative learning methods, namely that group learning in general improves the academic performance of students and also enhances their relationships with their peers.

Effects on Academic Performance of Students in Regular Classrooms.

Collaborative learning methods have been successful in improving the academic performance of students at various age and grade levels and subject areas, such as

- mathematics (Maheady, 1988a; Slavin et al., 1984b; Slavin, 1985c; Slavin 1989/90);

- reading (Greenwood et al., 1984; Slavin, 1989/90; Stevens et al., 1987; Topping, 1989);

- spelling (Delquadri et al., 1983; Greenwood et al., 1984);

- writing instruction (Slavin, 1989/90; Stevens et al., 1987);

- social studies (Maheady et al., 1988b; Maheady et al., 1991; Sharan et al., 1980; Sharan & Shackar, 1988); and

- science (Johnson et al., 1985; Lazarowitz & Karsenty, 1989).

While most studies have focused on the impact of collaborative learning methods on students' acquisition of fundamental skills such as mathematical procedures or spelling, some research results have pointed to the potential of group work to help students develop higher order thinking skills. For example, studies of reading comprehension and writing composition conducted by Slavin, Stevens, and their colleagues (Slavin et al., 1988; Stevens et al., 1987; Stevens & Slavin, 1991a) involved students in learning activities such as creative writing, drawing inferences, and identifying main ideas. Studies of the Group Investigation method have produced findings that students participating in group instruction performed better on assessments involving both recall and analysis of information than their peers taught through whole-class instruction. This was true when Group Investigation was used in history, geography, and biology instruction (Lazarowitz & Karsenty, 1989; Sharan & Shackar, 1988).

Effects on Academic Performance of Students with Learning Problems

Results of research indicate that for regular education students, collaborative learning generally yields positive results. However, results from studies involving students with learning problems have been mixed. A review of twenty-four peer tutoring studies involving learning disabled students, concluded that students with learning disabilities can and do learn in peer tutoring situations, but, it was not clear that tutoring is more effective than other instructional techniques (Scruggs and Richter, 1986). Tateyama-Sniezek (1990) reviewed twelve selected studies of cooperative learning that involved students with learning problems and concluded that generalizations about its effectiveness were difficult to make, since only half of the studies she reviewed reported significant results in favor of group learning.

These conclusions lead to a key question: "Are certain techniques used in collaborative learning more effective than others?" The answer appears to be yes. For example, students in general are more likely to meet with success when they are instructed in well-structured, more cognitively-oriented programs (Cohen et al., 1982), and when they are required as a part of their group work to give and receive explanations of answers (Webb, 1985).

Stevens and Slavin (1991b) contend that students with learning problems will show greater academic improvement in group learning situations when all group members are held individually accountable for their learning and when group reward is based upon the achievement of its members. Four of the studies analyzed by Tateyama-Sniezek met these reward conditions and measured academic impact, and four studies showed positive results in academic learning, although the findings in two studies did not reach significance. Clearly, determining what factors contribute most to successful group learning experiences merits more scrutiny (Fantuzzo, 1991; Scruggs & Richter, 1986).

Collaborative Learning's Influence on Peer Relationships

If findings regarding the academic benefits of using collaborative learning methods with students with learning problems are equivocal, why would a teacher of students with disabilities consider use of group approaches? The answer may be for the social benefits; group learning methods appear to improve relationships between students with disabilities and their nonhandicapped peers.

Two major concerns for teachers attempting to mainstream these students are helping them become comfortable in a regular classroom setting and helping them improve their relationships with their nonhandicapped peers. Research strongly supports the conclusion that collaborative learning methods are beneficial for improving communication and relationships between students with disabilities and their nonhandicapped classmates (Johnson & Johnson, 1982, 1984b, 1986; Johnson et al., 1985; Maheady et al., 1988a; Pigott et al., 1986; Rynders et al., 1981; Slavin, 1985b,1991b; Slavin et al., 1984; Wolfe et al., 1986) and for improving the social acceptance of mainstreamed special education students (Slavin, 1985c).

But successful social outcomes are not guaranteed. Cohen (1990) points out that while low-achieving students frequently do better academically in collaborative learning than in traditional instructional settings, they frequently are less active and influential in the group than their higher-achieving classmates. She stresses the importance of designing group work to help overcome status problems that may develop (Cohen, 1986).

HOW COLLABORATIVE LEARNING METHODS CONTRIBUTE TO THE DEVELOPMENT OF STRATEGIC LEARNERS

As was discussed in the above section, positive academic and social outcomes frequently are the result of collaborative learning methods. Several explanations have been offered as to why collaborative learning reaps these benefits. First, collaborative learning brings the politics of the playground into the classroom (Fantuzzo, 1991). In other words, it capitalizes on children's natural desire to be engaged in activity with each other. When instruction employs children's natural inclination to engage in activities with their peers, the chances for positive learning outcomes are enhanced. And when groups as well as individual students are rewarded for their academic achievement, peer norms will evolve that come to favor rather than oppose high achievement (Slavin 1986). Thus, collaborative learning methods can motivate students to learn (Good, 1989/90; Sharan, 1990).

Second, collaborative learning methods help students to learn how to work with others to achieve a common goal (Johnson et al., 1984). Group methods capture some of the dynamics of sports and team play loved by most students (Slavin, 1990b). Positive interdependence is required in many group approaches if success is to be realized by all (Johnson & Johnson, 1990; Male, 1986). Experiencing such interdependence leads students to understand that by working together they can be smarter and more powerful than they can be working on their own (Sapon-Shevin & Schniedewind, 1989/90). This is an important lesson to learn since more often than not workplace and family situations require cooperative efforts to achieve goals. Indeed, it has been suggested that the quality of one's adult life depends on one's ability to work with others (Johnson & Johnson, 1989/90).

Third, improvement in the self-esteem of students involved in collaborative learning groups has been noted (Johnson & Johnson, 1989b; Slavin, 1991b). Groups provide social support for efforts of their members (Brown & Palincsar, 1989). This support along with the student's knowledge that he or she has contributed to the group functioning and product no doubt contributes to enhancement of self-esteem.

Fourth, group learning provides students with an opportunity to talk among themselves about the learning task. This type of peer to peer exchange may help students to develop conceptual understanding, problem solving capabilities, and higher order thinking skills (Charles et al., 1987; Meyers, 1986). Students learn most effectively when they have ample opportunities to respond to others and receive immediate feedback on their performance (Maheady et al., 1988a). Such interaction appears to be particularly important for development of higher order skills. Theories of cognitive development emphasize that change in children's learning results from their internalizing cognitive activities originally experienced in the company of others (Brown & Palincsar, 1989). Teacher-student interaction can serve this purpose, but demands on the teacher's time in the classroom limits the opportunity for such exchanges. Cooperative learning and peer tutoring situations can offer at least a partial substitute for teacher-student interaction (Delquadri et al., 1986; Jenkins & Jenkins, 1985). In addition, group work provides students with the opportunity for meaningfully applying concepts and ideas (Cohen & Benton, 1988).

Fifth, group learning provides opportunities for social skills development among students with diverse abilities and provides teachers with an efficient instructional structure with which to accommodate the varying learning needs of students (Conway & Gow, 1988). Group learning methods also can help teachers adapt learning environments to better meet the instructional needs of students from diverse cultural backgrounds. Palincsar & Brown (1989) point out that in some cultures, learning may more naturally occur in collaborative situations than in the traditional, teacher directed classroom where teachers generate questions to which students are expected to respond.

EXAMPLES OF GROUP LEARNING METHODS

Numerous group learning programs have been developed over the past several years. These collaborative learning approaches generally fall within one of two categories: cooperative learning or peer tutoring. In cooperative learning methods, students work in small groups to help one another learn (Slavin, 1989). These groups may be formed to achieve an array of instructional objectives and often involve the production of a group product. Groups are generally composed of between three to six students (Davidson, 1985). Peer tutoring involves students directly teaching other children (Maheady et al., 1988b). Often this arrangement involves the assignment of one student to help a same-aged or younger student learn particular subject matter (Davidson, 1985).

Both cooperative learning and peer tutoring are characterized by active student involvement and require that students work together to accomplish a learning objective. In this sense one or all students in collaborative learning groups function as instructional agents for other group members. In the case of cooperative learning, group members often need to pool their expertise in order to accomplish the group goal.

Two of the most popular collaborative learning approaches emerging over the last few years have been developed by David Johnson and Roger Johnson at the University of Minnesota and Robert Slavin and his associates at Johns Hopkins University. The Johnsons' approach does not use a set curriculum nor is it targeted to a specific grade level or subject area. Rather it is a flexible approach that advocates the application of a set of principles when implementing cooperative learning in the classroom. Teachers are to design learning to foster positive interdependence in group work, give students a chance to interact face-to-face, establish individual accountability measures, and provide for time for students to reflect on their group work (Johnson & Johnson, 1986). The teacher monitors group behavior, provides assistance when needed, intervenes to teach cooperative skills, provides closure to lessons, evaluates students' learning, and assesses how well the group functioned (Johnson & Johnson, 1989a).

Robert Slavin and his associates at Johns Hopkins University's Center for Research on Elementary Schools have developed curriculum to use when implementing cooperative learning efforts within the heterogeneous classroom. Included are Team Accelerated Instruction (TAI) and Cooperative Integrated Reading and Composition (CIRC) (Slavin et al., 1988; Slavin et al., 1989/90; Slavin, 1990b). These methods rely on rewarding students with points earned based upon the performance of individual students within the group. Thus the Johns Hopkins' approaches stress both group rewards and individual accountability.

More details about both the Johnson and Johnson and Slavin programs and other collaborative learning approaches appear in Appendix D.

PRINCIPLES FOR DESIGNING AND IMPLEMENTING COLLABORATIVE LEARNING METHODS

The examples of collaborative learning methods described above and in Appendix D illustrate there is no one right way to incorporate collaborative learning into instructional practice. However, several factors have been identified that are believed to increase the chances for successful implementation of group learning. These factors, listed in Table 5-1, fall within three categories: preparing students and the classroom environment for group learning, designing instruction, and implementing collaborative learning approaches.

Preparing for Collaborative Learning

It is imperative that teachers not enter into collaborative learning without adequately preparing themselves and their students for doing so. The following factors are considered key to this preparation.

Prepare students to work collaboratively. It is a mistake to try to implement collaborative learning methods before students are ready to participate in them (Johnson & Johnson, 1986). Working with peers in a small group to achieve a learning goal or serving as a tutor or tutee in a peer tutoring arrangement may seem a strange and new undertaking for some youngsters. While playing with peers is a natural activity for children, play and camaraderie are not readily evident in traditional classrooms. Competition, not cooperation, has governed instructional practice. The first step in establishing a collaborative learning program is to prepare students to work effectively with others (Cohen, 1986; Cohen et al., 1990; Delquadri & Hightower, 1991; Johnson & Johnson et al., 1989; Manheimer & Washington, 1991; Putnam et al., 1989; Sharan, 1990; Schultz, 1989/90; Topping, 1989; Wilkinson, 1988).

Before doing so, teachers should ascertain what behaviors and skills students most need (Putnam et al., 1989). Observing students as they interact in groups is one way to do so. Teachers also are advised to determine if students have participated in group work previously.

What types of skills usually need to be taught? Learning to effectively and politely communicate with other children is first on the list. Students need to learn to be considerate of each other and to give everyone in the group a chance to talk (Cohen, 1990). They need

Table 5-1
Factors Contributing to the Successful Implementation of Collaborative Learning in the Classroom

Preparing for Collaborative Learning
- Prepare students to work together
- Provide counseling and training when students with disabilities are to be involved
- Create a classroom environment conducive to collaborative learning

Designing Instruction
- Select objectives to be accomplished through collaborative learning
- Decide on when to use collaborative learning and commit to doing so for a stated period of time
- Devise a schedule for group activity
- Select the appropriate group structure
- Design or select lessons
- Design, develop and/or select materials to be used in group work
- Determine criteria for success and how groups and students will be evaluated and rewarded for their efforts
- Decide on how the implementation of group methods will be evaluated

Implementing Collaborative Learning
- Arrange the classroom to accommodate group work
- Remind students of the desired group behavior
- Explain the assignment, criteria for success, and reward structure
- Provide ample opportunity for students to pursue group work
- Monitor group work
- Evaluate the group and its efforts

practice in listening and attending to others, in trying to understand what other students have to say, and in learning to listen to feelings as well as words (Manheimer & Washington, 1991). Younger children may need instruction in how to use language to give explanations and reasons for their ideas, while older students need practice in presenting their ideas concisely (Cohen, 1986) and communicating the rationale for their beliefs (Johnson & Johnson, 1984a).

Helping students learn to resolve conflicts among themselves should also be addressed when preparing students for group work. When children work together disagreements are likely to occur. Students need to try to appropriately resolve these conflicts themselves. Therefore, during training for group work, students need to be introduced to methods that will help them cope with and resolve conflicts (Delquadri & Hightower, 1991).

Students must also be introduced to methods that will help them to learn the most in group settings. Johnson and Johnson (1984a) stress that students need assistance

1. in learning behaviors that will help them and their fellow students acquire deeper levels of understanding of the content being studied;

2. in using reasoning strategies;

3. in how to conceptualize material being studied; and

4. in how to search for additional information (Johnson & Johnson, 1984a).

Most student training should occur before students begin to work in their groups. After group work begins, teachers may spot areas in need of additional attention and these should be addressed as needed.

Students who are to serve as tutors in peer tutoring arrangements also need special training to help them function in that role. They need to learn how to give clear directions, encourage and praise the children they are tutoring, confirm correct responses, correct errors, and avoid over prompting. Additional training should focus on areas such as: How to gather and replace instructional materials, measure and record student performance, and allocate time to specific tasks. Training in peer tutoring should not end when tutoring begins. Rather, as with all forms of collaborative learning, teachers need to monitor the tutoring sessions and determine what additional training may be required (Jenkins & Jenkins, 1985).

How should teachers instruct students in group skills? One suggested method is for teachers to model desired behaviors (Edwards, 1989/90; Johnson & Johnson, 1989/90). Teachers can demonstrate an array of behaviors such as how to provide positive reinforcement, listen to others, offer suggestions, and provide explanations.

A simple activity that can be used to help students to learn to listen and think about what other students are saying is to place students in a group and begin a discussion on a specific topic. Each student must paraphrase what the student who just spoke before had to say prior to presenting his or her own opinion (Manheimer & Washington, 1991).

Elizabeth Cohen in her book, *Designing Groupwork Strategies for the Heterogeneous Classroom* (1986), provides several examples for activities and games that can be used to help students acquire group work skills. One example offered, an activity called "Master Design," may be used in groups of five or fewer students to help them learn to help other students think for themselves and to illustrate the advantages of cooperative efforts.

EXAMPLE: Each group member receives an identical set of cardboard shapes containing, for example, squares, triangles, and parallelograms. The size of the shapes range from about 1/2" to 1-1/2" at the largest part, and several sizes of the same shape may be included in the set. A divider is needed which, when placed on a table, is low enough to allow each student in the group to see the faces of the other group members, but high enough to hide from view the table space in front of each of the other students.

The activity begins as one member of the group assumes the role of master designer and creates a design, which because of the divider, other group members cannot see. The master designer tells other group members how to replicate the design she has made. The master designer may answer questions posed by the other students, but she may not physically assist them to replicate the design. In other words, the task can only be accomplished through verbal directions and clarifications. When a group member thinks he has reconstructed the design, the master designer checks it. If it indeed matches, then that group member can also serve to help other students to guess the design solution. After everyone in the group succeeds in reconstructing the design, another student can play the role of master designer and the game cycle begins again (Cohen, 1986).

The three group behaviors illustrated by this activity are the importance of helping students do things for themselves explaining by telling how, and everybody helping. Cohen suggests that teachers who use this activity construct a sign or chart that lists these three behaviors and display it in the class before and during the activity. She also recommends that every time the master design game is played that one group member serve as an observer. The observer's job is to record and to report the number of times that desired group behaviors occurred. The observer may even be asked to provide examples of particularly good instances of the behavior. Having an observer draws the attention of all group members to the importance of the desired behaviors and helps students recognize when they occur.

Cohen (1986) further advises that certain key principles for teaching social learning be incorporated into activities developed for training students for collaborative learning. In particular, she cites those developed by Bandura (1969) which are listed in Figure 5-1.

Provide special counseling and training when collaborative learning is to involve students with learning problems. When students with learning problems are to be included in collaborative learning arrangements, particularly within a mainstreamed setting, teachers need to provide some additional consulting or training. Many of these students are anxious about taking part in groups with nonhandicapped peers. Regular education teachers can help alleviate some of these students' anxieties by following the steps suggested by Johnson and Johnson (1986). Teachers should

- *explain to these students the procedures that the learning group will follow;*
- *give students a structured role so that they understand what their responsibilities in the group will be;*
- *ask special education teachers to train and coach the students with learning problems in how to behave in collaborative learning situations; and*
- *ask special education teachers to teach students with learning problems the academic skills that will be needed to complete the group's work.*

Students who are not handicapped can experience anxiety when they know that they are going to be involved in collaborative learning with students with learning problems. In particular nonhandicapped members of cooperative learning groups may fear that these students

---

Figure 5-1
Principles of Social Learning

- label and discuss new, desired behaviors;
- teach students to recognize when new behaviors occur;
- teach students to label and discuss behaviors in an objective way;
- give students a chance to practice the new behaviors; and
- reinforce new behaviors when they occur.

From Bandura, 1969

may reduce the overall performance of the group. To alleviate these concerns, the Johnsons (1986) suggest that teachers train nonhandicapped students in how to tutor, teach, and share their skills and how to offer praise. Teachers are also advised to establish reasonable expectations for academic achievement by students with learning problems, as will be discussed later in this section. This will help alleviate concerns by nonhandicapped students that their group's effort will be negatively affected by the participation of students with learning problems. The Johnsons (1986) also recommend having the special education teacher talk to the nonhandicapped students to explain how best to teach students with disabilities.

Create a classroom environment conducive to collaborative learning. Group activities are most successful when they occur in a classroom environment where there exists a spirit of esprit de corp (Robertson et al., 1990). Robertson and her colleagues suggest several activities for helping to create such an atmosphere. Teachers are advised to have students participate in activities that help them to become acquainted with each other, that create an atmosphere of class unity, and that encourage mutual support. Getting acquainted activities could include having each student provide information about topics such as what they like to eat, if they have pets, and what hobbies they have. This information may be posted on wall charts and displayed around the room.

Whole-class unity can be built through class trips, projects, meetings, and social events such as class parties. Equally important is the creation of a class identity to guard against the development of factionalism among groups. Class identity can be strong through use of class mottos, logos, banners, or crests (Robertson et al., 1990).

Developing a sense of mutual support among group members is critical for effective group work. Youlanda Washington, a middle school teacher from Fort Knox, Kentucky, offers an example of an activity that she uses with her own students (Manheimer & Washington, 1991).

EXAMPLE: On the day that collaborative learning is to be introduced to the class, Washington has students write down on pieces of paper negative comments and put downs students may say to each other. She collects the papers and reads them all out loud to the class. The next day Washington comes to class dressed in black. Ceremoniously carrying the papers containing the negative comments, she leads her students in a funeral procession to the outside of the school. A hole is dug, and the put downs are buried, hopefully never to be heard again. On the following day, Washington has the children write down all the compliments and good comments that they like to hear. She collects them and reads them out loud. Then Washington, dressed this time in cheerful colors, leads the children outside the school where they joyously toss the positive comments to the wind. This activity dramatically symbolizes for students that understanding and support, not put downs and negativism, must characterize group work.

When attempting to create a positive, supportive environment, teachers should not overlook the power of example. Planning projects with other teachers and sharing materials with them are two ways the teacher can demonstrate a commitment to cooperative activity (Dees, 1990).

Designing Instruction

Besides introducing students to collaborative learning and educating them in appropriate group behaviors, teachers must also give careful consideration to planning and developing lessons. Numerous decisions must be made about when and why to use collaborative learning, how to structure groups and activities, and how group and individual outcomes will be evaluated.

Select objectives to be accomplished when using collaborative learning methods. Collaborative learning approaches have been utilized for a variety of instructional and social purposes as is indicated in Figure 5-2.

The first order of business for teachers planning group learning is to identify the objectives that they want to achieve by the group process. Teachers should be aware that some researchers disagree about when instructional group work should be used. Johnson and Johnson (1989a) contend that collaborative learning methods are appropriate for use whenever teachers want students to learn more, like school better, like each other better, have higher self-esteem, and learn more effective social skills. According to the Johnsons, collaborative learning can be used effectively throughout the curriculum. Similarly, Spencer Kagan (1989/90) has developed an array of collaborative learning structures that support various learning objectives and thus can be used in a variety of subjects and for practically all instructional purposes.

Other educators think collaborative learning initiatives should be confined to specific objectives and/or be more structured. Maheady and his colleagues (1988a) state that collaborative learning should only be used after information has been introduced, discussed, and reviewed by the classroom teacher. Cosden and Lieber (1986) think

Figure 5-2
Examples of Objectives for Collaborative Learning

- To present new subject content to students (Kagan, 1989/90);

- To assist students to learn vocabulary (Smith, 1987);

- To aid children in memorizing facts (Kagan, 1989/90);

- To help students master new content (Kagan, 1989/90);

- To encourage the development of problem-solving capabilities (Dees, 1990; Johnson & Johnson, 1990; Weissglass, 1990);

- To promote critical reading and comprehension skills (Flynn, 1989; Stevens et al., 1990);

- To practice the application and use of concepts (Cohen, 1986; Edwards, 1989/90; Kagan, 1989/90; Robertson, 1990);

- To check and review assignments (Kagan, 1989/90);

- To assist children in generating and revising hypotheses (Kagan, 1989/90);

- To provide students with an opportunity to review and critique each others' work and to share their reactions to stories and compositions (Bernagozzi, 1988; Kagan, 1989/90);

- To promote divergent thinking (Robertson, 1990); and

- To foster better social relations among students (Johnson & Johnson, 1989a).

students should work alone when they are building automaticity in basic academic skills, and then be brought together in small groups to work on activities requiring them to apply these skills. Cohen (1986, 1990) believes that while collaboration can assist students to master skills, it is even more effective in helping students practice and apply new concepts. She recommends that teachers select or design activities and problems that are open ended, have more than one right answer, and more than one way to solve them. This form of group activity provides an opportunity for active rehearsal of new concepts for students of all achievement levels (Cohen & Benton, 1988). Slavin (1991c) believes that collaborative learning programs are most effective when they are grounded within a specific subject area and supported by specially designed curricular materials.

Teachers will need to experiment to determine what uses of collaborative learning are most effective for them and their students.

What is important to remember is that lesson planning must begin with an identification of the objective for group work since this decision will influence so many others. Teachers should also note that a lesson may not be limited to a single objective; well-planned lessons can succeed in accomplishing multiple objectives (Manheimer & Washington, 1991).

Decide on when to use collaborative learning and commit to its use for a specified period of time. Teachers new to collaborative learning are urged to go slow when first trying group work (Robertson, 1990). Accordingly, teachers are advised to use group instruction only within one subject area initially (Johnson & Johnson, 1986; Watson & Rangel, 1989). This is to guard against the tendency of trying to do too much, too soon.

Skills involved in effective administration of collaborative learning are acquired over time. Teachers new to group learning find that sometimes activities do not achieve the intended results, conflicts develop among students, and parents may question the advisability of collaborative methods. These and other "problems" can be discouraging. Teachers need to remember that with experience they gain the insights and knowledge to anticipate and resolve many of these difficulties. Teachers who commit to trying group methods for a specific period of time may be more likely to work through problems and not "give up." At a minimum, teachers should pledge to try collaborative learning for at least one school year; however, some have recommended that teachers commit to this method for three years (Edwards, 1989/90). Making such a commitment will help teachers persevere on those days they may wish to abandon their efforts.

Devise a schedule for group activity. Teachers must be cognizant of the time necessary to implement collaborative learning methods (Bailey & Dyck, 1990) and make realistic time tables for doing so (Cohen, 1986). Scheduling of groups will depend largely upon the purpose for the group. Most often they will meet during regular school hours, during the time slot set aside for the subject matter to be addressed, and within a given class. On occasion teachers may wish to schedule groups to work before or after school. For example, peer tutoring, when undertaken to assist students who are having difficulty learning particular content, may be scheduled outside regular school hours (Hedin, 1987).

Select the appropriate group structure. The objectives for collaborative learning will guide the teacher in determining the group structure that should be used. For example, when a more able student is to help a less able peer to learn particular subject content, a peer tutoring format may be selected. When pairing students for tutoring, teachers generally select older, more able students to serve as tutors because they are easier to instruct in the ways of tutoring and can manage the tutoring situations with less supervision than their younger counterparts. However, younger students, those as young as seven, eight, and nine, have successfully participated in peer tutoring situations. Perhaps more important than age are the characteristics that tutors possess. Students should be dependable, responsible, sensitive, and caring or have the potential to develop these traits (Jenkins & Jenkins, 1985). Tutoring pairs may be composed of students within a given class or from students of different classes (Villa & Thousand, 1988).

When forming other groups, teachers need to keep in mind the general purpose for the grouping. According to Johnson and Johnson (1989b) cooperative learning groups fall into one of three general types: **base groups** are those which are long term and whose role is primarily providing peer support and long term accountability; **formal groups** are carefully structured and designed to complete assignments that could last for several hours, days, or even weeks; and **ad hoc groups** deal with brief and temporary tasks such as working together to formulate an answer to a question. Teachers may use any or all forms of group learning depending upon the purpose they are trying to achieve.

Generally groups should be formed so as to contain a cross section of students reflective of the class. In other words, groups should contain students with mixed abilities and varying capabilities, of different sexes, and, when possible, from different cultures (Johnson & Johnson, 1984).

As mentioned earlier, heterogenous groups appear to be instructionally more advantageous to students with learning problems than are homogeneous groups. But heterogeneous groups are not without potential problems that teachers need to confront if learning opportunities for the students are to be enhanced. Teachers need to be sensitive not only to the varying ability levels represented in the groups, but also to the status problems that can arise among students. It is not uncommon for hierarchies to emerge in groups with students of varying abilities. Students likely to be more influential or active are those who are perceived by their classmates to have higher status either by virtue of their higher social or societal standing, expertise within a particular subject area, and/or general academic capability—particularly their reading ability. Conversely, those students who do not share these characteristics generally are perceived by their classmates to have lower status (Cohen 1986, 1990).

According to Cohen (1986), several problems exist when such hierarchies are present. First, low-status youngsters do not interact as much and therefore learn less than their higher status peers; second, inequities in the group situation perpetuate inequities found in society in general; and third, groups do not function as well when each member does not have an equal opportunity to make a contribution.

It is natural for students strong in certain abilities or possessing expertise in a particular topic to talk and explain more in a group, concedes Cohen, and this is not necessarily a problem. It only becomes so when higher-status students dominate all aspects of group work. Ideally, groups should be structured and lessons designed so that over a series of group sessions different students will have an opportunity to play influential roles depending on their likes, abilities, and expertise (Cohen, 1986).

The optimal group size depends upon the purpose for collaborative learning. Base groups, for example, might be larger than formal groups. The latter requires considerable interaction which is facilitated in smaller groups. It has been suggested that such groups contain no more than five students (Cohen, 1986), but larger groups may be manageable. As a rule, the younger the student, the smaller the group recommended (Edwards, 1989/90).

Design or select lessons. Lessons need to be well organized and need to meet the specific instructional outcomes for which group work is being undertaken (e.g., concept practice, mastery of skills, research and investigation). Thus, as stressed earlier, teachers begin lesson design and/or selection by first identifying the objective to be pursued (Delquadri & Hightower, 1991; Johnson & Johnson, 1986, 1990; Male, 1986). This objective will most likely be academic but could also be social, particularly when dealing with students with learning problems (Kagan, 1989/90).

The teacher next should determine the group tasks and activities that will help achieve the desired outcomes (Johnson &Johnson, 1986, 1990). Tasks can be structured and designed in such a way as to minimize status problems frequently observed in groups containing students of mixed ability levels. For example, a collegial model can be used in which all members of the group work on the same task and where members are instructed to help each other to solve the problems (Cohen, 1986). An activity such as, "Building Story Maps" outlined in Figure 5-3 is an example of a lesson based upon this model.

In Figure 5-4 Dees (1990) provides a suggestion for another activity that could be used in a collegial model, this one focusing on practicing measurement skills.

Another way to involve all group members in a task is to assign each student a specific responsibility (Crabill, 1990; Johnson & Johnson, 1989/90). Students could be assigned roles such as facilitator, checker, reporter, setup person, cleanup person, and safety monitor (Cohen, 1986). An example of a multiple-role activity, "Space Travel: Launching and Landing Spacecrafts," has been offered by Lyman and Foyle (1990).

Figure 5-3
Building Story Maps

Subject Area: Reading

Grade Level: Primary

Instructional Objective: Help students understand story patterns

Directions for Group Activity: The teacher reads a story aloud to students and while doing so explains that stories usually pose a problem, contain events, and conclude with a solution to the problem. On the board, the teacher draws boxes in which he or she will record the problem, events, and solutions identified by the class from the book read. The teacher divides the class into pairs of students and gives each pair a different book and a worksheet containing a template of a story map such as follows

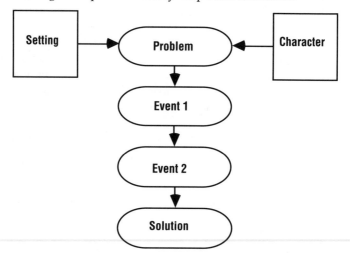

Students take turns reading the book to each other then work together to identify the characters, setting, problem, events and solutions and to complete the template. As an added activity, students may be asked to draw illustrations of the events or solution.

Materials: Selected books, worksheets, crayons, drawing paper, story map template.

Evaluation: The teacher circulates among students during the activity to observe students as they read, discuss, and work on the group product.

Figure 5-4
What Size Is It?

Subject Area: Math

Grade Level: Intermediate

Instructional Objective: Measuring using the metric system

Directions for group activity: After presenting information about taking measurements of length, width, and thickness using metric measures, the teacher divides students in pairs and gives them a handout containing the following information to be completed:

What is the	in centimeters	in millimeters
length	_____	_____
width	_____	_____
thickness	_____	_____
of your math book?		

What is the	in centimeters	in meters
length	_____	_____
width	_____	_____
of the chalkboard?		

What is the		
length	_____	_____
width	_____	_____
thickness	_____	_____
of the classroom door?		

What is the	in meters	in decimeters
length	_____	_____
width	_____	_____
of the classroom?		

Students are told to alternate measurement taking with, for example, one student completing the measurement in the first column and the other student doing the measurements required in the second column. Another option is to have each student take all the measurements individually and record them on his or her own worksheet. Then the student compares his or her answers with those of his or her partner and remeasures when a disagreement is noted. Students are instructed to compare their answers with those obtained from at least two other teams. When discrepancies are observed, team members are to figure out which if any of the answers are correct.

(Adapted from Dees, 1990.)

EXAMPLE: Students are placed in groups of four and assigned the roles of facilitator, writer, encourager, and reporter. This activity focuses on the study of the effects on spaceships of reentry into the earth's atmosphere. Prior to group work, the teacher provides an explanation of the forces that affect reentry. Once grouped, students work together to complete worksheets that require them to identify the factors affecting spaceship reentry and the ways astronauts must be protected during the process. Students also are asked to conduct an experiment. Before the experiment students must predict the outcome and afterwards discuss what they observed. Throughout the group process, the facilitator helps the students decide how to answer the questions; the writer records the answers on the sheet; the encourager makes positive comments about each student and the task; and finally, the reporter tells the class about the group's answers.

Another example of an activity that utilizes students in different roles is contained in Figure 5-5, Letter to the Editor.

A third method for involving all students in group work is to"jigsaw" materials so that each member is responsible for a "piece" of the assignment (Johnson & Johnson, 1989b). For example, Figure 5-6, Learn the States, provides an example of a jigsawed activity for learning the names and other information about states.

Another illustration of a jigsawed activity is suggested by Lyman and Foyle (1990).

EXAMPLE: "Cooperative Pumpkins," engages primary level children in constructing jack-o'-lanterns. Youngsters are divided into groups of threes. Drawings of pumpkins are divided into three parts— a top, middle, and bottom, and each child in the group is given a section of the pumpkin on which to draw a portion of a jack-o'-lantern's face. When the students have completed their work, the parts are pasted together.

Jigsawing can also be used for intergroup assignments. The teacher may divide the class into small groups and assign each responsibility for researching answers for a different set of questions. Each group member is responsible for becoming an "expert" on the questions assigned to the group. After the students complete their work, the teacher forms new groups, each containing a member from one of the original groups. Each student in the new group is an expert on one set of questions and assumes the responsibility to help fellow group members learn the answers to the questions for which she has special knowledge.

These examples illustrate how lessons can be structured to involve all group members. In general, the more challenging and complex the activity, the more opportunity to devise special roles for students and/or to jigsaw materials.

Figure 5-5
Letter to the Editor

Subject Area: Writing

Grade Level: Intermediate

Instructional Objective: Learning to write a letter stating an opinion and supporting evidence

Directions for group activity: After the teacher has presented lessons on editorial writing, which have included the reading and analyzing of letters to the editor, divide the class into groups of five students. Give each group the assignment of identifying and researching an issue and composing and sending a letter reflecting a position and supporting evidence to a newspaper or magazine editor. Explain to the students that this project will require that each group member perform a specific role although, as a group, they will need to agree on the issue to be addressed. One student will be responsible for identifying possible issues and appropriate newspapers and magazines to which to send the final letter. After the group decides on the issue to target, another student will be responsible for researching the issue. A third student will draft the letter. All group members will suggest revisions. A fourth student will be responsible for making revisions while a fifth student will be responsible for final editing and mailing the letter.

Materials: Library resources such as books, magazines, and newspapers; writing paper, blue and red pens, an envelope and stamp.

Evaluation: Each student is responsible for performing a particular function, which the teacher can assess.

Design, develop and/or select materials to be used in group work. Teachers need to prepare and/or locate any curricular materials, manipulatives, or any other items that will be needed for group activities. Teachers need to spend as much or more time readying materials for group learning as they do for other forms of instruction (Robertson et al., 1990).

Cohen (1990) contends that traditional materials will not suffice for use in collaborative learning situations because they generally do not encourage interaction—the factor that leads to success in group work. Because teachers are busy, it is difficult for them to create a lot of quality materials. Thus, Cohen suggests that teachers concentrate on developing only one new cooperative learning unit per year. After developing materials, teachers ideally should pretest them to ensure that they do what they are supposed to do and that they contain written instructions that students understand (Cohen, 1986).

Existing materials that reflect a sensitivity to the goals of collaborative learning and promote interaction can save teachers valuable time. Later in this chapter, features of media and materials that are believed to be supportive of collaborative learning are described. These can serve as guidelines for teachers and other school personnel as they design and/or select classroom resources.

Determine criteria for success and how groups and students will be evaluated and rewarded for their efforts. Teachers need to ascertain periodically if group activities are achieving desired outcomes. Further, teachers need to decide how they will reward successful group efforts.

Three ways for evaluating and rewarding students who participate in groups are: individual rewards for group work; group rewards for group work; and group rewards for individual learning. Slavin (1984, 1989, 1991b) strongly argues that the last evaluation and reward method is preferable to the others. Without individual accountability coupled with group rewards, states Slavin (1991b), there is little reason for more able students to help or involve less able students in the group activities.

Frequent evaluation of students is urged by the Johnsons and their colleagues (1984). When group work is being used as a way of helping students perform a specific procedure or develop an understanding of a particular concept, students' progress needs to be closely monitored.

Designing collaborative learning activities that incorporate accountability and evaluation activities between and among group members is one way to monitor individual student and group progress. For example, in the Cooperative Integrated Reading and Composition program (CIRC) developed by Slavin and his colleagues (1988), students are paired together to work on activities such as reading aloud to their partners, identifying story grammars, learning the meaning of new words, retelling stories, and spelling. Students must verify that the activities have been completed by their partners and/ or that their fellow students have met a predetermined criterion (Stevens et al., 1987).

Of course many teachers want or are required to include grades as a part of their evaluation process. Cohen (1986) suggests two ways to satisfy the need to give grades. One is to require that students produce individual products, the other is to test students for their understanding of concepts that the group work is intended to teach. One grading practice not advised by Cohen (1986) is the awarding of a student grade based upon what he or she contributed to the group. The reason

Figure 5-6
Learn the States

Subject Area: Social Studies and Writing

Grade Level: Intermediate

Instructional Objectives: Learning names of states, their capitals and their major industries; writing a report.

Directions for Group Activity: The teacher explains that the class will be divided into groups to study states within various regions of the country. Each group will be responsible for researching and reporting on states within a region. Each student within the group will be given responsibility for obtaining information about the capital and the major industry for a group of different states. Each group member will be responsible for sharing researched information with other members of the group and for assisting other group members to learn the information through use of drills, the computer, and paper and pencil games. Then the group will compile the information into a written report that will be delivered to the rest of the class. The teacher explains that at the conclusion of the study of the states, each student will be responsible for knowing the capitals of all states studied by the class not just those studied by the group.

Materials: note cards, maps, atlas, resource books, computer games, and writing paper

Evaluation: Each student will be tested on his or her ability to name states, capitals, and major industries.

for not doing so is that the teacher cannot be sure whether low or poor participation is really the fault of the student or of the dynamics of the group.

While determining ways to assess individual accountability, teachers must be sensitive to the needs of students with disabilities. Indeed, it may not be reasonable to hold a uniform standard for success for all group members. Johnson and Johnson (1986) offer the following advice to teachers utilizing groups that include students with different abilities: establish different criteria for success for each group member; vary the amount each group member is expected to master; give group members different assignments, lists, work, or problems and then use the average percentage worked correctly as the group's score; use improvement scores for students with disabilities.

In group discovery or other methods in which each student is assigned responsibility for performing specific functions, a student's performance of his or her role provides a form of individual accountability. These methods allow teachers to be sensitive to the individual capabilities of students and to customize evaluation criteria to the differing needs of students (Cohen, 1986).

How should groups be rewarded? Slavin (1991b) believes that groups should be rewarded based upon the extent to which individual members reach the group's learning goal. Several types of rewards have been suggested, such as allowing students to serve as a teacher's helper or messenger, giving the student time to work on a special project, praising the student, or giving tangible rewards such as certificates (Slavin, 1984; Slavin, 1991c).

Decide how the implementation of group methods will be evaluated. Not only do educators need to determine how students' learning and behavior will be evaluated, but they must also ascertain how well collaborative learning has been implemented. School district personnel need to determine how they will evaluate the processes of applying group learning techniques within the school setting.

Implementing Collaborative Learning

After preparing students and planning for instruction and assessment, teachers begin the actual implementation process. The following steps are recommended.

Arrange the classroom to accommodate group work. Flexible classroom furnishings are needed for group work (Cohen, 1986). Most grouping arrangements require that students sit so they are facing each other (Schultz, 1989/90). Tables may be used or desks may be arranged in circles or clusters (Edwards, 1989/90; Johnson et al., 1984).

Remind students of desired group behavior. Prior to beginning a group session, at least when collaborative learning is still new to the class, teachers should remind students of desired behaviors (Cohen, 1986; Johnson & Johnson, 1986, 1989a). For example, students should be reminded to

- *explain their actions to other group members;*
- *encourage other students;*
- *listen to others; and*
- *criticize ideas not people (Johnson & Johnson, 1984).*

Teachers need to make clear to students that they are responsible not just for their own learning but also for helping their peers (Watson & Rangel, 1987). Dees (1990) suggests that teachers explain to students that collaborative learning methods, besides being more fun or pleasant than other more individualistic methods of instruction, also will help them learn.

Teachers should stress that all group members should have an opportunity to participate. A teacher who suspects that one or two students may dominate the group, may wish to take preventive action by using a technique such as "talking chips." The teacher distributes a chip or token to each group member, and when a student speaks, he or she places his or her chip in the middle of the table. That student is not allowed to speak again until all other group members have spoken and placed their chips in the center of the table. After every student has spoken, the teacher redistributes the chips and the process starts a new (Manheimer & Washington, 1991).

Explain the assignment, criteria for success, and reward structure. Students must be clear about the exact nature of their group assignment. Teachers need to

- *provide background information (Robertson et al., 1990);*

- *specify and explain the goals and objectives for group work (Johnson & Johnson, 1986; Robertson et al., 1990; Villa & Thousand, 1988);*

- *explicitly explain the task to be accomplished (Cohen, 1986; Johnson & Johnson, 1989a);*

- *inform students of the expected outcomes (Cohen, 1986); and*

- *explain the evaluation criteria that will be used (Johnson & Johnson, 1986).*

Clear, written directions should be included on worksheets that students are expected to complete (Davidson, 1985). This will help students to work more independently of the teacher.

Provide ample opportunity for students to pursue group work. The strength of group work lies in the opportunity it offers for face-to-face interaction among students. Ample time must be set aside for this experience. Teachers must make judgments about the appropriate amount of time needed to accomplish group tasks. Too little time may lead to frustration; if too much time is allotted, students may become bored.

Monitor group work. The teacher serves as a facilitator and monitor once group work begins. As students engage in collaborative learning, teachers need to observe groups and identify and diagnose problems

(Crabill, 1990; Robertson et al., 1990; Schultz, 1989/90; Topping, 1989).

Teachers should particularly be concerned that groups are progressing toward the established objectives. When academic objectives are the focus of collaborative learning activities, teachers will need to provide corrective feedback on the products of group efforts (Cohen & Lotan, 1990; Delquadri & Hightower, 1991). When necessary, the teacher may need to intervene to change lessons to accommodate the needs of individual students (Jenkins & Jenkins, 1985) and/or to refine rules, roles, and norms (Cohen & Benton, 1988).

Teachers must also ensure that students are interacting appropriately (Robertson et al., 1990; Schultz, 1989/90). Occasionally conflict will arise in a group. When this happens, the teacher needs to remind students of appropriate, expected group behavior (Manheimer & Washington, 1991).

Teachers often involve students in the monitoring of group processes. For example, a teacher may ask group members to identify two things they did well as a group and one area in which they need improvement (Schultz, 1989/90). Students should be given an opportunity to develop and implement their own solution for a problem, when appropriate. At other times, the teacher may need to orchestrate a solution. For example, when lack of interaction by one group member is the problem, the teacher may select a student to work with the nonparticipating peer. Or the teacher might assign the passive student a highly structured role.

Teachers may wish to consider videotaping group members as they work together (Delquadri & Hightower, 1991). These tapes can be used to illustrate to group members their effective and ineffective group behaviors.

Evaluate group work. Assess the success of the group based upon criteria for group performance established at the onset of the collaborative learning effort (Johnson et al., 1984). Much of the evaluation effort will focus on how well students master the subject matter that is the focus for group attention. Other goals for collaborative learning, such as improving social relationships between students with disabilities and their nonhandicapped peers, also should be assessed. Observations of student interactions with their peers and interviews with students are two ways teachers can make some determination about collaborative learning's impact on social relations.

School personnel should not overlook the need to evaluate the role of the teaching staff in implementing collaborative learning. Cohen and Benton (1988) suggest that teachers observe and evaluate each other's work. Johnson and Johnson and their colleagues (1984) offer guidelines for teachers to follow when observing and evaluating their peers. These appear in Figure 5-7.

Collegial evaluations should focus on determining how effec-

Figure 5-7
Guidelines for Teachers' Observation and Evaluation
of Colleagues Using Collaborative Learning

- realize that they can learn from each other;

- ensure that observations and feedback are reciprocal;

- inquire of the teacher being observed if there is a particular area on which he or she wishes the observer to focus attention;

- confine feedback and comments to the actions of the observed teacher not to his or her competence;

- do not confuse a teacher's worth with his or her current level of expertise in implementing collaborative learning;

- provide concrete and practical suggestions; and

- communicate respect for the teacher's professionalism.

From Johnson & Johnson, 1984

tively and efficiently teachers apply group learning principles. In addition, they should determine how well the intervention was accepted and supported by other school staff and parents, and the perceived drawbacks, administratively, academically, or socially, of collaborative learning. This evaluation should be conducted by more than one staff member.

This discussion describes the factors and some approaches thought essential for incorporating collaborative learning into classroom instruction. The extent to which teachers implement those factors and their effectiveness in doing so depends largely upon the degree of support they receive. Of course, administrative and peer support is crucial. But so, too, is the assistance provided to the teacher by classroom materials. The next section discusses the role media and materials could/should play in implementing collaborative learning.

HOW MEDIA AND MATERIALS CAN SUPPORT THE USE OF COLLABORATIVE LEARNING METHODS

What features should school personnel look for when selecting materials to be used in collaborative learning instruction? How may media and materials be used to foster a better understanding among teachers of the purposes and goals of collaborative learning and the essential elements of its implementation? These issues are addressed in the next section.

How Can Materials Help Teachers Implement Collaborative Learning?

The first step in applying collaborative learning techniques in the classroom is preparing students for the experience. Classroom materials assist teachers when they contain activities to help youngsters develop social skills; incorporate exercises that help students enhance their abilities to express themselves orally and to listen to other youngsters; and illustrate, through video tapes, how collaborative learning works. Tapes could demonstrate frequently observed student behaviors and common problems that face youngsters new to group work (Anderson & Roe, 1991; Manheimer &Washington, 1991).

Teacher guides are helpful when they provide theory and background information that teachers need to wisely and appropriately use collaborative learning (Manheimer & Washington, 1991; Slavin, 1991c); describe and illustrate for teachers a few well-elaborated and well-researched techniques for grouping students for learning rather than providing numerous options which may prove overwhelming to the teacher new to group learning (Slavin, 1991c); and suggest ways to create a classroom environment conducive to group learning activities.

When they are designing and implementing collaborative learning teachers are helped by classroom resources that contain group activities for addressing a variety of objectives. Existing student materials are often not adaptable to group work because they are designed for completion by individual students working alone. Suggested activities should promote interaction; present challenging, open-ended, relevant tasks; and, when appropriate, engage youngsters in problem solving (Manheimer & Washington, 1991; Putnam & Wiederhold, 1991; Slavin, 1991c). For example, the resources utilized as a part of the Cooperative Integrated Reading and Composition program include group discussion questions about assigned passages and stories (Slavin, 1990a). These materials also include collaborative writing activities such as pre-writing conferencing and post-writing critiquing.

Materials also should include a clear indication of the learning objectives to be addressed, a description of the tasks involved in the activity, and a listing of additional materials needed (Anderson & Roe, 1991; Manheimer & Washington, 1991; Sandeen, 1991), and they should focus on those objectives that teachers are likely to teach as a part of their standard curriculum. Group learning can be used in any subject area. But teachers are most likely to want to utilize it to help youngsters learn key areas of the curriculum (Slavin, 1991c).

Classroom resources should provide suggestions for accommodating students of varying academic abilities. Activities should offer teachers guidance in how to ease status problems among students. Ideas for a variety of roles and responsibilities that can be assumed by students with varying talents should be included. Tasks not entirely dependent on students' abilities to read for their completion should be incorporated into group activities (Cohen et al., 1990). Otherwise, students with reading problems will be stymied in their efforts to participate.

To the extent possible, materials should allow students to pursue experimentation. More "hands on" materials are needed which are designed for group conducted experiments (Sandeen, 1991).

Activities suggested should be capable of being completed by students without undue reliance on or intervention by the teacher (Slavin, 1991c). The teacher who uses collaborative learning must not lose touch with what students are doing. But it is desirous, indeed necessary, that students working in groups function independently of the teacher. Therefore, it is important that materials contain clear, understandable, written instructions (Davidson, 1985).

Materials should prompt students to reflect on their own contributions to the group and the overall effectiveness of their group work. Occasional checklists or questions incorporated throughout materials can lead students to assess their behavior and identify areas in need of improvement.

Teachers would be helped by resources that provide elaborations of existing resources to make them usable in collaborative learning situations. It is true that many existing materials are not suitable for group work, but supplemental materials may transform original materials into group resources. Slavin and his colleagues (1990a) have done just that as a part of their Cooperative Integrated Reading and Composition program by producing materials intended to be used along with commonly available basal reading series. Mary Anderson's book, *Partnerships: Developing Teamwork at the Computer* (MAJO Press, 1988), also was written to guide teachers in the use of existing resources for group learning experiences. This guidebook provides cooperative learning activities that may be used with selected, commercially available software. Each lesson specifies goals, the grade level recommended for lesson use, time required, materials needed, group tasks, activities for closure, and ways the lesson could be extended.

Materials should offer activities across curriculum areas and multiple resources for use with students experienced in group work. Often teachers initially apply collaborative learning methods to basic skills instruction, but as they become more knowledgeable and sophisticated, teachers often wish to extend collaborative learning to other content areas such as science and social studies.

Figure 5-8
Checklist of Media and Material Features that Support Collaborative Learning

	Yes	No

Do the media and materials under consideration
for collaborative learning:

- contain activities that help students develop social skills including opportunities that help students express themselves when speaking to and listening to their peers?

- provide teachers with necessary background information about collaborative learning?

- describe or illustrate effective techniques for grouping students?

- suggest ways to create a classroom atmosphere that is conducive to collaborative learning?

- offer advice for planning and implementing group instruction?

Do media and materials offer the following to help
teachers design and implement lessons?

- group activities that are coordinated to content and objectives commonly taught in schools

- challenging, open-ended, relevant, and when possible hands-on activities

- clear descriptions for the teacher of the tasks that are involved in the activity

- guidelines for ways teachers can involve students of varying abilities

- activities that can be undertaken by students without undue reliance on the teacher

- suggestions for utilizing existing resources in collaborative learning situations

- activities that cut across the curriculum

- ways to construct instruments to assess students' actions in group learning situations

Teacher guides accompanying materials would be particularly helpful if they offered group learning activities coordinated to the content and objectives being addressed in the student materials (Manheimer & Washington, 1991). Some of these activities may be very explicit with guidelines indicating to the teacher what steps or parts could be modified. Other activities may be more descriptive than prescriptive, giving teachers considerable leeway to customize the activity to meet the needs of his or her students (Anderson & Roe, 1991). Guides should also provide guidelines for utilizing the activities with students of varying abilities. Common areas of difficulties experienced by students with disabilities should be noted and solutions suggested.

Practical advice should be offered for how to plan and implement group instruction. Guides could include suggestions for how to group students, prototypes of charts for tracking group progress, and prototypes of incentives that could be given to students, such as certificates of achievement.

Guides also should suggest ways teachers can help both students with disabilities and their nonhandicapped peers adjust to group work; provide guidelines for constructing instruments to evaluate student progress and group interactions; and offer advice and guidelines for establishing professional support groups and peer coaching among teachers using collaborative learning methods (Slavin, 1991c).

This chapter ends with Figure 5-8, which contains a checklist of features for media and materials thought to be supportive of collaborative learning methods.

APPENDIX A

Three Examples of Methods Designed to Increase Students' Strategic Reading Capabilities

RECIPROCAL TEACHING: LEARNING THROUGH DIALOGUES

Reciprocal Teaching, an interactive teaching approach, is based upon theories that social interactions play a prominent role in the learning process (Brown et al., 1983; Palincsar & Brown, 1988). Developed by Annemarie Palincsar and Ann Brown, Reciprocal Teaching is intended to improve the student's reading comprehension by teaching four strategies: summarizing the main content of what has been read, formulating potential test questions, clarifying ambiguities, and predicting what may come next (Palincsar, 1986b; Palincsar & Brown, 1984). These strategies are typically used by expert readers, while children with learning problems and new readers seldom employ them. The ultimate goal of Reciprocal Teaching is to influence how students interact with the learning situation. It aims not just to remediate an immediate educational deficiency but also to enhance students' problem-solving abilities (Brown & Palincsar, 1987; Palincsar, 1986b).

Strategies are taught to students through a series of dialogues between the teacher and students, with the dialogues centered on sections of text that students have first read silently. The teacher may begin by asking a student to summarize the passage that has just been read. After the first student responds, other students may refine, shorten or restate the answer. Next, a student may be asked by the teacher to think of a question that could be asked about the information in the passage. After a student responds, other students may again join in by refining the question.

Throughout this process, students may seek clarification of words or concepts they do not understand. The teacher may lead students to discover word-meanings or prompt them to apply previously learned strategies for gaining clarification (e.g., using context for identifying the meaning of unfamiliar words). Finally, students will be asked to think ahead and predict what information will follow in the next passage (Palincsar, 1986b).

Palincsar and Brown have published several sample dialogues. A review of these proves to be enlightening and is highly recommended (for example, see Palincsar & Brown, 1988; Brown & Palincsar, 1987; Palincsar & Brown, 1984).

Instructional Principles

Several important instructional principles underlie this instructional approach. The teacher informs students of the purpose and usefulness of the strategies to be taught, defines the strategies, and identifies situations in which the strategies could be applied. As mentioned earlier, knowledge of why the strategy is important and how it may be used has been shown to be related to students' use of the strategy beyond the training situation.

Teacher-modeling of the use of the strategies in appropriate contexts is another feature of Reciprocal Teaching. Modeling is intended to make explicit and concrete the ways in which students can use strategies to monitor their learning (Palincsar & Brown, 1988). The teacher's role changes, as instruction progresses, from that of mediator/facilitator to reflector/coach. In other words, when instruction using the Reciprocal Teaching approach begins, the teacher acts as the discussion leader. But through this interactive process, students gradually acquire proficiency in strategy use; over time, teacher involvement fades, and control of the discussions passes to the students (Palincsar & Brown, 1986). Throughout the period of instruction, appropriate feedback and encouragement is provided to students as well (Brown, 1985; Brown & Palincsar, 1987).

Ideally, this approach is used with small groups of six to eight students; however, it can be adapted for use with smaller and larger groups, including entire classes (Brown, 1985). The technique also can be employed in a peer-tutoring situation (Palincsar & Brown, 1988).

Research Studies

The Reciprocal Teaching approach has been used with a variety of students, including those categorized as learning disabled and hearing impaired (Andrews, 1988; Brown, 1985). While it has been employed at the elementary, secondary, and post-secondary levels, most of the research of this approach has been conducted on junior high school students with average reading decoding skills but below-average comprehension skills. Studies have taken place in laboratory settings, in classrooms with volunteer teachers, and in remedial reading classes with nonvolunteer teachers. As reported, in all cases, students taught reading strategies using Reciprocal Teaching made substantial, significant improvements over control groups on measures of reading comprehension. Furthermore, follow-up studies of students in these research settings indicate that improvements in reading performance were to a large extent maintained (Brown & Palincsar, 1987).

But do the effects of Reciprocal Teaching transfer? Some studies have attempted to answer that question. Students who were taught using Reciprocal Teaching did better than their peers who were not so trained on tests measuring comprehension of passages in social studies and science. These tests were given as a part of regular classroom activity outside of the research environment. These students also performed better on the Gates-McGinitie test of reading comprehension. Students were tested before and after four months of instruction, at which time a gain of four months would normally be expected in test scores. In fact, students instructed with Reciprocal Teaching, with the exception of one student who did not show a gain, averaged an increase of twenty months; the control group, on the other hand, only gained one month (Brown & Palincsar, 1987).

While used primarily with older students to enhance reading comprehension skills, Reciprocal Teaching has been tried with first graders in an effort to improve their listening comprehension. The approach once again produced significant improvements this time in listening comprehension (Brown & Palincsar, 1987).

According to the developers, preliminary findings from research suggest that both students with learning disabilities and those with a low average range of IQ could benefit from Reciprocal Teaching, but the method by which instruction is provided may need to be modified. What may work best with these students is to teach strategies one by one, as opposed to teaching them together as is usually done (Brown & Palincsar, 1987).

Andrews (1988) examined the Reciprocal Teaching method in teaching four prereading skills (spelling, book reading, story retelling, and word recognition) to five- to eight-year-old children with severe-to-profound hearing losses. Students taught these skills using Reciprocal Teaching significantly outperformed control group students taught by traditional methods. While Andrews' research focused on skills training as opposed to strategy instruction, the positive results with the young students naturally leads to speculation about this method's use in instructing older hearing-impaired students in higher-level reading strategies.

Role of The Teacher

Reciprocal Teaching is a very teacher-dependent approach. Teachers should undergo some formal training to learn to use this method and develop a coaching network of teachers using Reciprocal Teaching so teachers can support each other.

Fine (1988) reports that the presence of an "expert" teacher who can come into the classroom and teach a class using Reciprocal Teaching while the newly-trained teacher observes is a particularly valuable training method used in Reciprocal Teaching. Videotaping of teachers prior to their involvement in Reciprocal Teaching also has been helpful. Coaches use the tapes to analyze the teaching styles of the to-be-trained teachers, thus gaining a better understanding of the type of assistance each teacher will need.

While this type of training and ongoing support of teachers learning to use Reciprocal Teaching is the ideal, involvement in formal training is not thought absolutely necessary to employ this approach.

In summary, Reciprocal Teaching holds promise for instructing several categories of students in reading and listening. The developers believe that the method could be used within other content areas such as in mathematics to enhance arithmetic reasoning (Brown & Palincsar, 1987).

As a teaching method, Reciprocal Teaching requires teachers to think on their feet, to be sensitive to students' needs and, perhaps most essential but difficult of all, eventually to relinquish some control of the instructional process to students. If successful, Reciprocal Teaching can lead to enhanced thinking skills, not only for students but teachers as well.

For more information, see

Palincsar, A. S. (1986b). Metacognitive strategy instruction. Exceptional Children, 53, 118-124.

Palincsar, A., & Brown, A. (1986). Interactive teaching to promote independent learning from text. The Reading Teacher, 39, 771-777.

THE STRATEGIES INTERVENTION MODEL: HELPING LEARNING DISABLED STUDENTS DEVELOP LEARNING COMPETENCE

The Strategies Intervention Model was originally developed by Donald Deshler, Jean Schumaker and their colleagues, at the University of Kansas Institute for Research in Learning Disabilities. This model, which incorporates the Learning Strategies Curriculum, was specifically designed to help learning disabled adolescents cope with the rigorous demands of the secondary curriculum (Deshler & Schumaker, 1986). Since its development, the Learning Strategies Curriculum has been adapted by the Institute for use with younger learning disabled students and with older students at the college level.

The goal of the Learning Strategies Curriculum is to teach learning disabled students how to become more effective, efficient, and independent learners. Instruction is organized into three major strands: the **first** is reading-oriented and focuses on techniques for acquiring information from written materials. Strategies taught within this strand include Word Identification, Visual Imagery, Self-Questioning, Paraphrasing, Interpreting Visual Aids, and Multipass. The Multipass strategy is designed to help students to process information from textbooks (Deshler & Schumaker, 1986).

The **second strand** focuses on identifying and storing important information. Included are the Listening and Notetaking, First-Letter Mnemonic, and Paired-Associates Strategies (Deshler & Schumaker, 1986).

Strand three helps students to write and to demonstrate competence in academic tasks such as report writing and test taking. Included in this strand are Sentence Writing, Paragraph Writing, Theme Writing, Error Monitoring, Assignment Completion, and Test Taking Strategies (Deshler & Schumaker, 1986).

Students are taught a set of self-instructional steps for each strategy. When faced with an appropriate application for the strategy, students are to use it following the steps they have learned (Deshler et al., 1984b).

In teaching these strategies to students, teachers employ a multi-step process that includes

- *analyzing the current learning habits of the student;*
- *describing the strategy and the steps to using it;*
- *modeling the strategy using think-aloud techniques;*
- *requiring the student to rehearse verbally the steps of the strategy; and*
- *providing opportunities to apply the strategy in controlled materials similar to those found in school settings and, later, with actual classroom materials. During instruction and practice, teachers provide information and corrective feedback (Deshler et al., 1981; Deshler et al., 1984a).*

Throughout the instructional process, the teacher is cued to discuss when to use the strategy and how to identify situations related to strategy use. Students are prompted to become actively involved in the learning process; they are to describe how they are thinking about the use of the strategy, to identify situation-based modifications in the strategy, and to monitor their progress toward successful and independent use of the strategy.

Considerable attention is paid to instructing students explicitly in how to regulate their use of these learning strategies, as well as in describing when to use the strategies outside the training environment (Deshler & Schumaker, 1986). In fact, students are taught to generalize the learned strategies to appropriate situations in and out of the classroom (Ellis et al., 1987b).

This training for generalization is introduced during instruction, which often takes place in the resource room. Ideally, students will receive prompting and reinforcement for strategy use within their regular classroom as well. As Deshler and others have noted, for generalization to occur, the regular classroom teacher must prompt and reinforce students' strategy use (Deshler & Schumaker, 1986; Ellis et al., 1987b).

Under ideal conditions, resource-room and regular-classroom teachers collaborate and coordinate students' strategy instruction. The degree to which such collaboration occurs varies from school to school. While collaboration is more likely at the elementary level, it is possible at the secondary level, too (Lenz, 1988).

Instructional Principles

Several overriding principles guide the instruction in the Learning Strategies Curriculum. First among them is the need to create an environment in which students can experience success. This is a crucial feature of any program for students with learning disabilities, most of whom have experienced failures throughout their schooling. Motivational activities are also an integral part of the learning activities since these students often are lacking in this area as well (Deshler & Schumaker, 1986). A prominent feature of the Strategies Intervention Model is its acknowledgment that student learning is influenced by motivation and social skills as well as by academic factors. Therefore, this model includes components that specifically address these crucial areas of student need(Deshler & Schumaker, 1986).

The developers realize that the time available for students to be instructed in strategies decreases as they progress through the upper grades. Therefore this approach is designed to be as time-efficient as possible (Deshler & Schumaker, 1986).

Research Results

What results can be expected by teachers using this program? Most of the research of the Learning Strategies Curriculum has been conducted by the University of Kansas Institute for Research in Learning Disabilities. These studies generally employ repeated replications, multiple base-line designs to determine individual student progress over time. The Institute reports that prior to strategy training, students generally show little evidence of strategy use. However, following instruction, students exhibit marked gains, a finding of all studies conducted by the Institute (Deshler & Schumaker, 1986).

Results of research published in professional journals support this contention. For example, one study of the Multipass strategy—the strategy designed to help students acquire information from text—indicates that students instructed to use the strategy made major gains on teacher-designed tests to measure reading comprehension of grade-level text material. They also substantially improved their test grades in the regular classroom (Schumaker et al., 1982).

School District Involvement

Involvement in the Learning Strategies Curriculum requires that schools or districts desiring to have teachers trained in this approach commit to a thorough staff training program provided by trainers approved by the Institute. Often these trainers are from the district in question or another one close by. The developers point out that significant student gains are strongly related to the level of staff training (Deshler & Schumaker, 1986).

Training generally involves a three-year commitment, with three to five days per year devoted to staff inservice (Lenz, 1988). Instructed in one strategy at a time, teachers then teach that strategy to their students; after this, they share experiences in sessions designed to encourage mutual problem solving (Lenz, 1988).

In one year, teachers are usually trained in three strategies, with training structured to allow for competency to be reached in one strategy before the next is approached. Newly trained teachers are encouraged to consult with and learn from one another in informal support groups meeting between the formal training sessions (Lenz, 1988).

Teachers trained in the Learning Strategies Curriculum are usually special education teachers who instruct their students in a resource room. These students are most likely to be introduced to strategies and to practice their use.

A teacher manual for each strategy assists the teacher in instructing students. The manual directs the teacher to the types of curricular material to which the strategy should be applied; some of the manuals contain reproducible activity sheets (Lenz, 1988).

It is important to note that adolescent students should be reading at the 4th grade level to successfully learn and transfer use of the strategies to regular classroom material. However, for such strategies as Sentence-Writing, Test-Taking, and those designed for younger children, a lower reading level will suffice. Simple modifications of a number of the other strategies such as memorizing lists and paraphrasing text also allow for broader implementation (Lenz, 1988).

In summary, the Learning Strategies Curriculum has as a general goal the production of an independent learner. Its more immediate task is the improvement of students' performances on specific academic tasks required for school success. The fact that the Learning Strategies Curriculum is often used in a "fix it" situation should not detract from its ability to be used in a more comprehensive, prevention-oriented mode. Nor does its extensive use with learning disabled youngsters prohibit its use with other populations of students.

The Learning Strategies Curriculum provides a very structured, organized method of strategy instruction. Much of the demand for training in this approach—over 30,000 teachers throughout the country have been trained—is attributable to the positive results noted by teachers (Lenz, 1988). This success, one suspects, is related to both the required long-term commitment to formal teacher training and the deliberate teaching of one strategy at a time.

For more information, see:

Deshler, D., & Schumaker, J. (1986). Learning strategies: An instructional alternative for low-achieving adolescents. *Exceptional Children*, 52, 583-590.

Schumaker, J., Deshler, D., Alley, G., Warner, M., & Denton, P. (1982). Multipass: A learning strategy for improving reading comprehension. *Learning Disability Quarterly*, 15, 295-304.

DIRECT EXPLANATION MODEL: IMPROVING TEACHER TALK

The *Direct Explanation Model* focuses on the role of the teacher in explaining reading strategies and the reasoning processes behind them to elementary students, particularly those experiencing difficulty in comprehension. Duffy, Roehler, and the other developers of this method from the Institute for Research on Teaching at Michigan State University believe that low-ability readers need knowledge of strategies to become better readers. They point to research indicating that good readers use strategies to overcome comprehension problems in reading, but poor readers do not (Duffy et al., 1987c).

Duffy and his colleagues (1987b) believe that teachers need to be taught how to make effective decisions when teaching reading; in short, teachers need to learn how to modify basal text lessons by recasting the skills presented therein into useful strategies. According to Duffy and others, basal texts—the source of much reading instruction—seldom present reading skills in a strategic manner. Instead, these texts present skills without including the rationale for and reasoning behind the skill.

In addition, Duffy and Roehler (1987) stress that teachers should provide their strategy instruction by making explicit the reasoning associated with strategy use; i.e., that teachers need to think out loud while explaining reading strategies.

Role of the Teacher

Teachers are trained in Direct Explanation with a method similar to that which they will later use to teach their students. Teachers are given explicit instruction of what they should do, a rationale for why they should do it, a model of the thinking process involved when teaching strategies, an opportunity to practice, and coaching as they try implementing the teaching procedure (Roehler et al., 1986). In sum, teachers are taught how to plan explanations and how to respond to students' misunderstandings of the reading process (Roehler & Duffy, in press).

One technique used in implementing the Direct Explanation model at the school level is using the principal as the instructional leader and coach. John Busch (1988), an elementary school principal in the Hartford, Michigan, school system, has functioned in this capacity. To help teachers to learn and implement the Direct Explanation Model, Busch uses a four-step process recommended by the developers.

1. *Meet with a teacher to discuss the goal of the lesson: what the student should learn, when the student should use what is learned, and how the student should apply this knowledge.*

2. *Observe the teacher giving the lesson.*

3. *Following the lesson, students are interviewed: they are asked what they have learned, when they should use the knowledge, and how they might apply it.*

4. *The principal meets again with the teacher to review data collected from the observation and student interviews. Busch reports that this method has been exceptionally helpful to newly trained teachers for it encourages them to reflect upon their teaching and to refine their use of this method.*

Herrmann (1988b) has identified several decisions the teacher should make when planning for a direct explanation lesson. For example:

1. the teacher needs to decide what reasoning process to teach, why it is important, and when the student should use it;

2. determine how the reasoning process or strategy works;

3. identify passages and examples from text that do and do not illustrate the reasoning process to be taught;

4. assess the textbook's adequacy in presenting information about the reasoning process to be taught;

5. determine how the lesson should be introduced to the class and how its usefulness should be explained;

6. decide what to say and do while modeling when and how to use the reasoning process;

7. identify places in the text where students could apply the process;

8. try to anticipate the types of problems students may encounter learning when and how to use the reasoning process.

The teacher begins a Direct Explanation lesson by providing background vocabulary and creating interest for the basal story to be read (Roehler & Duffy, in press). The teacher then teaches a strategy by describing and modeling the reasoning process associated with the strategy. Students are given examples of how the strategy could be applied and are provided guided practice situations. Teachers gradually withdraw support as students become more proficient in strategy use (Duffy & Roehler, 1987).

The effective presentation of a Direct Explanation lesson is dependent upon the mental modeling provided by the teacher. By thinking out loud, teachers provide students with insights into the reasoning behind a strategy's use. Review of some of the published examples of mental modeling is highly recommended.

Research Results

Several studies of the Direct Explanation Model have been conducted. The first question researchers attempted to answer was, "Can teachers be taught to be more explicit in teaching students strategic reading skills?" These studies indicate they can. Teachers can be taught to recast textbook skills as strategies and to teach the reasoning processes associated with these strategies (Duffy et al., 1986a; Duffy et al., 1987c, Herrmann et al., 1985).

Next, studies examined the effect on students of being taught by the Direct Explanation Model. Poor readers increased their awareness of the strategies taught as well as their use of strategic reasoning (Duffy et al., 1986a). These children also significantly out performed control students on the word-study subtest of the Stanford Achievement Test. Interestingly, however, significant differences were not noted between these groups on the comprehension subtest. Reasons for this "no difference finding" could be explained by such factors as

1) the emphasis in basal texts on lower-level skill tasks, 2) the lack of suitability of the standardized test format for assessing students' reading behavior, and 3) the difficulty in showing growth over a short period of time with at-risk students (Duffy et al., 1987c).

Duffy and his colleagues (1986b) also studied variations among teachers trained in the Direct Explanation approach and the impact these variations had on student performance. While the Direct Explanation approach generally enhanced students' awareness of reading strategies when the instructed students were compared to those not receiving the intervention, considerable differences were noted in performance among the instructed classes. Transcripts of the teachers' lesson were analyzed to determine possible causes of these variations. Relatively subtle differences in what teachers say during instruction makes for marked differences in students' strategy awareness. The more effective teachers did not require strict memorization of steps in applying a strategy or memorization of arbitrary definitions. Instead, they described the new strategy as a cognitive process requiring flexibility and adaptation. They emphasized the reasoning associated with the strategy by both explaining and modeling the thinking processes involved. They also showed students how the strategy could be used in a variety of situations outside the school environment. These teachers provided more instruction at the beginning of a lesson and elaborated on responses given by **students** (Duffy et al., 1986b). These findings have great relevance for how this and other methods of strategy instruction are best taught.

The Direct Explanation Model is a challenging one. Mental modeling, one of the key components of this approach, can be troublesome for some teachers to master. Some teachers have difficulty conceptualizing the difference between skills and strategies (Roehler & Duffy, in press; Roehler et al., 1986). Busch (1988) reports that the anxiety level of teachers tends to be very high as they begin to work with this method. As teachers meet with success, their anxiety quickly subsides. Establishing collaborative teams and effective instructional leadership should provide the support that teachers need as they learn to apply the Direct Explanation Model in their classroom (Duffy, 1988).

For more information, see:

Duffy, G., & Roehler, L. (1987). Teaching reading skills as strategies. *Reading Teacher, 40,* 414-421.

Duffy, G., Roehler, L., & Herrmann, B. A. (1988). Modeling mental processes helps poor readers become strategic readers. *The Reading Teacher, 41,* 762-767.

APPENDIX B

Three Examples of Composition Instruction

SELF-INSTRUCTIONAL STRATEGY DEVELOPMENT

The goal of strategy instruction in writing is to help students to become more independent learners by explicitly assisting them to develop processes and techniques used by good writers (Harris & Pressley, 1991). Steve Graham and Karen Harris of the University of Maryland have developed and utilized a self-instructional strategy development approach (SISD) to teach students with learning problems an array of strategies and self-management routines to be employed when writing (Graham & Harris, 1987; Graham & Harris, 1989c; Graham et al., 1987; Harris & Graham, 1988; Harris & Graham 1992).

Many of the writing strategies developed by Graham and Harris have focused on prewriting activities. For example students have been taught strategies that focus on the following:

- *brainstorming ideas or words in advance of writing. This strategy is particularly useful because it gives students a means for searching their memory for relevant information prior to story writing (Graham et al., in press; Harris & Graham, 1985);*

- *generating and organizing ideas before and during writing. This strategy includes a series of prompts that urges students to reflect on their purpose for writing, consider the intended audience, develop a plan, evaluate possible content through considering its impact on the reader, and continue the process of content generation and planning while writing (Graham & Harris, 1989c); and*

- *planning their stories through asking a series of questions designed to prompt their thinking (Graham & Harris, 1989a). This strategy helps students to stop and think about what the content for their stories should be before beginning to write.*

Harris and Graham (1992) have summarized their approaches to writing in a recent book, *Helping Young Writers Master the Craft*-in this series.

The SISD approach also has been used successfully to teach strategies for use with other writing processes such as revision (Graham & MacArthur, 1988).

How Are Strategies Taught?

Seven basic but recursive and flexibly applied stages provide the structural frame for this approach.

1. Preskill development involves developing skills students may be lacking that are necessary to understand, acquire and execute the strategy to be taught.

2. An initial conference is held to establish instructional goals and the significance of the strategies and self-regulation abilities to be developed;

3. Discussion of the strategy includes considerations of the strategy, its purpose, strengths and limitations, and when and where to use it;

4. Modeling the strategy by the teacher or a peer is a key step in which use of the strategy is mastered;

5. Mastery of the strategy involves the student's learning of the strategy steps;

6. Collaborative practice comprises applying the strategy in scaffolded situations;

7. Independent performance is the step in which students are encouraged to use the strategy and self-instructions independently (Graham et al., 1987).

The goal of this interactive instructional process is to aid the student who is having difficulty with writing to internalize, execute, modify, and maintain use of the instructed strategies (Graham et al., in press).

Harris (1990) stresses that students involved in SISD are not treated as passive recipients of instruction. Rather, they are expected to be active collaborators in determining the goals of their instruction, completing the task, evaluating the strategy and task performance, and planning for transfer and maintenance. Teachers utilizing SISD are expected to form a collaborative relationship with students. For SISD to be successful, the teacher must be responsive to each child and provide individually tailored feedback.

In recent years, SISD has been used by some special education teachers within programs that rely primarily on a process approach to writing (Danoff, 1990). Within the process framework students write frequently and regularly, make decisions about their writing, share their work with other students and the teacher, receive responses to their work from teachers or other students, and confer with teachers.

Teachers provide instruction to students in the cognitive processes that underlie writing during conferences and direct instruction. Typically teachers assist students in understanding the processes used in writing by modeling strategies and the thinking that accompany their use. While these procedures are thought valuable components in a writing program, Graham, Harris and their colleagues believed that students with learning disabilities need direct, structured instruction in *how to apply* writing processes and strategies (Graham et al., in press).

Barbara Danoff (1990), a special education teacher, found that this was the case with her fourth and fifth grade students who were in need of special education. These children had been involved in a process-oriented writing program in their regular classroom for three to four years. As a result, they were very comfortable writing and wrote frequently. But Danoff observed that these youngsters still experienced difficulties frequently observed in students with learning problems. For example, they wrote stories that typically included only two or three of the common story elements. Danoff taught these children a strategy to help them remember to incorporate all seven common story elements in their pieces. Following their learning of the strategy, the students began to write stories with all seven story elements included, and their stories were judged to be of higher quality than the stories produced prior to strategy instruction.

Danoff (1990) instructed her students using a "plug-in" model where she worked with both normally achieving students and students who needed special education within the regular classroom. Strategy approaches have been used within resource room settings.

For more information, see:

Harris, K. & Graham, S. (1992). *Helping young writers master the craft: Strategy instruction & self-regulation in the writing process.* Cambridge, MA: Brookline Books.

Graham, S., & Harris, K. (1989c). Improving learning disabled students' skills at composing essays: Self-instructional Strategy Training. *Exceptional Children*, 55, 201-214.

COGNITIVE STRATEGY INSTRUCTION IN WRITING

Cognitive Strategy Instruction in Writing (CSIW), developed by Carol Sue Englert and her colleagues at Michigan State University, is founded on two major beliefs. The social context of writing should not be ignored during teaching, so students should be made sensitive to audience concerns when writing. Second, knowledge of text structure plays a key role in planning, organizing, drafting and revising compositions, and can serve as the basis for producing a series of questions or strategies for use in guiding writing. The intent of this program, then, is to instruct students in how to monitor and control strategies for planning, drafting, peer editing and revising compositions (Englert et al., 1988a).

How Is The CSIW Program Implemented?

One of the first steps usually taken when implementing CSIW is for the teacher to present examples of both poorly and well-organized compositions within various writing genres. As teachers read the compositions to students, they ask key questions that good writers would ask as they write and revise. With this approach, the teacher models monitoring behavior and also illustrates how different kinds of writing are designed to answer different types of questions (Englert & Raphael, 1988). The teachers also model writing behaviors, such as how to decide what changes should be made in a composition during revision.

Besides strategy modeling, the CSIW approach relies heavily on the use of "Think Sheets" to prompt students to think about their audience and the intended text structure as they organize and revise their texts. For example, the Think Sheet used during the planning of a composition prompts students to consider their purpose for writing the piece and their audience. Students are reminded to search their memory to identify what they know about the topic they have selected and are guided in grouping their ideas (Englert & Raphael, 1988; Englert et al., 1988a).

The Think Sheet prompting organized thought includes questions based on the specific type of composition being produced. For example, when writing a compare and contrast essay, students are guided in determining **what** is being compared or contrasted, and with what results (Englert et al., 1988a; Englert & Raphael, 1988).

The editing Think Sheet provides checklists that help students judge the content and organization of their composition, and another Think Sheet is designed for use in a peer-editing situation (Englert & Raphael, 1988). Finally, the Think Sheet for revision helps students focus on decisions to be made during that process, such as how to decide whether to make recommended changes (Englert et al., 1988a).

Englert and Raphael (1988) have identified several features they believe are essential for the implementation of the CSIW program. They include

- *teacher modeling of strategies and the thinking that accompanies their use;*

- *student rehearsal of strategies and use of Think Sheets;*

- *interactive teaching and classroom dialogues about strategies and how problems encountered in writing may be addressed;*

- *gradual internalizing of strategies by students particularly through self and peer editing activities;*

- *group work used for peer coaching and cooperative learning; and*

- *monitoring of student thinking and of their use of strategies.*

Although mechanics and grammar teaching are not emphasized in the CSIW, the teacher works with students in writing conferences to help them identify and correct spelling and grammatical errors in their compositions (Englert et al., 1988a).

For more information, see:

Englert, C., & Raphael, T. (1988). Constructing well-formed prose: Process, structure and metacognitive knowledge. *Exceptional Children, 54,* 513-520.

Englert, C. S., & Raphael, T. (1989). Developing successful writers through cognitive strategy instruction. In J. Brophy (Ed.), *Advances in research on teaching* (Vol. 1) (pp. 105-151). Greenwich, CT: JAI Press.

PROCESS WRITING

The basic principles of process writing approaches were described in a study conducted about ten years ago by Donald Graves and his associates at the University of New Hampshire (Graves, 1982). After observing six and nine-year-old students as they wrote, Graves formulated several hypotheses that have served to guide the development of process writing programs. He observed the following

- *behaviors of writers are highly variable, and until a writer writes or speaks, it is impossible for the teacher to know what to do instructionally;*

- *teachers need to observe clusters of behaviors before making decisions about a student's writing;*

- *scope and sequence of skill acquisition have little relevance to how writers develop;*

- *a conference approach to writing instruction is the best way to help students develop as writers;*

- *students should be given the opportunity for sustained writing in class and at predictable times;*

- *students should be allowed to select most of their writing topics; and*

- *skills are best taught within the context of the student's own writing.*

Process writing programs depend on a high degree of teacher-student interaction. Graves (1985) believes that teachers teach most by sharing how they learn and that this instruction can best occur within an instructional environment that is highly structured and predictable.

How is the Process Approach Implemented?

A workshop type of environment where students discover and act upon their own intentions, and where reading, writing and other language arts instruction is integrated typifies process writing classrooms (Atwell, 1988). For example, Susan Stires (1988) reports that she designed her instruction for primary level students in need of special education to provide numerous opportunities for them to talk, question, and listen. Reading instruction was centered around children's literature. Students read to themselves and each other, and time was taken for students to discuss their reading with their classmates. Writing instruction complemented the reading program as students wrote daily about what they had read (Stires, 1983).

Instructional programs based upon process approach principles share several characteristics. First, adequate and predictable instructional time needs to be set aside for writing (Sunstein, 1990). Graves (1985) advises that teachers should teach writing at least four days a week, as compared to the national average of one day in eight. Taking enough time for writing is thought to be particularly important for students with learning problems.

Second, students' control of their own writing is instilled through practices such as allowing them to select the topics for their compositions. Graves (1985) reminds that all children have important experiences and interests they can use as the basis for their writing. Journal writing, where students record their thoughts daily, is frequently used as a way of encouraging children to think about topics they may write.

Third, a responsive environment for writing is essential for supporting children in their efforts to communicate through the written word. Responsiveness is conveyed through teacher-student conferences in which a teacher guides students' writing by being sensitive to their learning needs, asking questions about their writing, and providing comments and feedback on their ideas (Graves, 1985). Teachers model effective writing behavior, but such modeling usually occurs at the point and time that an individual student needs assistance with a particular point (Stires, 1990).

Fourth, in the process writing classroom, the social nature of writing is strongly emphasized (Wansart, 1988). Students share their writing with their classmates and in turn listen and learn from them (Sunstein, 1990). It is believed that a supportive environment assists students to take responsibility for their writing (Graves, 1985).

Fifth, teachers and students become equal partners in the learning process (Sunstein, 1990). Teachers write along with their students, sharing their thinking about their own writing processes as they do (Graves, 1985; Stires, 1989).

Sixth, while teachers in the process writing program do not emphasize instruction in grammar, spelling, and mechanics, neither do they ignore the need for children to develop these proficiencies. But it is believed that skill instruction is best presented within the context of writing instruction and as a means of making writing clearer to the intended audience (Stires, 1990).

Stires (1989) stresses that although the individual teacher's guidance and involvement in authentic writing experiences can assist students to become better writers, the ultimate responsibility for writing must be placed on the writer. At all stages in the writing process, students are expected to conduct self-evaluations.

While developed for use with regular education students, process writing programs have been used successfully in both resource room and regular classroom settings with students who are experiencing learning problems (Atwell, 1988). Susan Stires (1988) has remarked that her experiences teaching writing to children in need of special education have taught her that disabled writers are distinguishable from other student writers only to the degree to which certain parts of the writing process are difficult for them. She has come to see that all disabled writers have strengths.

In recent years, extensive efforts have been made to offer knowledge of and training in process writing approaches to teachers throughout the country. Workshops are offered by Graves and his colleagues at the University of New Hampshire, Lucy Calkins of Teacher's College, Columbia University, and through the National Writing Project headquartered at University of California at Berkeley.

For more information, see:

Atwell, N. (1988). A special writer at work. In T. Newkirk, & N. Atwell (Eds.), *Understanding writing: Ways of observing, learning, and teaching* (pp. 114-129). Portsmouth, NH: Heinemann.

Graves, D. (1983). *Writing: Teachers and children at work.* Exeter, NH: Heinemann.

APPENDIX C

Two Examples of Approaches Designed to Enhance Student's Problem Solving Capabilities

Cognitively Guided Instruction

Cognitively Guided Instruction (CGI) is basically a teacher education program which provides teachers with knowledge about how children think and learn in specific mathematical domains. This knowledge is the result of findings from studies exploring children's addition and subtraction learning (Carpenter & Moser, 1982). Teachers determine the type of instruction that occurs in their classrooms. Thus, instructional decisions are influenced by what teachers know and what they believe to be the best way to teach specific subject matter (Fennema et al., 1989).

Some examples of important teacher knowledge and beliefs are ways to best present a subject; knowledge of effective examples, demonstrations, and media and materials that illustrate principles; an understanding of what makes learning particular topics within a subject easy or difficult; and knowledge of conceptions or misconceptions that youngsters may possess (Shulman, 1986). Major areas of teacher knowledge that influence mathematics instruction include an understanding of the conceptual and procedural knowledge students possess; familiarity with techniques for assessing students' understanding and for determining their misconceptions; and cognizance of the stages of understanding that students pass through as they move from knowing little about a topic to their mastery of it (Fennema et al., 1989).

Studies of Teachers' Knowledge and Beliefs About Mathematics

Research findings illustrate the importance of knowledge and beliefs on teachers' instructional decisions. Peterson and her colleagues (1988/89) found that first grade teachers varied widely in their beliefs and that the differences in teachers' beliefs about how young children should be taught mathematics are reflected in content and strategies that teachers reported selecting.

Teachers identified as having more cognitive-based perceptions—those believing that children construct math knowledge, that math skills should be taught in relation to problem solving, that instruction should be sequenced to build on children's development of mathematical ideas, and that instruction should be organized to facilitate children's knowledge construction—reportedly emphasized problem solving and the development of mathematical understanding in their teaching and de-emphasized the teaching of number facts. Students of those teachers scored higher on word problem solving than did children of teachers who had a less cognitive-oriented perspective (Peterson et al., 1989).

Carpenter and his colleagues (1988a) determined that first grade teachers also varied in their knowledge of how children solve addition and subtraction word problems. Most could identify the differences among problem types and the major strategies children use to solve problems. But teachers had not organized this knowledge into a framework that related problem type, problem difficulty, and children's solution strategies to one another. Consequently, this information did not influence teachers' instructional decisions.

Objectives of the CGI Program

The CGI program is designed to help teachers learn, organize, and use knowledge about children's mathematical thinking in their teaching. During workshops, participating teachers are presented with recent findings about children's learning and cognition in mathematics. Workshop time is allotted for teachers to discuss the principles of CGI instruction and to design their instructional program for classroom use. Teachers are also given the opportunity to examine teaching materials that could be used during instruction (Carpenter et al., 1988b).

While manipulatives are frequently used in CGI classrooms, this program does not require the use of specific materials. Instead, teachers are expected to make their own decisions about how and when media and materials can be intelligently and meaningfully incorporated into instruction (Fennema et al., 1989).

The CGI program does not prescribe a specific teaching method. The developers of this approach do anticipate that teachers will modify their behavior in certain directions when they gain insight into how children think about mathematics. First it is expected that teachers will become more adept at assessing children's thinking. Assessment is crucial if instruction is to be based on what students currently know and understand. Listening to children's explanations of their problem-solving processes and questioning children about their understanding are key assessment techniques (Fennema et al., 1989). For example, Barbara Marten, a CGI teacher from Madison, Wisconsin, reports that she frequently attempts to gauge the thought processes of her students as they work by asking them to explain how they solved particular problem types or how they know what they know. By listening to students, Marten acquires information that helps her design and pace instruction to meet student learning needs (Marten, 1989).

Second, teachers in the program learn how to design instruction based on what children know. Mathematics instruction needs to be meaningful to students and to be presented in a way that guides them to use more productive strategies when solving increasingly complex problems. Providing students with ample opportunities to engage in problem solving is one way this is accomplished. Therefore, CGI teachers place an early and continuing emphasis on word problems as the basis for teaching computational skills (Fennema et al., 1989).

Do the behaviors of CGI trained teachers change as a result of this program? Formal observations reveal that most teachers do indeed spend more time listening to children's explanations of problem solving, and they utilized word problems as the basis for instruction considerably more than non-trained teachers.

Classroom Implementation of CGI

Cognitively Guided Instruction can be used with whole classes or in small group settings (Fennema et al., 1989). Marten (1989) indicates that she groups children by their abilities to solve certain problem types and by their use of specific solution strategies. When placed in the groups, students are given problems to solve. While they are doing so, Marten observes them and through these observations she is able to diagnose difficulties.

An example of a CGI lesson was included in a recent edition of WCER Highlights, a newsletter published by the Wisconsin Center for Education Research (1989). Mazie Jenkins, a CGI teacher, began the lesson by posing an addition problem to her students. She told students she had prepared 15 word problems while her student teacher had written seven. She asked the students to tell her the total number of word problems prepared. When a controversy over the correct answer ensued (22 or 23), Jenkins challenged the class to find ways to determine what the correct answer might be. When a student stated that it must be 22 because two odd numbers equal an even number, Jenkins directed students to test the theory, which they did. This brief example illustrates how ideally the CGI teacher identifies problems from everyday situations, builds upon student responses, prompts students to call forth their knowledge and apply it to problem-solving situations, challenges students to test their conclusions, and leads them to explore new concepts and strategies.

Research Results

What is known about the effectiveness of the CGI approach? In one major study of this program conducted by Carpenter, Fennema and their colleagues (1988b), first grade CGI teachers devoted significantly more classroom time than other teachers to word problem solving and to listening to children explain the reasoning used in problem solving. In addition, these teachers expected and accepted from students a greater variety of problem-solving strategies (Fennema et al., 1989).

Significantly, students of CGI teachers did as well on standardized tests of computation and on tests of recall of number facts as did students of teachers not involved in the program, even though CGI teachers spent less time directly teaching math facts and computational skills (Fennema et al., 1989). Furthermore, students taught by CGI teachers performed better on problem-solving measures, had a greater understanding of problem solving, and were more confident of their ability to solve problems than students taught by non-CGI teachers. Interestingly, classes designated as lower achieving as a result of their scores on the pretest measure, the Iowa Test of Basic Skills, performed better than did lower achieving classes of non-CGI teachers on simple arithmetic word problems (Carpenter et al., 1988b).

For more information:

Peterson, et. al. (1988/89) Using knowledge of how children think about mathematics. *Educational Leadership*, 46, 42-46.

Fennea, et. al. (1989) Learning mathematics with understanding: cognitively guided instructions. In: J. Brophy (Ed.). Advances in research in teaching, 1, 195-221. Greenwich , CT: VAI Press.

THE VERBAL PROBLEM SOLVING FOR MILDLY HANDICAPPED STUDENTS PROJECT

The Verbal Problem Solving for Mildly Handicapped Students Project, shares with Cognitively Guided Instruction (CGI) the view that children need to learn mathematics in a meaningful manner, and that problem solving should stimulate and be the reason for learning an array of mathematical skills, including basic fact recall and computation. Unlike CGI, The Verbal Problem Solving project and its predecessor, Project Math, also developed by Cawley and his colleagues, are designed specifically for use with students with learning problems and rely heavily on the use of specially-designed materials oriented to problem solving. Also unlike CGI, this project includes components for teaching students from kindergarten through twelfth grade (Cawley, 1989).

Program Principles

Several instructional principles have guided the development of both The Verbal Problem Solving Project and Project Math. First, students with language arts deficiencies should not be delayed or hindered in their mathematics learning because of these problems (Cawley, 1989), nor should students experiencing difficulties with formal computations or basic fact recall be prohibited from engaging in more challenging problem-solving activities (Cawley & Miller, 1986). The developers believe that instructional modifications should be made to help circumvent students' learning problems. For example, The Verbal Problem Solving Project utilizes materials that direct student activities through visual communications and oral explanations by the teacher (Cawley, 1989).

Second, to the extent possible, mathematics instruction should be provided within the context of other subject content (Cawley, 1989). For example, The Verbal Problem Solving Project has produced materials that include an array of science-based activities, most of which are designed around group work. These activities not only provide students with opportunities for mathematics and science learning, but also help youngsters develop interpersonal skills through group activity (Cawley et al., 1988).

Third, students need to be active participants in their learning. Traditional mathematics instruction that places primary emphasis on drill and practice type of activities, the use of worksheets, and memorization often spawns a passive approach to learning. In contrast, Cawley and his colleagues (1988) believe that instruction stressing problem solving leads students to active involvement in math learning since effective problem solving requires students to plan and monitor solutions, apply a variety of cognitive strategies involved with thinking and reasoning, and execute procedures and skills. According to Cawley (1989), problem solving instruction is in keeping with the ultimate purpose of mathematics teaching for most youngsters—to help them learn to solve mathematical problems that they will face daily as adults.

Fourth, mathematics instruction for students who are disabled should be comprehensive and not focus on computational skills alone. Students with learning problems need to be introduced to an array of mathematical concepts and topics, including measurement, geometry, and fractions. Since the lifelong mathematical needs of these students transcend computation, mathematics instruction should as well (Cawley et al., 1988).

Role of Media and Materials

The Verbal Problem Solving Project, like Project Math, utilized an array of materials as the basis for instruction. Object cards and story mats depicting scenes such as wildlife and zoo settings are used with elementary-level children. The mat containing the wildlife environment scenes, for example, uses object cards with pictures of endangered animals (e.g., pandas and wild horses) and extinct creatures (dinosaurs).

A typical lesson using the wildlife mat would begin with the teacher engaging students in a discussion of the meaning of endangered and extinct. Next, the teacher may place some of the cards picturing pandas and wild horses on the mat and ask students to determine the number of pandas, the number of wild horses, and the number of endangered animals altogether. Students may then be asked to use the cards to perform a variety of computational operations, including division (Cawley, 1989).

While The Verbal Problem Solving Project requires students to perform computations, the focus of the project is not on the direct instruction of these skills. Rather, it focuses on supplementing students' regular mathematics instruction, where such skills are directly and formally taught (Baker, 1989), and on stressing conceptual development (Cawley, 1989).

Other materials have been produced that are used in this program. Cards containing graphic information that must be "read" and analyzed are included to help youngsters learn to interpret graphic material, and a series of activity sheets containing word problems are used to engage students in higher level thinking such as reflecting, synthesizing, and evaluating. These problem-solving activities are intended for use with junior and senior high school-aged students.

The program also includes Social Utilization Units built around science situations that require students to apply a variety of mathematical processes over time. For example, one such unit requires students to measure plant growth. Students plant seeds and identify conditions related to plant growth that they wish to evaluate. During the course of the unit, students make a variety of measurements at given intervals to assess the height and breadth of the plants, and they chart the results of these measurements. Students then evaluate their observations and draw conclusions. Thus, a student taking part in this unit has an opportunity to perform a variety of mathematical functions including measuring, computing, recording data, and graphing (Cawley, 1989).

The Verbal Problem Solving Project materials provide youngsters with an opportunity to apply a variety of mathematical skills, process information, analyze data, and develop their metacognitive capabilities. Cawley and his colleagues have published samples of some of the activities used in the project (see, for example, Cawley et al., 1988; Cawley & Miller, 1986). All the materials are accompanied by teacher manuals. These manuals are intended to help teachers structure their lessons by including background information, examples, and sample scripts (Baker, 1989).

Program Implementation

By design, little teacher training is offered through this program, since one of its goals is to provide materials that can readily be used by teachers who have little background in teaching mathematics or science. Teachers who participate in the project are provided with an initial overview of the program and materials. Site coordinators make periodic visits to participating teachers. At the end of the school year, participating teachers are interviewed to ascertain their opinions about the usefulness of the materials and the program in general (Baker, 1989).

For more information, see:

Cawley, J., Fitzmaurice, A. & Shaw, R. (1988) Mathematics for the mildly handicapped: A guide to curriculum & instruction. Boston, MA: Allyn & Bacon

Cawley J. & Miller J. (1986) Selected views on metacognation, arithmetic problems solving, & Learning Disabilities, *Learning Disabilities Focus*, 2, 1, 36-48.

Examples of Collaborative Learning Methods

Study Buddy

The Study Buddy program, a peer tutoring approach primarily for older elementary students, was developed by Dirk Hightower and Rachael Robb Avery of the Primary Mental Health Project in Rochester, New York (Hightower & Avery, 1987). The stated purpose of this intervention is to enhance social relations, school adjustment, and academic success of students and by so doing prevent youngsters from developing difficulties with interpersonal relationships later in life.

Students are placed with one or two other students of the same sex. Ideally, students are grouped with other youngsters who have complementary, interpersonal skills and learning styles. Study buddies meet regularly to develop ongoing peer relationships, learn successful academic and social skills, receive feedback, and practice learned skills.

Students are introduced to the Study Buddy program through a two-part curriculum. The first part, which takes about four weeks to implement, is called "Reciprocal Peer Learning." Students work with their partners toward an agreed-to goal in subjects such as math or spelling. Partners meet twice a week in 35-45 minute sessions.

The second part of the curriculum titled, "Cooperative Peer Relations," introduces skills needed for good interpersonal relations. Study Buddy partners assist each other to learn these skills over a period of eight weeks during biweekly 35-45 minute sessions.

After students have completed the curriculum, study groups continue to meet together twice a week. At this point, teachers assign the students work in a variety of subject areas such as math, social studies, science, language arts, and art.

Teachers learn to implement the program by attending a series of training sessions. They are taught strategies for grouping students, techniques for helping troubled Study Buddy groups, and ways to overcome problem areas. The curriculum units are also explained to teachers during these sessions.

After they begin implementing the Study Buddy program teachers are supported in their efforts by consultants who meet with them once every three weeks. These meetings are intended to provide a forum for discussing problems and exchanging information, and to foster cohesiveness among teachers implementing the program.

Classwide Peer Tutoring

Developed by the Juniper Gardens Children's project, the Classwide Peer Tutoring program is intended to improve instruction for minority, disadvantaged, and/or disabled students. The program has been used at both the elementary and secondary level (Maheady et al., 1988b) and with several categories of special education students including those who are learning disabled, educable mentally retarded, or behaviorally disordered (Delquadri et al., 1986).

This approach is based upon the belief that opportunity for frequent interaction in an educational setting is an important antecedent to achievement for at-risk students. Teacher responses that involve high levels of correction and feedback are particularly effective when instructing students with disabilities. The developers of this approach recognized that opportunities for the teacher to provide such interactions are limited. Therefore, they designed a program that enables students to provide their peers with this form of instructional interaction (Greenwood et al., 1984).

Classwide Peer Tutoring does not utilize a prepared curriculum, but most often employs materials currently used by the school district. This approach and variations of it have been used in the instruction of oral reading, reading comprehension, spelling, vocabulary development, and social studies (Delquadri et al., 1986; Maheady et al., 1988b).

Students undergo training before becoming involved with peer tutoring. The teacher explains the approach and then models the procedures that students will use in their peer tutoring sessions. Within a class, students are assigned to one of two teams and then students are separated into pairs within the teams.

Tutoring occurs during 30-minute sessions. Each student receives 10 minutes of tutoring from the other student. The remaining 10 minutes of the session are used to add and post points that are awarded in the tutoring sessions as a form of motivation.

During the tutoring sessions the student serving as tutor observes the tutee performing whatever skill is being practiced. For example, for oral reading, the tutee reads an assigned passage and the tutor awards the tutee a specified number of points for every sentence read correctly. The tutor corrects any errors made by the student. For example, if the tutee mispronounces a word, the tutor provides the correct pronunciation. The tutee then rereads the sentence in which the error had occurred until he or she does so correctly. Points are awarded for corrected performance and for working cooperatively. Earned points are recorded, team scores computed, and the winning team recognized and applauded (Delquadri et al., 1986).

Maheady and his colleagues (1988b) developed a variation of Classwide Peer Tutoring to teach social studies to secondary level students. In this program, regular and special education teachers together identify topics for tutoring and develop study guides containing a series of questions to serve as the focus for peer tutoring.

Teachers learn to use Classwide Peer Tutoring either through formal training or through reading a manual produced to explain the procedures that should be implemented when using this approach (Greenwood et al., 1984).

For more information, see:

Maheady, L., Harper, G., & Sacca, M. (1988). Peer-mediated instruction: A promising approach to meeting the diverse needs of LD adolescents. *Learning Disabilities Quarterly, 11,* 108-113.

Program for Complex Instruction

The Program for Complex Instruction was developed by Elizabeth Cohen and her associates at Stanford University (Cohen, 1990). The program is designed for use with elementary-aged students in grades two through five. The intent of this approach is to involve students in activities that are intrinsically motivating and challenging. In so doing, the program is designed to facilitate the development of thinking skills and to improve the linguistic and academic functioning of children in heterogeneous classrooms (Lotan & Benton, 1990).

Especially designed curricular materials are employed with Complex Instruction such as the Finding Out/Descubrimiento bilingual math and science curriculum developed by Edward DeAvila and his associates. This curriculum is organized around the following themes: measurement, change and measurement, shapes, crystals and powders, balance and structures, coordinates and measurement, clocks and pendulums, time and shadows, reflection/ refraction and optical illusions, estimation, probability and estimation, sound, water, water measurement, magnetism, electricity, and heat. The materials that help teach these themes include activity cards, worksheets, and manipulatives (Lotan & Benton, 1990).

Groups in the Complex Instruction program are structured so that each student plays a specific role. One student, for example, may be the facilitator, the student who seeks help from the teacher when the group is having difficulties; another student may be the checker, the one who makes sure the children have completed assigned worksheets; a third student may be responsible for reporting the results of the group work to the class; a fourth student assumes responsibility for cleaning up and putting away the materials used for the activity.

A specific role is identified for each student in the group to involve all students and to overcome status problems that often develop in heterogeneous groups (Cohen, 1986, 1990).

Complex Instruction stresses the importance of individual accountability, in other words, each student is held responsible for completing assigned tasks (Cohen, 1990). Equally important is the concept that all group members should be actively involved in the learning activity assigned. Because students in heterogeneous groups have different strengths and weaknesses, activities used in this approach require the application of a variety of abilities and skills for their completion—strengths in reasoning, observing, and detecting spatial relationships, as well as the traditional academic skills of reading, writing, and arithmetic are needed to complete a group assignment (Lotan & Benton, 1990).

Ideally, the teacher implementing the Complex Instruction Program will organize the class into learning centers. When this is done, a maximum of five children work at each center on a specified activity.

Teachers using Complex Instruction must create an environment that allows students to experiment, discover, and make mistakes. At the onset, the teacher makes it clear to children that multiple abilities are needed for performing the group's activity and helps students develop respect for each child's capabilities (Cohen, 1990; Lotan & Benton, 1990). Teachers make a special effort to "assign competence" to low-status students, often the youngsters who have below average reading and math skills. In other words, the teacher looks for opportunities to publicly praise these students for their valuable contribution to the group.

The teachers participating in the Program for Complex Instruction take part in a two-week training program usually held in the summer. Teachers are trained in how to delegate authority to groups and how to encourage students to engage in group learning (Cohen, 1990). They also learn about the theory behind the program, have the chance to watch experienced teachers use the method, practice the approach with students, and receive feedback (Lotan & Benton, 1990).

Teachers not able to go through the training can learn to implement parts of this program by reading *Designing Groupwork* (1986), written by the program's developer, Elizabeth Cohen. Before implementing the program on their own, teachers are urged to consider whether or not Complex Instruction meets their instructional goals. This approach is particularly effective for conceptual learning and thus should be used to achieve those types of learning goals. In addition, teachers must give thought to the curricular materials that will be needed. Materials should contain activities that are open-ended and require higher order thinking. Typical drill and practice textbook and workbook items would not be suitable for use. Too, activities need to be structured to accommodate the varying abilities of group participants

For more information, see:

Lotan, R., & Benton, J. (1990). Finding out about complex instruction: Teaching math and science in heterogeneous classrooms. In N. Davidson (Ed.), *Cooperative learning in mathematics: A handbook for teachers* (pp. 47-68). Menlo Park, CA: Addison Wesley.

Cohen, E. (1986). *Designing groupwork: Strategies for the heterogeneous classroom.* New York: Teachers College Press.

Cohen, E. (1990, October). Continuing to cooperate: Prerequisites for persistence. *Phi Delta Kappan, 72,* 134-136+.

JOHNSON AND JOHNSON COOPERATIVE LEARNING

The Johnsons' approach to cooperative learning can and has been applied across several subject areas and grade levels and with a variety of students including youngsters with disabilities. The Johnsons believe that group learning experiences should incorporate several elements. Thus, along with their colleagues, they have formulated a set of guidelines for establishing and using cooperative learning. These include the following:

1. Students need to be taught collaborative skills.

2. There should be positive interdependence in group work. Students must perceive that the goal of the group is to make sure that everyone in the group learns, that group members are rewarded based on their overall achievement, that tasks are designed so that their completion depends upon each member's contribution, that group members have complementary roles to play, and that the division of labor is designed so that the actions of one member have to be completed before the next member can complete his or her task.

3. Students need a chance to interact face-to-face. Interactions among students are believed to be the most powerful aspects of group learning experiences.

4. Individual accountability must exist. That is to say each group member must fulfill his/her responsibilities and obligations.

5. Time must be set aside for groups to reflect on their activities, to determine areas of success, and to correct those areas in need of improvement. (Johnson & Johnson, 1986; Johnson & Johnson, 1989a)

The Johnsons stress the importance of students being adequately prepared to work in groups. Students need to be taught social skills or what could be described as group etiquette. Too, they need to learn how to use learning processes that will help them to build deeper understandings of the material being studied and skills that will help them further investigate material, resolve controversies, and reconceptualize what is being studied. When teaching group skills, teachers must ensure that students know what is to be learned, understand the need for it, and have an opportunity to practice its use (Johnson et al., 1984).

The teacher assumes the role of academic expert and classroom manager when implementing the Johnson and Johnson approach. He or she specifies objectives for the lesson, makes decisions about how students should be placed in the group, explains the tasks and activities the students will engage in, structures positive goal interdependence, structures individual accountability, structures intergroup cooperation, explains criteria for success, and specifies desired behaviors (Johnson & Johnson, 1989a).

As students work in groups, the teacher monitors their behavior, provides assistance when needed, intervenes to teach cooperative skills, provides closure to lessons, evaluates students' learning, and assesses how well the group functioned (Johnson & Johnson, 1989a). Since no materials are specifically developed for use with this approach, teachers must design, prepare, and/or evaluate the suitability of classroom materials to be used (Johnson et al., 1984).

Direct training in use of these methods is provided by the Johnsons and other trainers. While this training can provide an introduction to the techniques and processes, perfecting the method occurs over time with practice. Collegial support is particularly useful in helping teachers do so. The Johnsons believe it is preferable for a group of teachers from the same school to be trained together so that when they begin to implement cooperative learning they can support each other (Brandt, 1987).

For more information, see:

Johnson, D., Johnson, R., Holubec, E., & Roy, P. (1984). *Circles of learning: Cooperation in the classroom.* Alexandria, VA: ASCD.

Johnson, D., & Johnson, R. (1989b). Cooperative learning: What special education teachers need to know. *The Pointer, 33*(2), 5-10.

JOHNS HOPKINS APPROACHES TO COOPERATIVE LEARNING

Robert Slavin and his associates at Johns Hopkins University's Center for Research on Elementary Schools have developed cooperative learning programs to support instruction within the heterogeneous classroom. Included are Team Accelerated Instruction (TAI) and Cooperative Integrated Reading and Composition (CIRC). These approaches are intended for use in the regular classroom and as alternatives to ability grouping or remedial or special education pull-out programs (Slavin et al., 1988). They combine cooperative instruction with other curriculum and domain-specific learning thereby producing an instructional approach intended for use throughout the school year in the appropriate subject area. Thus the Johns Hopkins programs include materials that teachers can readily use when implementing these approaches (Slavin et al., 1989/90).

Both TAI and CIRC stress the importance of use of both group rewards and individual accountability. Team Accelerated Instruction combines the motivational power of peer teaching with individualized instruction (Slavin, 1990b). The program is designed primarily for students in grades three through six, but it has been used at higher grade levels. Topics covered in the program include addition, substraction, multiplication, division, numeration, decimals, fractions, word problems, statistics, and algebra (Slavin et al., 1989/90).

Students are assigned to four to five member mixed ability learning teams, and every eight weeks, students are reassigned to a new team. A placement test is administered and each student is initially placed at the appropriate level in the program. Students are given self-instructional curriculum materials for the topic being addressed. These materials include explanations of the skill to be learned; step-by-step examples for solving problems; practice pages; tests; and answer sheets (Slavin et al., 1989/90).

Prior to beginning work in these materials, students are given an explanation of the concepts that underlie the skills to be learned. The teacher does this by bringing together from the teams those students who are at the same point in the curriculum. While the teacher is instructing a group of students, the other children continue to work on the self-instructional materials (Slavin et al., 1989/90; Slavin, 1990b).

When in teams, students work on problems and their solutions are checked by other team members. When students get four problems in a row correct they take a quiz and if they score 80% or better they are given a longer test. A score of 80% or better on this test is recorded on a Team Summary sheet. Whenever students fail to met the 80% standard either on the quiz or test, they receive individual attention from the teacher (Slavin et al., 1989/90).

Each week the team score is computed based on the average number of units covered by each student on the team and the scores on the tests. Teams that meet certain levels of achievement are awarded certificates (Slavin et al., 1989/90).

In addition to work on the units, students are given three minute tests of math facts twice a week. Every three weeks the teacher instructs the entire class in skills such as geometry, measurement, sets, and problem-solving strategies (Slavin et al., 1989/90).

The Cooperative Integrated Reading and Composition (CIRC) program consists of three components—basal-related activities, direct instruction in reading comprehension, and integrated language arts and writing instruction. As with the TAI program, students of mixed abilities work together (Slavin et al., 1988; Slavin et al., 1989/90).

To implement this program, the teacher first establishes two or more reading groups based upon student reading ability. Then teams are formed containing members from each group. For example, when the class has been divided into two reading groups—one containing higher and the other lower reading ability students—a four member team would contain two students from each group.

Some of the CIRC activities require students to work in pairs, others require all the members of the team to take part. As with TAI, scores are assigned for quizzes and other assignments such as compositions and book reports (Slavin et al., 1989/90).

Several activities to be used with basals have been incorporated into this program. Partner reading involves students reading silently to themselves then taking turns reading with their partner. Partners correct each other's errors. In the story structure identification activity, students identify the major components of stories. During story-related writing, the student writes a reaction to the story, writes about a topic related to it, or writes another section of the story such as an alternate ending. The word study activity aims to assist students in learning words that appear in stories they are reading, and the story retelling activity involves students in summarizing the main points in a story (Slavin et al., 1988).

Students verify when their partners have completed assignments and/or achieved a specified criterion for the activity. Periodically tests are given to check student progress (Slavin et al., 1988; Slavin et al., 1989/90).

Teachers using CIRC provide a lesson in reading comprehension skills one day a week. The teachers use specially developed curriculum materials that include worksheets and/or games. Students are also asked to read trade books every evening at home and must complete one book report every two weeks (Slavin et al., 1988; Slavin et al., 1989/90).

The integrated language arts and writing component of CIRC also employs a specifically designed curriculum. During three one-hour sessions each week, students write compositions on topics of their choice. Prior to these writing activities, teachers take ten minutes to present a mini lesson on writing processes, style, or mechanics. The next forty minutes is spent by students utilizing writing processes as they produce their own compositions, and the last ten minutes of the hour is spent sharing the writing products with classmates. In addition the teacher devotes two one-hour sessions per week to the teaching of specific aspects of writing such as how to organize narrative writing, noun-verb agreement, and so on (Slavin et al., 1988).

Training for these programs usually is provided on site over the period of one or two days. Training also is available through conferences that are held twice a year in Baltimore. TAI and CIRC materials are only available to school districts that have arranged for training (Slavin, 1991c).

For more information, see:

Slavin, R. (1989/1990). Research on cooperative learning: Consensus and controversy. *Educational Leadership, 47*(4), 52-55.

Slavin, R. (1985a). An introduction to cooperative learning research. In R. Slavin, S. Sharan, S. Kagan, R. Hertz-Lazarowitz, C. Webb, & R. Schmuck (Ed.), *Learning to cooperate, cooperating to learn* (pp. 5-15). New York: Plenum Press.

GROUP INVESTIGATION

Group Investigation developed by Sharan & Sharan (1998/90) attempts to merge democratic with academic inquiry processes. The method is designed to allow students to take an active part in determining what they will study and how. No set curriculum or materials are used as a part of this program. Carrying out investigations requires students to engage in problem-solving; to gather, interpret, and synthesize data; and to apply information. This method has been used at the elementary and junior high school levels and with students of varying abilities (Hertz-Lazarowitz et al., 1980; Sharan & Shackar, 1988; Sharan et al., 1984).

Students in groups practicing Group Investigation follow six steps: identifying the topic to be studied, planning the investigation, carrying out the investigation, preparing the final report, presenting the final report, and evaluating the group work (Sharan & Shackar, 1988; Sharan & Sharan, 1989/90). Areas to be investigated may be selected by one of two ways: students may be allowed to select their own areas to explore or the teacher may assign a broad topic, often one that coincides with the curriculum being studied. If the latter, students will then select the particular area for study. For example, a teacher may introduce a topic such as, "What can we learn about Arizona Indians?" Students will then identify areas and questions within this topic that they want to investigate. During this process, the teacher can stimulate questioning by identifying and bringing to the attention of the students materials such as magazine articles, films, books, and other items that relate to the topic.

Each student selects areas he or she would like to investigate. Students then meet in a series of progressively larger groups sharing their ideas. As a result of these meetings, a list of interest areas is developed. The teacher organizes the suggested areas for study into categories. A group is then formed to investigate each category. An example of such a category for the major topic referred to earlier is, "How did the different Indian tribes adapt their dwellings to their environment?" (Sharan & Sharan, 1989/90). Students are given the opportunity to choose which category they want to investigate and, thus, which group they will join.

Once in their group, students work to develop a researchable question. Each group member identifies a specific question or area that he or she will be responsible for researching alone or with a partner. An example of such a question may be, "How did the nomadic Apaches design their shelters?" Each group determines how it will proceed with its investigation. Teachers sometimes have students complete worksheets that reflect what will be studied by the group, which students will be investigating which areas, and the resources the group members anticipate using (Sharan & Sharan, 1989/90). At this planning stage the teacher monitors group activities and offers help when it is needed.

When students start their investigations, the teacher plays a different role. At the start of each class period, the teacher reviews what each group hopes to accomplish that day. Students then conduct the investigations, obtain answers to their questions, and discuss their findings with fellow group members. Sometimes these discussions will raise new questions that will be investigated (Sharan & Sharan, 1989/90).

When the group is ready to prepare its report, the members meet with the teacher to discuss intended contents and request any special materials or equipment needed. The teacher provides feedback about the proposed report and plans for presenting it. The groups then prepare and present their final reports to the class as a whole (Sharan & Sharan, 1989/90).

Teachers use progress interviews with students and observations of them working in the group to determine the extent to which students are using higher order thinking processes. Teachers may assess students' content learning by administering tests containing questions suggested by each group. The teacher also evaluates the group product (Sharan et al., 1984; Sharan & Sharan, 1989/90).

Teachers are trained in Group Investigation through a series of workshops. Topics for these training sessions include basic principles of cooperative learning; techniques for training pupils to conduct small group work and for developing their communication and listening skills; and methods for training pupils to plan a study project, to use learning resources, and to prepare and present their reports. Simulations and small group work are features of teacher training (Sharan & Shackar, 1988).

For more information,see:

Sharan, Y., & Sharan, S. (1989/1990). Group investigation expands cooperative learning. *Educational Leadership, 47*(4), 17-21.

Structural Approach to Cooperative Learning

This approach to cooperative learning advocated by Spencer Kagan and his colleagues is intended to provide teachers with a knowledge of several group learning structures that they can apply to achieve specific learning objectives across subject areas (Kagan, 1989/90). This approach does not rely on a particular curriculum and can be used within a variety of subject areas (Brandt, 1989/90). Nor does it provide teachers with detailed directions of what and how to teach (Kagan, 1989/90). Examples of a few of the group structures taught include

Round Robin. Each member of the group shares information or a thought with fellow group members. This structure helps group members become acquainted with each other. It fosters equal participation and is useful for team building.

Numbered Heads Together. The teacher using this structure asks a question. Group members consult with each other to make sure that everyone knows the answer. The teacher then will call upon one student to respond. Teachers most often use this structure to review and check knowledge and comprehension and to determine mastery.

Think-Pair-Share. This method is used for concept development. Students think about a topic by themselves, then they pair up with another student to discuss it. This structure helps students to generate and revise hypotheses, reason, and apply knowledge.

Co-op Co-op. Students work together in groups to produce a product that they will share with the entire class. Each student makes a specific contribution to the group. This structure promotes learning and sharing of complex material, as well as skills in evaluation, application, analysis, and synthesis. Thus it can be used for a variety of objectives.

Training and materials used in the Structural Approach to Cooperative Learning are provided by Resources for Teachers in San Juan

Capistrano, California (Kagan 1989/90). Training focuses on teaching teachers the structures and helping them to match structures to instructional or social goals (Brandt, 1989/90).

For more information, see:

Kagan, S. (1989/1990). The structural approach to cooperative learning. *Educational Leadership, 47*(4), 12-15.

References

Albion, F., & Salzberg, C. (1982). The effect of self-instructions on the rate of correct addition problems with mentally retarded children. *Education and Treatment of Children, 5,* 121-131.

Allardice, B., & Ginsburg, H. (1983). Children's psychological difficulties in mathematics. In H. Ginsburg (Ed.), *The development of mathematical thinking* (pp. 319-350). New York: Academic Press.

Allington, R. (1988). *Report from small group one.* Presentation at the First Annual ICSEMM Instructional Methods Forum, Washington, D.C.

Anderson, M. (1988). *Partnerships: Developing teamwork at the computer.* Arlington, VA: MAJO Press.

Anderson, M., & Roe, T. (1991). *Report from small group three.* Presentation at the Fourth Annual Instructional Methods Forum,. Washington, D.C.

Anderson, V., & Hidi, S. (1988/89). Teaching students to summarize. *Educational Leadership, 46,*(4), 42-46.

Andrews, J. (1988). Deaf children's acquisition of prereading skills using the reciprocal teaching procedure. *Exceptional Children, 54,* 349-35.

Applebee, A. (1981). *Writing in the secondary school: English and the content areas.* Urbana, IL: National Council of Teachers of English.

Applebee, A., Langer, J., Jenkins, L., Mullis, I., & Foertsch, M. (1990). *Learning to write in our nation's schools.* Princeton, NJ: ETS.

Applebee, A., Langer, J., & Mullis, I. (1986). *The Writing Report Card: Writing achievement in American schools.* Princeton, NJ: ETS.

Arbitman-Smith, R., Haywood, H.C., & Bransford, J.D. (1984). Assessing cognitive change. In P. Brooks, R. Sperber, & M. McCauley (Eds.), *Learning and cognition in the mentally retarded* (pp. 433-471). Hillsdale, NJ: Erlbaum.

Atwell, N. (1984, December). Having a writing conference with yourself. *Livewire,* 1041.

Atwell, N. (1988). A special writer at work. In T. Newkirk & N. Atwell (Eds.), *Understanding writing: Ways of observing, learning, and teaching* (pp. 114-129). Portsmouth, NH: Heinemann.

Atwell, N. (1990). Introduction. In N. Atwell (Ed.), *Coming to know: Writing to learn in the intermediate grades* (pp. xi-xxiii). Portsmouth, NH: Heinemann.

Au, K., & Kawakami, A. (1984). Vygotskian perspectives in discussion processes in small group reading lessons. In P. Peterson, L. Wilkinson, & M. Hallinan (Eds.), *The social context of instruction: Group organization and group processes* (pp. 209-225). Orlando, FL: Academic Press.

Augustine, D., Gruber, K., & Hanson, L. (1989/1990). Cooperation works. *Educational Leadership, 47*(4), 4-7.

Avery, C. (1987). Traci: A learning disabled child in a writing process classroom. In G. Bissex, & R. Bullocks (Eds.), *Seeing for ourselves* (pp. 59-75). Portsmouth, NH: Heinemann.

Bailey, G., & Dyck, N. (1990). The administrator and cooperative learning: Roles and responsibilities in instructional leadership. *Clearinghouse, 64*(1), 39-43.

Baker, J. (1989). *Verbal problem solving for mildly handicapped students in the Pittsburgh Public Schools.* Presentation at the Second Annual ICSEMM Instructional Methods Forum, Washington, D.C.

Baker, L., & Brown, A.L. (1984). Cognitive monitoring in reading. In J. Flood (Ed.), *Understanding reading comprehension* (pp. 21-44). Newark, DE: International Reading Association.

Bandura, A. (1969). *Principles of behavior modification*. New York: Holt, Rinehart & Winston.

Barenbaum, E. (1990). *Strategy training in composing with learning disabled children*. Presentation at the Third Annual ICSEMM Instructional Methods Forum, Washington, D.C.

Barenbaum, E., Newcomer, P., & Nodine, B. (1987). Children's ability to write stories as a function of variation in task, age, and developmental level. *Learning Disabilities Quarterly, 10,* 175-188.

Baroody, A. (1985). Basic counting principles used by mentally retarded children. *Journal of Research in Mathematics Education, 17,* 382-389.

Baroody, A. (1986). Counting ability of moderately and mildly handicapped children. *Education and Training of the Mentally Retarded, 21,* 289-300.

Baroody, A. (1987). *Children's Mathematical Thinking: A Developmental Framework for Preschool, Primary, and Special Education Teachers*. New York: Teachers College Press.

Baroody, A. (1988a). Mental-addition development of children classified as mentally handicapped. *Educational Studies in Mathematics, 19,* 369-388.

Baroody, A. (1988b). Number comparison learning by children classified as mentally retarded. *American Journal of Mental Retardation, 92,* 461-471.

Baroody, A. (1989a). *A guide to teaching mathematics in the primary grades*. Boston: Allyn and Bacon.

Baroody, A. (1989b). *Designing instruction to foster meaningful learning and problem-solving ability*. Presentation at the ICSEMM Publishers Workshop, Washington, D.C.

Baroody, A. (1989c). One point of view: manipulatives don't come with guarantees. *Arithmetic Teacher, 37,* October, 4-5.

Baroody, A. (in press). Teaching mathematics developmentally to children classified as learning disabled. In D. Reid, W. Hresko and H. Swanson (Eds.) *A cognitive approach to learning disabilities*. Austin, TX: Pro-ED.

Baroody, A., & Ginsburg, H. (1984, April). *TMR and EMR Children's Ability to Learn Counting Skills and Principles*. Paper presented at the annual meeting of American Educational Research Association, New Orleans (ED 249 681).

Baroody, A., & Ginsburg, H. (1986). The relationship between initial meaningful and mechanical knowledge of arithmetic. In J. Hiebert (Ed.), *Conceptual and procedural knowledge: The case of mathematics* (pp. 75-112). Hillsdale, NJ.: Erlbaum.

Baroody, A., & Snyder, P. (1983). A cognitive analysis of basic arithmetic abilities of TMR children. *Education and Training of the Mentally Retarded, 18,* 253-259.

Baroody, A., & Standifer, D. (in progress). Addition and subtraction. In R. Jensen (Ed.), *Early Childhood* volume of the National Council of Teachers of Mathematics Research Interpretation Project. New York: Macmillan.

Beck, I. (1989). Improving practice through understanding reading. In L. Resnick and L. Klopfer, *Toward the thinking curriculum: Current cognitive research* (40-58). Alexandria, VA: Association for Supervision and Curriculum Development.

Belmont, J., Butterfield, E., & Borkowski, J. (1978). Training retarded people to generalize memorization methods across tasks. In M.M. Gruneberg, P.E. Morris, & R.N. Sykes (Eds.), *Practical aspects of memory.* London: Academic Press.

Bereiter, C. (1980). Development in writing. In L. Gregg & E.R. Steinberg (Eds.), *Cognitive processes in writing* (pp. 73-93). Hillsdale, NJ: LEA.

Bereiter, C., & Scardamalia, M. (1982). From conversation to composition: The role of instruction in a developmental process. In R. Glaser (Ed.), *Advances in instructional psychology*, Vol. 2 (pp. 1-64). Hillsdale, NJ: LEA.

Bereiter, C., & Scardamalia, M. (1986). Levels of inquiry into the nature of expertise in writing. *Review of Research in Education* (Vol. 13, pp. 259-282). Washington, DC: AERA.

Bereiter, C., & Scardamalia, M. (1987). *The psychology of written composition*. Hillsdale, NJ: LEA.

Bernagozzi, T. (1988). The new cooperative learning: One teacher's approach. *Learning, 16*(6), 39-43.

Blankenship, C. (1984). Curriculum and instruction: An examination of models in special and regular education. In J. Cawley (Ed.), *Developmental teaching of mathematics for the learning disabled* (pp. 29-53). Rockville, MD: Aspen.

Bley, N. (1987). Problem solving and learning disabilities. *Arithmetic Teacher, 34, April,* 35.

Bley, N. (1989). *Topics and issues.* Presentation at the Second Annual ICSEMM Instructional Methods Forum, Washington, D.C.

Bley, N., & Thornton, C. (1981). *Teaching mathematics to the learning disabled.* Rockville, MD: Aspen.

Borkowski, J., Estrada, M., Milstead, M., & Hale, C. (1989). General problem solving skills: Relations between metacognition and strategic processing. *Learning Disabilities Quarterly, 12,* 57-70.

Borkowski, J.G., & Cavanaugh, J.C. (1979). Maintenance and generalization of skills and strategies by the retarded. In N.R. Ellis (Ed.), *Handbook of mental deficiency: Psychological theory and research,* (pp. 569-608), 2nd ed. Hillsdale, NJ: Erlbaum.

Borkowski, J.G., Reid, M.K., & Kurtz, B. (1984). Metacognition and retardation: Paradigmatic, theoretical, and applied perspectives. In D. Brooks, R. Sperber, & C. McCauley (Eds.), *Learning and cognition in the mentally retarded* (pp. 55-75). Hillsdale, NJ: Erlbaum.

Borkowski, J.G., Weyhing, R., & Turner, L. (1986). Attributional retraining and the teaching of strategies. *Exceptional Children, 53,* 130-137.

Bos, C. (1988). Process-oriented writing: Instructional implications for mildly handicapped students. *Exceptional Children, 54,* 521-527.

Bos, C.S., & Filip, D. (1984). Comprehension monitoring in learning disabled and average students. *Journal of Learning Disabilities, 17,* 229-233.

Bossert, S. (1989). Cooperative activities in the classroom. *Review of Research in Education* (pp. 225-250). Washington: American Educational Research Association.

Bossert, S., Barnett, B., & Filby, N. (1984). Grouping and instructional organization. In P. Peterson, L. Wilkinson, & M. Hallinan (Eds.), *The social context of instruction: Group organization and group processes* (pp. 39-51). Orlando, FL: Academic Press.

Boynton, R. (1988, December). Somewhere over the rainbow: Textbooks and English classes. *English Education,* 206-214.

Bracewell, R. (1980). Writing as a cognitive activity. *Visible Language, 14,* 400-422.

Brady, S., & Jacobs, S. (1988). Children responding to children: Writing groups and classroom community. In T. Newkirk, & N. Atwell (Eds.), *Understanding writing: Ways of observing, learning, and teaching* (pp. 142-150). Portsmouth, NH: Heinemann.

Brainin, S.S. (1985). Mediating learning pedagogic issues in the improvement of cognitive functioning. In E.W. Gordon (Ed.), *Review of research in education* (Vol. 12, pp. 121-154). Washington, DC: AERA.

Brandt, R. (1987). On cooperation in schools: A conversation with David and Roger Johnson. *Educational Leadership, 45*(3), 14-19.

Brandt, R. (1989/1990). On cooperative learning: A conversation with Spencer Kagan. *Educational Leadership, 47*(4), 8-11.

Brennan, C. (1988). How to cover a language arts text. In T. Newkirk, & N. Atwell (Eds.), *Understanding writing: Ways of observing, learning, and teaching* (pp. 274-283). Portsmouth, NH: Heinemann.

Bridge, C., & Hiebert, E. (1985). A comparison of classroom writing practices, teachers' perceptions of their writing instruction, and textbook recommendations on writing practices. *Elementary School Journal, 86,* 155-172.

Brown, A.L. (1974). The role of strategic behavior in retardate memory. In N.R. Ellis (Ed.), *International review of research in mental retardation* (Vol. 7). New York: Academic Press.

Brown, A.L. (1980). Metacognitive development and reading. In R.S. Spiro, B.B. Bruce, & W.L. Brewer (Eds.), *Theoretical issues in reading comprehension.* Hillsdale, NJ: Erlbaum.

Brown, A.L. (1985). *Teaching students to think as they read: Implications for curriculum reform.* (Reading Education Report No. 58). Urbana: University of Illinois, Center for the Study of Reading.

Brown, A.L., & Barclay, C.R. (1976). The effects of training specific mnemonics on the metamnemonic efficacy of retarded children. *Child Development, 47,* 71-80.

Brown, A.L., Bransford, J., Ferrara, R., & Campione, J. (1983). Learning, remembering, and understanding. In J. Flavell & E. Markman (Eds.), *Handbook of child psychology, Vol. 3: Cognitive development* (pp. 77-166). New York: John Wiley.

Brown, A.L., & Campione, J. (1986). Psychological theory and the study of learning disabilities. *American Psychologist, 41,* 1059-1068.

Brown, A.L., Campione, J.C., & Barclay, C.R. (1979). Training self-checking routines for estimating test readiness: Generalizations from list learning to prose recall. *Child Development, 50,* 501-512.

Brown, A.L., & Palincsar, A.S. (1982). Inducing strategic learning from text by means of informed self-control training. *Topics in Learning and Learning Disabilities, 2,* 1-17.

Brown, A.L., & Palincsar, A.S. (1987). Reciprocal teaching of comprehension strategies: A natural history of one program for enhancing learning. In J. Day & J. Borkowski (Eds.), *Intelligence and exceptionality: New directions in theory, assessment and instructional practices* (pp. 81-132). Norwood, NJ: Ablex.

Brown, A., & Palincsar, A. (1989). Guided cooperative learning and individual knowledge acquisition. In L. Resnick (Ed.), *Knowing, learning, and instruction: Essays in honor of Robert Glaser* (pp. 393-447). Hillsdale, NJ: LEA.

Brown, C., Carpenter, T., Kouba, V., Lindquist, M., Silver, E., & Swafford, J. (1988a, April). Secondary school results for the fourth NAEP mathematics assessment: Discrete mathematics, data organization and interpretation, measurement, number and operations. *Mathematics Teacher, 81,* 241-248.

Brown, C., Carpenter, T., Kouba, V., Lindquist, M., Silver, E., & Swafford, J. (1988b, May). Secondary school results for the fourth NAEP mathematics assessment: Algebra, geometry, mathematical methods and attitudes. *Mathematics Teacher, 81,* 337-347, 397.

Bulgren, J., & Montague, M. (1989). *Report from small group four.* Presentation at the ICSEMM Instructional Methods Forum. Washington, D.C.

Burns, M. (1985, February). The role of questioning. *Arithmetic Teacher, 32,* 14-17.

Busch, J. (1988, September). Interviewed by Karen Scheid via telephone.

Bush, W. (1987, November). Mathematics textbooks in teacher education. *School Science and Mathematics, 87,* 558-564.

Byrd, D. (1990). Peer tutoring with the learning disabled: A critical review. *Journal of Educational Research, 84(2),* 115-118.

Calkins, L. (1983). *Lessons form a Child: On the Teaching and Learning of Writing.* Exeter, NH: Heinemann.

Callahan, L., & MacMillan, D. (1981). Teaching mathematics to slow learning and mentally retarded children. In *The mathematical education of exceptional children and youth* (pp. 146-190). Reston, VA: National Council of Teachers of Mathematics.

Campbell, B., Brady, M., & Linehan, S. (1991). Effects of peer-mediated instruction on the acquisition and generalization of written capitalization skills. *Journal of Learning Disabilities, 24,* 6-14.

Campione, J.C., & Brown, A.L. (1977). Memory and metamemory development in educable retarded children. In V. Kail, Jr., and J.W. Hagen (Eds.), *Perspectives on the development of memory and cognition* (pp. 367-406). Hillsdale, NJ: Erlbaum.

Carlson, S., & Alley, G. (1981). *Performance and competence of learning disabled and high achieving high school students on essential cognitive skills research report No. 53.* Lawrence, KS: University of Kansas Institute for Research in Learning Disabilities.

Carnine, D. (in progress). At risk students: Making the math connection.

Carnine, D., & Vandegrift, J. (1989). *Report from small group three.* Presentation at the Second Annual ICSEMM Instructional Methods Forum, Washington, D.C.

Carpenter, R. (1985). Mathematics instruction in resource rooms: Instructional time and teacher competence. *Learning Disabilities Quarterly, 8,* 95-100.

Carpenter, T. (1985). Learning to add and subtract: An exercise in problem solving. In E. Silver (Ed.), *Teaching and learning mathematical problem solving: Multiple research perspectives* (pp. 17-40). Hillsdale, NJ: Erlbaum.

Carpenter, T., Fennema, E., Peterson, P., & Carey, D. (1988a). Teachers' pedagogical content knowledge of students' problem solving in elementary arithmetic. *Journal for Research in Mathematics Education, 19,* 385-401.

Carpenter, T., Fennema, E., Peterson, P., Chiang, C., & Loef, M. (1988b). *Using knowledge of children's mathematics thinking in classroom teaching: An experimental study.* Paper presented at the annual meeting of the American Educational Research Association, New Orleans (ED 292 983).

Carpenter, T., & Moser, J. (1982). The development of addition and subtraction problem solving skills. In T. Carpenter, J. Moser, & T. Romberg (Eds.), *Addition and subtraction: A cognitive perspective* (pp. 9-24). Hillsdale, NJ: Erlbaum.

Carpenter, T., & Moser, J. (1984). The acquisition of addition and subtraction concepts in grades one through three. *Journal for Research in Mathematics Education, 15,* 179-202.

Case, L., & Harris, K. (1988). *Self-instructional strategy training: Improving the mathematical problem solving skills of learning disabled students.* Paper presented at the annual meeting of the American Educational Research Association, New Orleans.

Cawley, J. (1970). Teaching arithmetic to mentally handicapped children. *Focus on Exceptional Children, 2*(4), 1-8.

Cawley, J. (1984a). An integrative approach to needs of learning disabled children: Expanded use of mathematics. In J. Cawley (Ed.) *Developmental teaching of mathematics for the learning disabled* (pp. 81-94). Rockville, MD: Aspen.

Cawley, J. (1984b). Learning disabilities: Issues and alternatives. In J. Cawley (Ed.), *Developmental teaching of mathematics for the learning disabled* (pp. 1-28). Rockville, MD: Aspen.

Cawley, J. (1984c). Selection, adaptation, and development of curricular and instructional materials. In J. Cawley (Ed.), *Developmental teaching of mathematics for the learning disabled* (pp. 227-252). Rockville, MD: Aspen.

Cawley, J. (1985a). Cognition and the learning disabled. In J. Cawley (Ed.), *Cognitive strategies and mathematics of the learning disabled* (pp. 1-32). Rockville, MD: Aspen.

Cawley, J. (1985b). Thinking. In J. Cawley (Ed.), *Cognitive strategies and mathematics for the learning disabled* (pp. 139-161). Rockville, MD: Aspen.

Cawley, J. (1989). *Qualitative enhancement of mathematics performance among the mildly handicapped.* Presentation at the Second Annual ICSEMM Instructional Methods Forum, Washington, D.C.

Cawley, J., Fitzmaurice-Hayes, A., & Shaw, R. (1988). *Mathematics for the mildly handicapped: A guide to curriculum and instruction.* Boston: Allyn Bacon.

Cawley, J., & Goodman, J. (1969). Arithmetical problem solving: A demonstration with the mentally handicapped. *Exceptional Children, 36,* 83-90.

Cawley, J., & Miller, J. (1986). Selected views on metacognition, arithmetic problem solving, and learning disabilities. *Learning Disabilities Focus, 2*(1) 36-48.

Cawley, J., & Miller, J. (1989). Cross-sectional comparisons of the mathematical performance of children with learning disabilities: Are we on the right track toward comprehensive programming? *Journal of Learning Disabilities, 22,* 250-254, 259.

Cawley, J., Miller, J., & School, B. (1987). A brief inquiry of arithmetic word-problem-solving among learning disabled secondary students. *Learning Disabilities Focus, 2*(2), 87-93.

Cawley, J., & Vitello, S. (1972). Model for arithmetical programming for handicapped children. *Exceptional Children, 39,* 101-111.

Ceci, S., & Baker, J. (1987). Commentary: How should we conceptualize the language problems of learning disabled children? In S. Ceci (Ed.), *Handbook of cognitive, social, and neuropsychological aspects of learning disabilities* (Vol. 2, pp. 103-112). Hillsdale, NJ: Erlbaum.

CGI math teachers tune in to students' thinking. (1989). *WCER Highlights, 1*(1), 1-3.

Chan, L., & Cole, P. (1986). The effects of comprehension monitoring training on the reading competence of learning disabled and regular class students. *RASE, 7*(4), 33-40.

Chan, L., Cole, P., & Barfett, S. (1987). Comprehension monitoring: Detection and identification of text inconsistencies by LD and normal students. *Learning Disability Quarterly, 10,* 114-124.

Charles, R., Lester, F., & O'Duffer, P. (1987). *How to evaluate progress in problem solving.* Reston, VA: National Council of Teachers of Mathematics.

Cherkes-Julkowski, M. (1985a). Information processing: A cognitive view. In J. Cawley (Ed.), *Cognitive strategies and mathematics for the learning disabled* (pp. 117-138). Rockville, MD: Aspen.

Cherkes-Julkowski, M. (1985b). Metacognitive consideration in mathematics instruction for the learning disabled. In J. Cawley (Ed.), *Cognitive strategies and mathematics for the learning disabled* (pp. 99-116). Rockville, MD: Aspen.

Christenson, S., Thurlow, M., Ysseldyke, J., & McVicar, R. (1989). Writing language instruction for students with mild handicaps: Is there enough quantity to ensure quality. *Learning Disabilities Quarterly, 12,* 219-229.

Ciborowski, Jean (1992). *Textbooks and the students who can't read them: A guide for the teaching of content.* Cambridge, MA: Brookline Books.

Clark, F., Deshler, D., Schumaker, J., Alley, G., & Warner, M. (1984). Visual imagery and self-questioning strategies to improve comprehension of written material. *Journal of Learning Disabilities, 17,* 145-149.

Cobb, P. (1988). The tension between theories of learning and instruction in mathematics education. *Educational Psychologists, 23,* 87-103.

Cohen, E. (1984). Talking and working together: Status, interaction, and learning. In P. Peterson, L. Wilkinson, & M. Hallinan (Eds.), *The social context of instruction: Group organization and group processes* (pp. 171-187). Orlando, FL: Academic Press.

Cohen, E. (1986). *Designing groupwork: Strategies for the heterogeneous classroom.* New York: Teachers College Press.

Cohen, E. (1990, October). Continuing to cooperate: Prerequisites for persistence. *Phi Delta Kappan, 72,* 134-136+.

Cohen, E., & Benton, J. (1988). Making groupwork work. *American Educator, 12,* 10-17, 45-46.

Cohen, E., & Lotan, R. (1990). Teacher as supervisor of context technology. *Theory Into Practice, 29*(2), 78-84.

Cohen, E., Lotan, R., & Catanzarite, L. (1990). Treating status problems in the cooperative classroom. In S. Sharan (Ed.), *Cooperative learning theory and research* (pp. 203-229). New York: Praeger.

Cohen, E., Lotan, R., & Leechor, C. (1989). Can classrooms learn? *Sociology of Education, 62,* 75-94.

Cohen, P., Kulik, J., & Kulik, C. (1982). Educational outcomes of tutoring: A meta-analysis of findings. *American Educational Research Journal, 19*(2), 237-248.

Conway, R., & Gow, L. (1988). Mainstreaming special class students with mild handicaps through group instruction. *RASE, 9*(5), 34-41.

Cosden, M. (1989). Cooperative groups and microcomputer instruction: Combining technologies. *The Pointer, 33*(2), 21-26.

Cosden, M., & Lieber, J. (1986). Grouping students on the microcomputer. *Academic Therapy, 22,* 165-172.

Cosden, M., Pearl, R., & Bryan, T. (1985). The effects of cooperative and individual goal structures on learning disabled and nondisabled students. *Exceptional Children, 52,* 103-114.

Crabill, C. (1990). Small-group learning in the secondary mathematics classroom. In N. Davidson (Ed.), *Cooperative learning in mathematics: A handbook for teachers* (pp. 201-227). Menlo Park, CA: Addison Wesley.

Crosswhite, J. (1987). Cognitive science and mathematics education: A mathematics educator's perspective. In A. Schoenfeld (Ed.), *Cognitive science and mathematics education* (pp. 265-277). Hillsdale, NJ: Erlbaum.

Cruickshank, W. (1948). Arithmetic ability of mentally retarded children, II. *Journal of Educational Research, 42,* 279-288.

Dalton, B. (1989, November). Computers and writing. *Tech Use Guide: Using Computer Technology.* Reston, VA: Center for Special Education Technology.

Danoff, B. (1990). *Implementing a writing program with youngsters with learning problems.* Presentation at the ICSEMM Third Annual Instructional Methods Forum, Washington, DC.

Davidson, N. (1985). Small-group learning and teaching in mathematics: A selective review of the research. In R. Slavin, S. Sharan, S. Kagan, R. Hertz-Lazarowitz, C. Webb, & R. Schmuck (Eds.), *Learning to cooperate, cooperating to learn* (pp. 211-230). New York: Plenum Press.

Davidson, N., & Solomon, R. (1991). *Instructional decision making for cooperative learning.* Maryland School Performance Program Academy.

Davis, B., Scriven, M., & Thomas, S. (1987). *The evaluation of composition instruction* (Second Edition). New York: Teachers College Press.

Davis, R., & Hajicek, J. (1985). Effects of self-instructional training and strategy training on a mathematics task with severely behaviorally disordered students. *Behavioral Disorders, 10,* 275-282.

De Corte, E., & Vershaffel, L. (1981). Children's solution processes in elementary arithmetic problems: Analysis and improvement. *Journal of Educational Psychology, 73,* 765-779.

Dees, R. (1990). Cooperative in the mathematics classroom: A user's manual. In N. Davidson (Ed.), *Cooperative learning in mathematics: A handbook for teachers* (pp. 160-200). Menlo Park, CA: Addison Wesley.

Delclos, V., Bransford, J., & Haywood, C. (1984). A program for teaching thinking: Instrumental enrichment. *Childhood Education, 60,* 256-259.

Delquadri, J., Greenwood, C., Stretton, K., & Hall, R. (1983). The peer tutoring game: A classroom procedure for increasing the opportunity to respond and spelling performance. *Education and Treatment of Children, 6,* 225-239.

Delquadri, J., Greenwood, C., Whorton, D., Carta, J., & Hall, R. (1986). Classwide Peer Tutoring. *Exceptional Children, 52,* 535-542.

Delquadri, J., & Hightower, D. (1991). *Report from small group one.* Fourth Annual Instructional Methods Forum, Washington, D.C.

Derber, S. (1988). *Reciprocal teaching: A teacher's perspective.* Presentation at the ICSEMM Instructional Methods Forum, Washington, D.C.

Derry, S., Hawkes, L., & Tsai, C. (1987). A theory for remediating problem-solving skills of older children and adults. *Educational Psychologist, 22,* 55-87.

Deshler, D. (1978). Issues related to the education of learning disabled adolescents. *Learning Disabilities Quarterly, 1,* 2-10.

Deshler, D., Alley, G., Warner, M., & Schumaker, J. (1981). Instructional practices for promoting skill acquisition and generalization in severely learning disabled adolescents. *Learning Disability Quarterly, 4,* 415-421.

Deshler, D., & Schumaker, J. (1986). Learning strategies: An instructional alternative for low-achieving adolescents. *Exceptional Children, 52,* 583-590.

Deshler, D., Schumaker, J., & Lenz, K. (1984). Academic and cognitive interventions for LD adolescents: Part I. *Journal of Learning Disabilities, 17,* 108-117.

Deshler, D., Schumaker, J., & Lenz, B.K. (1984a). Academic and cognitive interventions for LD adolescents: Part I. *Journal of Learning Disabilities, 17,* 108-117.

Deshler, D., Schumaker, J., Lenz, B.K., & Ellis, E. (1984b). Academic and cognitive interventions for LD adolescents: Part II. *Journal of Learning Disabilities, 17,* 120-129.

DiPardo, A., & Freedman, S. (1988). Peer response groups in the writing classroom: Theoretic foundations and new directions. *Review of Educational Research, 58,* 119-149.

Donahoe, K., & Zigmond, N. (1986). *High school grades of urban LD students and low achieving peers.* Unpublished Manuscript. Pittsburgh, PA: Program in Special Education, University of Pittsburgh.

Dowd, M. (1988). *Report from small group 3.* First Annual Instructional Methods Forum. Washington, D.C.

DuCharme, C., Earl, J., & Poplin, M. (1989). The author model: The constructionist view of the writing process. *Learning Disabilities Quarterly, 12,* 237-242.

Duffy, G. (1988, September). Interviewed by Karen Scheid via telephone.

Duffy, G., & Roehler, L. (1987). Teaching reading skills as strategies. *Reading Teacher, 40,* 414-421.

Duffy, G., Roehler, L., & Herrmann, B.A. (1988). Modeling mental processes helps poor readers become strategic readers. *The Reading Teacher, 41,* 762-767.

Duffy, G., Roehler, L., Meloth, M., Polin, R., Rackliffe, G., Tracy, A.& Vaurus, L.B.A. (1987a). Developing and evaluating measures associated with strategic reading. *Journal of Reading Behavior, 19,* 223-246.

Duffy, G., Roehler, L., Meloth, M., Vaurus, L., Book, C., Putnam, J., & Wesselman, R. (1986a). The relationship between explicit verbal explanations during reading skill instruction and student awareness and achievement: A study of reading teacher effects. *Reading Research Quarterly, 21,* 237-252.

Duffy, G., Roehler, L., & Putnam, J. (1987b). Putting the teacher in control: basal reading textbooks and instructional decision making. *The Elementary School Journal, 87,* 357-366.

Duffy, G., Roehler, L., & Rackliffe, G. (1986b). How teachers' instructional talk influences students' understanding of lesson content.

The Elementary School Journal, 87, 3-16.

Duffy, G., Roehler, L., Sivan, E., Rackliffe, G., Book, C., Meloth, M., Vaurus, L., Wesselman, R., Putnam, J., Bassiri, D. (1987c). Effects of explaining the reasoning associated with using reading strategies. *Reading Research Quarterly, 22,* 347-368.

Durkin, D (1979). What classroom observations reveal about reading comprehension instruction. *Reading Research Quarterly, 14,* 481-533.

Durkin, D. (1981). Reading comprehension instruction in five basal readers. *Reading Research Quarterly, 16,* 515-546.

Durkin, D. (1984). Is there a match between what elementary teachers do and what basal reader manuals recommend? *Reading Teacher, 37,* 734-745.

Educational Testing Service. (1989). *A world of differences: An international assessment of mathematics and science.* Princeton, NJ: Educational Testing Service.

Edwards, C., & Stout, J. (1989/1990). Cooperative learning: The first year. *Educational Leadership, 47*(4), 38-41.

Eiserman, W. (1988). Three types of peer tutoring: Effects on the attitudes of students with learning disabilities and their regular class peers. *Journal of Learning Disabilities, 21,* 249-252.

Ellis, E.S. (1986). The role of motivation and pedagogy on the generalization of cognitive strategy training. *Journal of Learning Disabilities, 19,* 66-70.

Ellis, E.S. (1988). *Suggestions for incorporating the principles of cognitive and metacognitive theories in the design of media and materials.* Presentation at the ICSEMM Publishers Workshop, Washington, D.C.

Ellis, E.S., Lenz, B.K., & Sabornie, E.J. (1987a). Generalization and adaptation of learning strategies to natural environments: Part 1: Critical agents. *RASE, 8*(1), 6-20.

Ellis, E.S., Lenz, B.K., & Sabornie, E.J. (1987b). Generalization and adaptation of learning strategies to natural environments: Part 2: Research into practice. *RASE, 8*(2), 6-23.

Ellis, S. (1989/1990). Introducing cooperative learning. *Educational Leadership, 47*(4), 34-37.

Englert, C., & Raphael, T. (1988). Constructing well-formed prose: Process, structure and metacognitive knowledge. *Exceptional Children, 54,* 513-520.

Englert, C.S. (1987). Writing disorders. In *Encyclopedia of special education* (Vol. 3) (pp. 1673-1676). New York: John Wiley and Sons, Inc.

Englert, C.S., Hiebert, E., & Stewart, S. (1985). Spelling unfamiliar words by an analogy strategy. *Journal of Special Education, 19,* 291-306.

Englert, C.S., & Raphael, T. (1989). Developing successful writers through cognitive strategy instruction. In J. Brophy (Ed.), *Advances in research on teaching* (Vol. 1) (pp. 105-151). Greenwich, CT: JAI Press.

Englert, C.S., Raphael, T., Anderson, L., Anthony, H., Fear, K., & Gregg, S. (1988a). A case for writing intervention: Strategies for writing informational text. *Learning Disabilities Focus, 3,* 98-113.

Englert, C.S., Raphael, T., Fear, K., & Anderson, L. (1988b). Students' metacognitive knowledge about how to write informational text. *Learning Disability Quarterly, 11,* 18-46.

Englert, C.S., Stewart, S., & Hiebert, E. (1988c). Young writers use of text structure in expository text generation. *Journal of Educational Psychology, 80,* 143-151.

Englert, C.S., & Thomas, C. (1987). Sensitivity to the text structure in reading and writing: A comparison between learning disabled and non-learning disabled students. *Learning Disability Quarterly, 10,* 93-105.

Erickson, M. (1987). Deaf readers reading beyond the literal. *American Annals of the Deaf, 132,* 291-294.

Fantuzzo, J. (1991). *Collaborative learning methods: Instructionally sailing Scylla and Charybdis.* Presentation at the Fourth Annual Instructional Methods Forum, Washington, DC.

Fantuzzo, J., Dimeff, L., & Fox, S. (1989). Reciprocal peer tutoring: A multimodal assessment of effectiveness with college students. *Teaching of Psychology, 16*(3), 133-135.

Fantuzzo, J., King, J., & Heller, L. (in preparation). Effects of reciprocal peer tutoring in mathematics and school adjustment: A component analysis.

Fantuzzo, J., Polite, K., & Grayson, N. (1990). An evaluation of reciprocal peer tutoring across elementary school settings. *Journal of School Psychology, 28,* 309-323.

Fantuzzo, J., Riggio, R., Connelly, S., &

Dimeff, L. (1989). Effects of reciprocal peer tutoring on academic achievement and psychological adjustment: A component analysis. *Journal of Educational Psychology, 89*(2), 173-177.

Farley, J. (1986). An analysis of written dialogue of educable mentally retarded writers. *Education and Training of the Mentally Retarded, 21,* 181-191.

Farnsworth, L. (1990). In the schema of things. In N. Atwell (Ed.), *Coming to know: Writing to learn in the intermediate grades* (pp. 77-85). Portsmouth, NH: Heinemann.

Fear, K. (1990). *The relationship between teacher conceptions and student perceptions and performance in writing.* Presentation at the American Educational Research Association Annual Meeting, Boston, MA.

Fear, K. (in progress). *An examination of differences in teacher conceptions related to practices in writing instruction.*

Fear, K., & Fox, D. (1990). *Report from small group 2.* Third Annual ICSEMM Instructional Methods Forum, Washington, DC.

Feldman, K. (1988). *Report from small group 2B.* First Annual Instructional Methods Forum, Washington, D.C.

Fennell, F. (1983). Focusing on problem solving in the primary grades. In G. Shufelt & J. Smart (Eds.), *The agenda in action.* 1983 NCTM Yearbook (pp. 33-40). Reston, VA: National Council of Teachers of Mathematics.

Fennema, E. (1989, June). *Cognitively Guided Instruction.* Presentation at the Second Annual ICSEMM Instructional Methods Forum, Washington, D.C.

Fennema, E., Carpenter, T., & Peterson, P. (1989). Learning mathematics with understanding: Cognitively Guided Instruction. In J. Brophy (Ed.), *Advances in research on teaching,* Vol. 1 (pp. 195-221). Greenwich, CT: JAI.

Fine, C. (1988, August). *Reciprocal Teaching: Staff Development Issues.* Presentation at the ICSEMM Instructional Methods Forum, Washington, DC.

Fitzgerald, J. (1989, October). Enhancing two related thought processes: Revision in writing and critical reading. *The Reading Teacher, 43,* 42-48.

Fitzgerald, J., & Markham, L. (1987). Teaching children about revision in writing. *Cognition and Instruction, 4,* 3-24.

Fitzgerald, J., Spiegel, D., & Teasley, A. (1987). Story structure and writing. *Academic Therapy, 22,* 255-262.

Fitzmaurice, A. (1980). LD teachers' self-ratings on mathematics education competencies. *Learning Disabilities Quarterly, 3,* 90-94.

Fitzmaurice-Hayes, A. (1984). Curriculum and instructional activities pre-K through grade 2. In J. Cawley (Ed.), *Developmental teaching of mathematics for the learning disabled* (pp. 95-114). Rockville, MD: Aspen.

Fitzmaurice-Hayes, A. (1985a). Assessment of the severely impaired mathematics student. In J. Cawley (Ed.), *Practical mathematics appraisal of the learning disabled* (pp. 249-277). Rockville, MD: Aspen.

Fitzmaurice-Hayes, A. (1985b). Classroom implications. In J. Cawley (Ed.), *Cognitive strategies and mathematics for the learning disabled* (pp. 209-236). Rockville, MD: Aspen.

Fitzmaurice-Hayes, A. (1985c). Whole numbers: Concepts and skills. In J. Cawley (Ed.), *Secondary school mathematics for the learning disabled,* (pp. 83-114). Rockville, MD: Aspen.

Fitzmaurice-Hayes, A. (1989). *Math instruction for students with learning disabilities.* Presentation at the 1989 ICSEMM Instructional Methods Forum, Washington, D.C.

Flavell, J. (1979). Metacognition and cognitive monitoring: A new area of cognitive development inquiry. *American Psychologist, 34,* 906-911.

Fleischner, J., Garnett, K., & Preddy, D. (1982). *Mastery of the basic number facts by learning disabled students: An intervention study.* Research Institute for the Study of Learning Disabilities, Teachers College, Columbia University, New York.

Fleischner, J., Nuzum, M., & Marzola, E. (1987). Devising an instructional program to teach arithmetic problem-solving skills to students with learning disabilities. *Journal of Learning Disabilities, 20,* 214-217.

Fleischner, J., & O'Loughlin, M. (1985). Solving story problems: implications of research for teaching the learning disabled. In J. Cawley, (Ed.), *Cognitive strategies and mathematics for the learning disabled* (pp. 163-181). Rockville, MD: Aspen.

Flower, L., & Hayes, J.R. (1981). A cognitive process theory of writing. *College Composition and Communication, 32,* 365-387.

Flynn, L. (1989). Developing critical reading skills through cooperative problem solving. *The Reading Teacher, 42*, 664-668.

Fowler, S. (1986). Peer monitoring and self-monitoring: Alternatives to traditional teacher management. *Exceptional Children, 52*, 573-581.

Freedman, S., & Mcleod, A. (1988). *National surveys of successful teachers of writing and their students: The United Kingdom and the United States* (Technical Report No. 14). Berkeley, CA: Center for the Study of Writing.

Fridriksson, T., & Stewart, D. (1988). From the concrete to the abstract: Mathematics for deaf children. *American Annals of the Deaf, 133*, 51-55.

Fuson, K., & Secada, W. (1986). Teaching children to add by counting on with one-handed finger patterns. *Cognition and Instruction, 3*, 229-260.

Gallegos, R. (1980). The effect of a reward-based counseling system on self-concept, achievement, and attendance patterns of minority high school students. *Dissertation Abstracts International, 40*, No. 8311391.

Gardner, M. (1985). Cognitive psychological approaches to instructional task analysis. In E.W. Gordon (Ed.), *Review of Research in Education* (Vol. 12, pp. 157-195). Washington, D.C.: AERA.

Garnett, K., & Fleischner, J. (1983). Automatization and basic fact performance of normal and learning disabled children. *Learning Disabled Quarterly, 6*, 223-230.

Garofalo, J. (1987, May). Research report: Metacognition and school mathematics. *Arithmetic Teacher, 34*, 22-23.

Garofalo, J., & Lester, F. (1985). Metacognition, cognitive monitoring, and mathematical performance. *Journal for Research in Mathematics Education, 16*, 163-176.

Garofalo, J., & Standifer, D. (1989). *Report from small group one.* Presentation at the ICSEMM Instructional Methods Forum, Washington, D.C.

Gaskins, I., Downer, M., Anderson, R., Cunningham, P., Gaskins, R., Schommer, M., & Teachers of Benchmark School. (1988). A metacognitive approach to phonics: Using what you know to decide what you don't know. *RASE, 9*(1), 36-41.

Gaskins, I., & Elliott, T. (1991). *Implementing cognitive strategy instruction across the school: The Benchmark manual for teachers.* Cambridge, MA: Brookline Books.

Gere, A., & Abbott, R. (1985). Talking about writing: The language of writing groups. *Research in the Training of English, 19*, 362-385.

Gerleman, S. (1987). An observational study of small-group instruction in fourth grade mathematics classrooms. *The Elementary School Journal, 88*, 3-28.

Gettinger, M., Byrant, N., & Fayne, H. (1982). Designing spelling instruction for learning disabled children: An emphasis on unit size, distributed practices, and training for transfer. *Journal of Special Education, 16*, 439-448.

Ghatala, E. (1986). Strategy-monitoring training enables young learners to select effective strategies. *Educational Psychologist, 21*(1-2), 43-54.

Giacobbe, M.E. (1988). Choosing a language arts textbook . In T. Newkirk, & N. Atwell (Eds.), *Understanding writing: Ways of observing, learning and teaching* (pp. 253-273). Portsmouth, NH: Heinemann.

Ginsburg, H. (1989). *Children's Arithmetic* (2nd ed.). Austin, Texas: PRO-ED.

Goldman, S. (1989). Strategy instruction in mathematics. *Learning Disabilities Quarterly, 12*, 43-55.

Goldman, S., Pellegrino, J., & Mertz, D. (1988). Extended practice of basic addition facts: Strategy changes in learning disabled students. *Cognition and Instruction, 5*, 223-265.

Good, T., & Brophy, J. (1989). Teaching the Lesson. In R. Slavin (Ed.), *School and classroom organization* (pp. 25-66). Hillsdale, NJ: LEA.

Good, T., Grouws, D., & Ebmeier, H. (1983). *Active mathematics teaching.* New York: Longman.

Good, T., Grouws, D., Mason, D., Slavings, R., & Cramer, K. (1990). An observational study of small group mathematics instruction in elementary schools. *AER Journal, 27*, 755-782.

Good, T., & Marshall, S. (1984). Do students learn more in heterogeneous or homogeneous groups? In P. Peterson, L. Wilkinson, & M. Hallinan (Eds.), *The social context of instruction: Group organization and group processes* (pp. 15-38). Orlando, FL: Academic Press.

Good, T., Reys, B., Grouws, D., and Mulryan, C. (1989/1990). Using work groups in mathematics instruction. *Educational Leadership*, 47(4), 56-62.

Goodstein, H., Bessant, H., Thibodeau, G., Vitello, S., Vlahakos, I. (1972). The effect of three variables on the verbal problem solving of educable mentally handicapped children. *American Journal of Mental Deficiency*, 76, 703-709.

Goodstein, H., Cawley, J., Gordon, S., & Helfgott. (1971). Verbal problem solving among educable mentally retarded children. *American Journal of Mental Deficiency*, 76, 238-241.

Gottlieb, J., & Leyser, Y. (1981). Facilitating the social mainstreaming of retarded children. *Exceptional Education Quarterly*, 1(4), 57-69.

Graham, S. (1982). Composition research and practice: A united approach. *Focus on Exceptional Children*, 14(8), 1-16.

Graham, S. (1987). Writing assessment. In *Encyclopedia of special education* (Vol. 3) (pp. 1671-1673). New York: John Wiley and Sons, Inc.

Graham, S. (1988). *Report from small group four.* First Annual Instructional Methods Forum, Washington, D.C.

Graham, S. (1990). *Effective writing instruction for special education students.* Presentation at the ICSEMM Third Annual Instructional Methods Forum, Washington, DC.

Graham, S., & Harris, K. (1987). Improving composition skills of inefficient learners with self-instructional strategy training. *Topics in Language Disorders*, 7, 66-77.

Graham, S., & Harris, K. (1988a). *Improving learning disabled students' skills at generating essays: Self-instructional strategy training.* Paper presented at the 1988 annual meeting of the American Educational Research Association, New Orleans.

Graham, S., & Harris, K. (1988b). Instructional recommendations for teaching writing to exceptional students. *Exceptional Children*, 54, 506-512.

Graham, S., & Harris, K. (1989a). A components analysis of cognitive strategy instruction: Effects on learning disabled students' compositions and self-efficacy. *Journal of Educational Psychology*, 81, 353-361.

Graham, S., & Harris, K. (1989b). Cognitive training: Implications for written language.

In J. Hughes, & R. Hall (Eds.), *Cognitive behavioral psychology in the schools: A comprehensive handbook* (pp. 247-279). New York: Guilford.

Graham, S., & Harris, K. (1989c). Improving learning disabled students' skills at composing essays: Self-instructional Strategy Training. *Exceptional Children*, 55, 201-214.

Graham, S., & Harris, K. (in progress). Cognitive strategy instruction in written language for learning disabled students.

Graham, S., Harris, K., MacArthur, C., & Schwartz, S. (in press). In B. Wong (Ed.), *Learning about learning disabilities.* New York: Academic Press.

Graham, S., Harris, K., & Sawyer, R. (1987). Composition instruction with learning disabled students: Self-instructional Strategy Training. *Focus on Exceptional Children*, 20(4), 1-11.

Graham, S., & Johnson, L. (1989). Teaching reading to learning disabled students: A review of research-supported procedures. *Focus on Exceptional Children*, 21(4), 1-12.

Graham, S., & MacArthur, C. (1987). Written language of handicapped. In *Encyclopedia of special education* (Vol. 3) (pp. 1678-1681). New York: John Wiley and Sons, Inc.

Graham, S., & MacArthur, C. (1988). Improving learning disabled students' skills at revision essays produced on a word processor: Self-instructional Strategy Training. *Journal of Special Education*, 22, 133-151.

Graham, S., & Miller, L. (1980). Handwriting research on practice: A unified approach. *Focus on Exceptional Children*, 13, 1-16.

Graves, A. (1990). *Narrative story writing research: A summary.* Presentation at the ICSEMM Third Annual Instructional Methods Forum, Washington, DC.

Graves, A., Montague, M., & Wong, Y. (1990). The effects of procedural facilitation on story composition of learning disabled students. *Learning Disabilities Research*, 5, 88-93.

Graves, D. (1977). Language arts textbooks: A writing process evaluation. *Language Arts*, 54, 817-823.

Graves, D. (1978). *Balance the basics: Let them write.* New York: Ford Foundation.

Graves, D. (1982). *A case study observing the development of primary children's composing, spelling, and motor behaviors during the writing process. Final report.* Durham, NH: New Hampshire University.

Graves, D. (1983). *Writing: Teachers and children at work*. Exeter, NH: Heinemann.

Graves, D. (1985). All children can write. *Learning Disabilities Focus, 1*(1), 36-43.

Graves, D., & Giacobbe, M.E. (1982). Questions for teachers who wonder if their writers can change. *Language Arts, 59*, 495-503.

Greenwood, C., Delquadri, J., & Hall, R. (1984). Opportunity to respond and student academic performance. In W. Howard, T. Heron, J. Porter, & D. Hill (Eds.), *Focus on behavior analysis in education* (pp. 58-88). Columbus, OH: Charles Merrill.

Greenwood, C., Dinwiddie, G., Terry, B., Wade, L., Stanley, S., Thibodeau, S., & Delquadri, J. (1984). Teacher versus peer-mediated instruction: An ecobehavioral analysis of achievement outcomes. *Journal of Applied Behavioral Analysis, 17*, 521-538.

Gregory, J., Shanahan, T., & Walberg, H. (1985). Learning disabled 10th graders in mainstreamed settings: A descriptive analysis. *RASE, 6*(4), 25-33.

Guskey, T. (1990). Cooperative mastery of learning strategies. *Elementary School Journal, 91*, 33-42.

Harris, K. (1988). *Implications of learning strategy research for special education students.* Presentation at the ICSEMM Instructional Methods Forum, Washington, D.C.

Harris, K. (1990). *Self-instruction strategy training: Summary remarks.* Presentation at the ICSEMM Third Annual Instructional Methods Forum, Washington, D.C.

Harris, K., & Graham, S. (1985). Improving learning disabled students' composition skills: Self-control strategy training. *Learning Disabilities Quarterly, 8*, 27-36.

Harris, K., & Graham, S. (1987). Improving learning disabled students' skills at generating essays: Self-instructional strategy training. Unpublished data.

Harris, K., & Graham, S. (1988, Winter). Self-instructional strategy training. *Teaching Exceptional Children, 20*, 35-37.

Harris, K., & Graham, S. (1992). *Helping young writers master the craft: Strategy instruction & self-regulation in the writing process.* Cambridge, MA: Brookline Books.

Harris, K., Graham, S., & Freeman, S. (1988). Effects of strategy training on metamemory among LD. *Exceptional Children, 54*, 332-338.

Harris, K., & Pressley, M. (1991). The nature of cognitive strategy instruction: Interactive strategy construction. *Exceptional Children, 57*, 392-404.

Hasselbring, T., Goin, L., & Bransford, J. (1987). Developing automaticity. *Teaching Exceptional Children, 19*(3), 30-33.

Hasselbring, T., Goin, L., & Bransford, J. (1988). Developing math automaticity in learning handicapped children: The role of computerized drill and practice. *Focus on Exceptional Children, 20*(6), 1-7.

Hayes, J., & Flower, L. (1980). Writing as problem-solving. *Visible Language, 14*, 388-399.

Hayes, J., & Flower, L. (1983). Uncovering cognitive processes in writing: An introduction to protocol analysis. In P. Mosenthal, L. Tamor, & S. Walmsley (Eds.), *Research on writing principles and methods* (pp. 207-220). New York: Longman.

Hayes, J., & Flower, L. (1986). Writing research and the writer. *American Psychologist, 41*, 1106-1113.

Hedin, D. (1987, December). Expanding the use of cross-age/peer tutoring. *Educational Digest*, 39-41.

Henderson, R. (1986). Self-regulated learning: Implications for the design of instructional media. *Contemporary Educational Psychology, 11*, 405-427.

Hendrickson, A. (1983). Prevention or cure? Another look at mathematics learning problems. In D. Carnine, D. Elkind, A.D. Hendrickson, D. Meichenbaum, R.L. Sieben, & F. Smith (Eds.), *Interdisciplinary voices in learning disabilities and remedial education* (pp. 93-107). Austin, TX: Pro-ED.

Herrmann, B.A. (1988a). *Report from Small Group 2A.* First Annual Instructional Methods Forum, Washington, D.C.

Herrmann, B.A. (1988b). Two approaches for helping poor readers become more strategic. *The Reading Teacher, 42*, 24-28.

Herrmann, B.A. (1989, Spring). Characteristics of explicit and less explicit explanations of mathematical problem solving strategies. *Reading Research and Instruction, 28*, 1-17.

Herrmann, B.A. (in progress). An exploratory study of the effects of peer-monitoring and peer collaboration on preservice teachers' knowledge structure.

Herrmann, B.A., Duffy, G., & Roehler, L.

(1985). A descriptive study of the effects and characteristics of direct teacher explanation in a clinical setting. *Research on teaching.* Michigan State University, East Lansing, Michigan.

Herrmann, B.A., & Marshall, K., (in progress). An exploratory study of the effects of peer monitoring on the regular and special education teachers' abilities to collaborate.

Hertz-Lazarowitz, R., Sharan, S., & Steinberg, R. (1980). Classroom learning style and cooperative behavior of elementary school children. *Journal of Educational Psychology,* 72(1), 99-106.

Hiebert, J. (1984). Children's mathematics learning: The struggle to link form and understanding. *Elementary School Journal,* 84, 497-513.

Hiebert, J., & Wearne, D. (1988). Instruction and cognitive change in mathematics. *Educational Psychologist,* 23, 105-117.

Hightower, D., & Avery, R. (1987). *Study Buddy Program.* Rochester, NY: Primary Mental Health Project.

Hillocks, G. (1984, November). What works in teaching composition: A meta-analysis of experimental treatment studies. *American Journal of Education,* 93, 133-170.

Hillocks, G. (1987). Synthesis of research on teaching writing. *Educational Leadership, 44,* 71-82.

Hittleman, D. (1978). *Developmental reading: A psycholinguistic perspective.* Chicago: Rand McNally.

Hittleman, D., & Moran, M. (1990). *Report of small group four.* Third Annual ICSEMM Instructional Methods Forum, Washington, D.C.

Hock, M. (1988). *The strategies intervention model: A plan for student academic and social independence.* Presentation at the ICSEMM Instructional Methods Forum, Washington, D.C.

Holmes, E. (1985). *Children learning mathematics: A cognitive approach to teaching.* Englewood Cliffs, NJ: Prentice Hall.

Hughes, T. (1978). *What the British tell the U.S. about writing and reading.* Paper presented at the Third Great Lake Regional Conference of the International Reading Association, Cincinnati, OH. (ED 175020).

Hull, G. (1989). Research on writing: Building a cognitive and social understanding of composing. In L. Resnick, & L. Klopfer (Eds.), *Toward the thinking curriculum: Current cognitive research.* Alexandria, VA: ASCD.

Idol, L. (1987a). A critical thinking map to improve content area comprehension of poor readers. *RASE 8*(4), 28-40.

Idol, L. (1987b). Group story mapping: A comprehension strategy for both skilled and unskilled readers. *Journal of Learning Disabilities 20,* 196-205.

Idol, L. (1988). Johnny can't read: Does the fault lie with the book, the teacher, or Johnny? *RASE 9*(1), 8-25, 35.

Isaacson, S. (1987). Effective instruction in written language. *Focus on Exceptional Children, 19*(6), 1-12.

Isaacson, S. (1988, Winter). Teaching written expression. *Teaching Exceptional Children,* 20, 32-33.

Isaacson, S. (1989). Role of secretary vs. author: Resolving the conflict in writing instruction. *Learning Disability Quarterly, 12,* 209-217.

Isaacson, S. (1990). *Implementing a writing program for students with learning problems.* Presentation at the ICSEMM Third Annual Instructional Methods Forum, Washington, DC.

Jenkins, J., Heliotis, J., Haynes, M., & Beck, K. (1986). Does passive learning account for disabled readers' comprehension deficits in *Learning Disabilities Quarterly, 9,* 69-76.

Jenkins, J., & Jenkins, L. (1985). Peer tutoring in elementary and secondary programs. *Focus on Exceptional Children, 17*(6), 1-12.

Jenkins, M., & Rivera, D. (1989, June). *Report from small group two.* Second ICSEMM Instructional Methods Forum, Washington, D.C.

Jensen, J., & Roser, N. (1987). Basal readers and language arts program. *Elementary School Journal,* 87, 374-383.

Johnson, D., & Johnson, R. (1982). The effects of cooperative and individualistic instruction on handicapped and non-handicapped students. *Journal of Social Psychology, 118,* 257-268.

Johnson, D., & Johnson, R. (1984a). *Cooperation in the classroom.* Edina, MN: Interaction Book Company.

Johnson, D., & Johnson, R. (1984b, October). The effects of intergroup cooperation and intergroup competition on ingroup and outgroup cross-handicap relationships. *The Journal of Social Psychology, 124,* 85-94.

Johnson, D., & Johnson, R. (1986). Mainstreaming and cooperative learning strategies. *Exceptional Children, 52,* 553-561.

Johnson, D., & Johnson, R. (1989a). Cooperative learning and mainstreaming. In R. Gaylord-Ross (Ed.), *Integration strategies for students with handicaps* (pp. 233-248). Baltimore: Paul H. Brookes.

Johnson, D., & Johnson, R. (1989b). Cooperative learning: What special education teachers need to know. *The Pointer, 33*(2), 5-10.

Johnson, D., & Johnson, R. (1989/1990). Social skills for successful group work. *Educational Leadership, 47*(4), 29-33.

Johnson, D., & Johnson, R. (1990). Using cooperative learning in mathematics. In N. Davidson (Ed.), *Cooperative learning in mathematics: A handbook for teachers* (pp. 103-125). Menlo Park, CA: Addison Wesley.

Johnson, D., Johnson, R., Holubec, E., & Roy, P. (1984). *Circles of learning: Cooperation in the classroom.* Alexandria, VA: ASCD.

Johnson, R., Johnson, D., Scott, L., & Ramolae, B. (1985). Effects of single-sex and mixed-sex cooperative interaction on science achievement and attitudes of cross-handicapped and cross-sex relationships. *Journal of Research in Science Teaching, 22*(3), 207-220.

Johnson, D., Johnson, R., Warring, D., & Maruyama, G. (1986). Different cooperative learning procedures and cross-handicap relationship. *Exceptional Children, 53,* 247-252.

Johnson, L., & Pugach, M. (1991). Peer collaboration: Accommodating students with mild learning and behavior problems. *Exceptional Children, 57,* 454-461.

Johnston, M., Whitman, T., & Johnson, M. (1981). Teaching addition and subtraction to mentally retarded children: A self-instructional program. *Applied Research in Mental Retardation, 1,* 141-160.

Jones, B., Palincsar, A., Ogle, D., & Carr, E. (1987). *Strategic teaching and learning: Cognitive instruction in the content areas.* Alexandria, Virginia: ASCD.

Jones, B., Pierce, J., Hunter, B. (1988/89). Teaching students to construct graphic representations. *Educational Leadership, 46*(4), 20-25.

Kagan, S. (1989/1990). The structural approach to cooperative learning. *Educational Leadership, 47*(4), 12-15.

Karweit, N. (1989). Time and learning: A review. In R. Slavin (Ed.), *School and classroom organization* (pp. 69-95). Hillsdale, NJ: LEA.

Kehle, T., & Guidubaldi, J. (1978). Effects of EMR placement models on affective and social development. *Psychology in the Schools, 15,* 275-282.

Kellas, G., Ashcraft, M.H., & Johnson, N.S. (1973). Rehearsal processes in the short-term memory performance of mildly retarded adolescents. *American Journal of Mental Deficiency, 77,* 670-679.

Kendall, C., Borkowski, J., & Cavanaugh, J. (1980). Metamemory and the transfer of an interrogative strategy by EMR children. *Intelligence, 4,* 255-270.

Kennedy, L. (1986, February). A rationale. *Arithmetic Teacher, 33,* 6-7.

Kilpatrick, J. (1985). A retrospective account of the past 25 years of research on teaching mathematical problem solving. In E. Silver (Ed.), *Teaching and learning mathematical problem solving: Multiple research perspectives* (pp. 1-15). Hillsdale, NJ: Erlbaum.

Kirby, D., Latta, D., & Vinz, R. (1988). Beyond interior decorating: Using writing to make meaning in elementary school. *Phi Delta Kappan, 69,* 718-724.

Kirby, J., & Becker, L. (1988). Cognitive components of learning problems in arithmetic. *RASE, 9*(5), 7-16.

Klausmeier, H., & Ripple, R. (1971). *Learning and human abilities.* New York: Harper and Row.

Knudson, R. (1989). Effects of instructional strategies on children's informational writing. *Journal of Educational Research, 83,* 91-96.

Kohn, A. (1991a). Don't spoil the promise of cooperative learning: Response to Slavin. *Educational Leadership, 48*(5), 93-94.

Kohn, A. (1991b). Group grade grubbing versus cooperative learning. *Educational Leadership, 48*(5), 83-87.

Kolligian, J., Jr., & Sternberg, R.S. (1987). Intelligence, information processing, and specific learning disabilities: A triarchic synthesis. *Journal of Learning Disabilities, 20,* 8-17.

Kouba, V., Brown, C., Carpenter, T., Lindquist, M., Silver, E., & Swafford, J.

(1988a, April). Results of the fourth NAEP assessment of mathematics: Number, operations, and word problems. *Arithmetic Teacher, 35*, 14-19.

Kouba, V., Brown, C., Carpenter, T., Lindquist, M., Silver, E., & Swafford, J. (1988b, May). Results of the fourth NAEP assessment of mathematics: Measurement, geometry, data interpretation, attitudes and other topics. *Arithmetic Teacher, 33*, 10-16.

Lane, B. (1980). The relationship of learning disabilities to juvenile delinquency: Current status. *Journal of Learning Disabilities, 13*, 425-434.

Langer, J., & Applebee, A. (1986). Reading and writing instruction: Toward a theory of teaching and learning. In E. Rothkopf (Ed.), *Review of Research in Education* (Vol. 13) (pp. 171-194). Washington, DC: AERA.

Lazarowitz, R., & Karsenty, G. (1989). Cooperative learning and students' academic achievement, process skills, learning environment, and self-esteem in tenth grade biology classroom. In S. Sharan (Ed.), *Cooperative learning: Theory and practice.* New York: Praeger Publishing Company.

Lazerson, D., Foster, H., Brown, S., & Hummel, J. (1988). The effectiveness of cross-age tutoring with truant, junior high school students with learning disabilities. *Journal of Learning Disabilities, 21*, 253-255.

Leinhardt, G., Zigmond, N., & Cooley, W. (1980). *Reading instruction and its effects.* Presentation at the American Educational Research Association Annual Meeting, Boston, MA.

Lenz, B.K. (1988). *The learning strategies curriculum of the strategies intervention model.* Presentation at the ICSEMM Instructional Methods Forum, Washington, D.C.

Leon, J., & Pepe, H. (1983). Self instructional training: Cognitive behavior modification for remediating arithmetic deficits. *Exceptional Children, 50*, 54-60.

Lester, F. (1985). Methodological considerations in research on mathematical problem solving instruction. In E. Silver (Ed.), *Teaching and learning mathematical problem solving: Multiple research perspectives* (pp. 41-69). Hillsdale, NJ: Erlbaum.

Lester, F., & Garofalo, J. (1987, April). *The influence of affects, beliefs, and metacognition on problem solving behavior: Some tentative speculations.* Paper presented at the annual meeting of the American Educational Research Association, Washington, D.C. (ED 281 758).

Levin, J. (1986). Four cognitive principles of learning-strategy instruction. *Educational Psychologist, 21*(1-2), 3-17.

Lieber, J., & Semmel, M. (1985). Effectiveness of computer application to instruction with mildly handicapped learners: A review. *RASE, 6*(5), 5-12.

Lieber, J., & Semmel, M. (1987a). The effects of group size on attitudes toward microcomputers. *RASE, 8*(5), 29-33.

Lieber, J., & Semmel, M. (1987b). The relationship between group size and performance on a microcomputer problem-solving task for learning handicapped and non-handicapped students. *Journal of Educational Computing Research, 3*, 171-187.

Lieber, J., & Semmel, M. (1989). The relationship of group configuration to the interactions of students using microcomputers. *Journal of Special Education Technology, 10*(1), 14-23.

Lindquist, M. (1987). Strategic teaching in mathematics. In B. Jones, A. Palincsar, D. Ogle, & E. Carr (Eds.), *Strategic teaching and learning: Cognitive instruction in the content areas* (pp. 111-134). Alexandria, VA: ASCD.

Lloyd, J., & Keller, C. (1989). Effective mathematics instruction: Development, instruction, and programs. *Focus on Exceptional Children, 21*(7), 1-10.

Lloyd, J., Saltzman, N., & Kauffman, J. (1981). Predictable generalizations in academic learning as a result of preskills and strategy training. *Learning Disability Quarterly, 4*, 203-216.

Lotan, R., & Benton, J. (1990). Finding out about complex instruction: Teaching math and science in heterogeneous classrooms. In N. Davidson (Ed.), *Cooperative learning in mathematics: A handbook for teachers* (pp. 47-68). Menlo Park, CA: Addison Wesley.

Lubin, D., & Forbes, D. (1984). Children's reasoning and peer relations. In B. Rogoff, & J. Lave (Eds.), *Everyday cognition: Its development in social context* (pp. 220-237, 298-299). Cambridge, MA: Harvard University Press.

Luftig, R., & Johnson, R. (1980, September). *Identification and recall of structurally important units in verbal discourse as a function of metacognitive processing of mentally retarded children*. U.S. Special Education Programs Report. Lafayette, IN: Purdue University.

Lyman, L., & Foyle, H. (1990). *Cooperative grouping for interactive learning: Students, teachers, and administrators*. Washington, D.C.: National Education Association.

MacArthur, C., & Graham, S. (1986). *LD students' writing under three conditions: Words processing, dictation, and handwriting*. Paper presented at the American Educational Research Association in San Francisco. San Francisco.

MacArthur, C., & Graham, S. (1987). Learning disabled students' composing under three methods of text production: Handwriting, word processing, and dictation. *Journal of Special Education, 21*(3), 22-42.

Maheady, L., Harper, G., & Sacca, M. (1988). Peer-mediated instruction: A promising approach to meeting the diverse needs of LD adolescents. *Learning Disabilities Quarterly, 11*, 108-113.

Maheady, L., Mallette, B., Harper, G., & Sacca, K. (1991). Heads Together: A peer-mediated option for improving the academic achievement of heterogeneous learning groups. *RASE, 12*(2), 25-33.

Maheady, L., Sacca, M.K., & Harper, G. (1988). Classwide peer tutoring with mildly handicapped high school students. *Exceptional Children, 55*, 52-59.

Male, M. (1986). Cooperative learning for effective mainstreaming. *The Computing Teacher, 14*, 35-37.

Male, M. (1990). Cooperative learning and computers in elementary and middle school math classroom. In N. Davidson (Ed.), *Cooperative Learning in Mathematics: A Handbook for Teachers* (pp. 126-159). Menlo Park, CA: Addison-Wesley.

Manheimer, M., & Washington, Y. (1991). *Report from small group four*. Fourth Annual ICSEMM Instructional Methods Forum, Washington, DC.

Marten, B. (1989). *CGI in the classroom*. Presentation at the Second Annual ICSEMM Instructional Methods Forum, Washington, D.C.

Martin, P., & Carnahan, S. (1989). Teaching hands-on science and math: What hinders and what helps. *Connect, March*, 1-4.

Marzano, R., Brandt, R., Hughes, C., Jones, B., Presseisen, B., Rankin, S., & Subor, C.

(1988). *Dimensions of thinking: A framework for curriculum and instruction*. Alexandria. VA: ASCD.

Marzano, R., Paynter, D., Kendall, J., Pickering, D., and Marzano, L. (1991). *Literacy Plus: An integrated approach to teaching reading, writing, vocabulary and reasoning teacher Guide*. Columbus, OH: Zaner-Bloser, Inc.

Mastropieri, M., & Scruggs, T. (1991). *Teaching students ways to remember: Strategies for learning mnemonically*. Cambridge, MA: Brookline Books.

Mathias, C. (1988). *Using strategy instruction in the classroom: A teacher's perspective*. Presentation at the ICSEMM Publishers Workshop. Washington, D.C.

Maurer, S. (1987). New knowledge about errors and new views about learners: What they mean to educators and more educators would like to know. In A. Schoenfeld (Ed.), *Cognitive science and mathematics education* (pp. 165-187). Hillsdale, NJ: Erlbaum.

Mayer, R. (1982). The psychology of mathematical problem solving. In F. Lester & J. Garofalo (Eds.), *Mathematical problem solving: Issues in research* (pp. 1-13). Philadelphia: Franklin Institute.

Mayer, R. (1985). Implications of cognitive psychology for instruction in mathematical problem solving. In E. Silver (Ed.), *Teaching and learning mathematical problem solving: Multiple research perspectives* (pp. 123-138). Hillsdale, NJ: Erlbaum.

McCutchen, D. (1986). Domain knowledge and linguistic knowledge in the development of writing ability. *Journal of Memory and Language, 25*, 431-444.

McLeod, T., & Armstrong, S. (1982). Learning disabilities in mathematics: Skill deficits and remedial approaches. *Learning Disability Quarterly, 5*, 305-311.

Meichenbaum, D. (1977). *Cognitive-behavioral modification: An integrative approach*. Plenum Press, New York.

Meichenbaum, D. (1985). Teaching thinking: A cognitive-behavioral perspective. In S. Chipman, J. Segal, & R. Glaser (Eds.), *Thinking and learning skills: Vol 2. Research and open questions* (pp. 407-426). Hillsdale, NJ: Erlbaum.

Messerer, J., & Lerner, J. (1989). Word processing for learning disabled students. *Learning Disabilities Focus, 5*, 13-17.

Meyer, B.J.F. (1975). *The organization of prose and its effects in memory.* Amsterdam, Holland: North Holland Publishing Co.

Meyers, C. (1986). *Teaching students to think critically.* San Francisco: Jossey Bass.

Miller, T. (1988). *A publisher's perspective: Decision to publish materials incorporating cognitive/metacognitive strategies.* Presentation at the ICSEMM Instructional Methods Forum, Washington, DC.

Montague, M. (in press). Strategy instruction & mathematical problem solving. *Journal of Reading, Writing, and Learning Disabilities.*

Montague, M., & Bos, C. (1986). The effects of cognitive strategy training on verbal math problem solving performance of learning disabled adolescents. *Journal of Learning Disabilities, 19,* 26-33.

Montague, M., & Bos, C. (in press). Cognitive and metacognitive characteristics of eighth grade students' mathematical problem solving. *Learning and Individual Differences.*

Montague, M., Maddux, C., & Dereshiwsky, —. (1990). Story grammar and comprehension and production of narrative prose by students with learning disabilities. *Journal of Learning Disabilities, 23,* 190-197.

Moran, M. (1981). Performance of learning disabled and low achieving secondary students on formal features of a paragraph writing task. *Learning Disabilities Quarterly, 4,* 271-280.

Morocco, C. (1990). *The role of media and materials in the teaching of writing to special education students.* Presentation at the ICSEMM Third Annual Instructional Methods Forum, Washington, DC.

Morocco, C., Dalton, B., & Tivnan, T. (1990). *The impact of computer-supported writing instruction on the writing quality of 4th grade students with and without learning disabilities.* Presentation at the American Educational Research Association Annual Meeting. Boston, MA.

Morocco, C., & Neuman, S. (1986). Word processors and the acquisition of writing strategies. *Journal of Learning Disabilities, 19,* 243-247.

Morocco, C., Neuman, S., Cushman, H., Packard, D., & Neale, A. (1987). *Teachers, children, and the magical writing machine: Instructional contexts for word processing with learning disabled children.* Newton, MA: Education Development Center.

Mosenthal, J., & Englert, C.S. (1987). The beginning capacity to teach. *RASE, 8*(6), 38-47.

Mosenthal, P. (1989, April). The whole language approach: Teachers between a rock and a hard place. *The Reading Teacher, 42,* 628-629.

Mosenthal, P., Davidson-Mosenthal, R., & Krieger, V. (1981). How fourth graders develop points of view in classroom writing. *Research in the Teaching of English, 15*(3), 197-214.

Murray, D. (1982). *Learning by teaching: Selected articles on writing and teaching.* Portsmouth, NH: Heinemann.

Myers, M. (1983). The relationship between the teacher and the researcher. In M. Myers, & J. Gray (Eds.), *Theory and practice in the teaching of composition: Processing, distancing, and modeling.* Urbana, IL: National Council of Teachers of English.

Myers, M. (1984). Shifting standards of literacy: The teacher's catch 22. *English Journal, 73,* 26-32.

Myers, M., & Paris, S. (1978). Children's Metacognitive Knowledge About Reading. *Journal of Educational Psychology, 70,* 680-690.

Myklebust, H. (1973). *Development and disorders of written language: Studies of normal and exceptional children.* New York: Grune and Stratton.

National Council of Teachers of English. *How to help your child become a better writer.* Urbana, IL: NCTE.

National Council of Teachers of Mathematics. (1989). *Curriculum and evaluation standards for school mathematics.* Reston, VA: National Council of Teachers of Mathematics.

National Research Council (1989). *Everybody counts.* Washington, D.C.: National Academy Press.

Nevin, A. (1989). Cooperative learning with adults. *Teaching Exceptional Children, 21*(3), 66-67.

Nevin, A., Johnson, D., & Johnson, R. (1982). The effects of group and individual contingencies on academic performance and social relations of special needs students. *Journal of Social Psychology, 116,* 41-59.

Nevin, A., Polewski, C., & Skieber, E. (1984). The impact of cooperative learning in a regular classroom. *The Pointer, 28,* 19-21.

Newcomer, P., Barenbaum, E., & Nodine, B.

(1988a). Comparison of the story production of LD, normal achieving and low achieving children under two modes of production. *Learning Disabilities Quarterly*, 11, 82-96.

Newcomer, P., Nodine, B., & Barenbaum, E. (1988b). Teaching writing to exceptional children: Reaction and recommendations. *Exceptional Children, 54*, 559-564.

Newmann, F., & Thompson, J. (1987). *Effects of cooperative learning on achievement in secondary schools: A summary of research.* Madison: University of Wisconsin.

Nijhof, W., & Kommers, P. (1985). An analysis of cooperation in relation to cognitive controversy. In R. Slavin, S. Sharan, S. Kagan, R. Hertz-Lazarowitz, C. Webb, & R. Schmuck (Eds.), *Learning to cooperate, cooperating to learn* (pp. 125-145). New York: Plenum Press.

Nodine, B., Barenbaum, E., & Newcomer, P. (1985). Story composition by learning disabled, reading disabled, and normal children. *Learning Disabilities Quarterly, 8*, 167-179.

Oka, E., & Paris, S. (1987). Patterns of motivation and reading skills in underachieving children. In S. Ceci (Ed.), *Handbook of cognitive, social, and neuropsychological aspects of learning disabilities* (pp. 115-145). Hillsdale, NJ: Erlbaum.

Palincsar, A.S. (1986a). *Interactive cognition to promote listening.* Paper presented at the annual meeting of AERA, San Francisco, CA.

Palincsar, A.S. (1986b). Metacognitive strategy instruction. *Exceptional Children, 53*, 118-124.

Palincsar, A.S. (1988). *Reciprocal teaching: An instructional method for teaching comprehension and comprehension monitoring strategies.* Presentation at the ICSEMM Instructional Methods Forum, Washington, D.C.

Palincsar, A. (1990). Providing the context for intentional learning. *RASE 11*(6), 36-39.

Palincsar, A., & Brown, A. (1984). Reciprocal teaching of comprehension-fostering and comprehension-monitoring activities. *Cognition and Instruction, 1*, 117-175.

Palincsar, A., & Brown, A. (1986). Interactive teaching to promote independent learning from text. *The Reading Teacher, 39*, 771-777.

Palincsar, A., & Brown, A. (1988). Teaching and practicing thinking skills to promote comprehension in the context of group problem solving. *RASE, 9*(1), 53-59.

Palincsar, A., & Brown, A. (1989). Instruction for self-regulated reading. In L. Resnick and L. Klopfer, *Toward the thinking curriculum: Current cognitive research*, (pp. 19-39). Alexandria, VA: Association for Supervision and Curriculum Development.

Palincsar, A., Brown, A., & Martin, S. (1987). Peer interaction in reading comprehension instruction. *Educational Psychologist, 22*(3 & 4), 231-253.

Paolucci-Whitcomb, P. (1985). Preparing consulting teachers through a collaborative approach between university faculty and field-based consulting teachers. *Teacher Education and Special Education, 8*(3), 132-143.

Paris, S., Cross, D., & Lipson, M. (1984). Informed strategies for learning: A program to improve children's reading awareness. *Journal of Educational Psychology, 76*, 1239-1252.

Paris, S., & Jacobs, J. (1984). The benefits of informed instruction for children's reading awareness and comprehension skills. *Child Development, 55*, 2083-2093.

Paris, S., & Meyers, M. (1981). Comprehension monitoring, memory, and study strategies of good and poor readers. *Journal of Reading Behavior, 13*, 5-24.

Paris, S., & Oka, E. (1986a). Children's reading strategies, metacognition, and motivation. *Developmental Review, 6*, 25-56.

Paris, S., & Oka, E. (1986b). Self-regulated learning among exceptional children. *Exceptional Children, 53*, 103-108.

Paris, S., Wixson, K., & Palincsar, A.S. (1986). Instructional approaches to reading comprehension. In E. Rothkopf (Ed.), *Review of Research in Education* (Vol 13, pp. 91-128). Washington, D.C.: AERA.

Payne, J., Polloway, E., Smith, J., & Payne, R. (1981). *Strategies for teaching the mentally retarded*, 2nd ed. Columbus, Ohio: Merrill.

Pellegrino, J., & Goldman, S. (1987). Information processing and elementary mathematics. *Journal of Learning Disabilities, 20*, 23-32.

Peters, E., Lloyd, J., Hasselbring, T., Goin, L., Bransford, J., & Stein, M. (1987). Effective mathematics instruction. *Teaching Exceptional Children, 19*(3), 30.

Peterson, P., Fennema, E., & Carpenter, T. (1988/1989). Using knowledge of how students think about mathematics. *Educational Leadership, 46*(4), 42-46.

Peterson, P., Fennema, E., Carpenter, T., and Loef, M. (1989). Teaching pedagogical content beliefs in mathematics. *Cognition and Instruction, 6*, 1-40.

Peterson, P., Wilkinson, L., Spinelli, F., & Swing, S. (1984). Merging the process-product and the sociolinguistic paradigm: Research on small group processes. In P. Peterson, L. Wilkinson, & M. Hallinan (Eds.), *The social context of instruction: Group organization and group processes* (pp. 125-152). Orlando, FL: Academic Press.

Peterson, S., Mercer, C., & O'Shea, L. (1988). Teaching learning disabled students place value using concrete to abstract sequence. *Learning Disabilities Research, 4*, 52-56.

Pigott, H., Fantuzzo, J., & Clement, P. (1986). The effects of reciprocal peer tutoring and group contingencies on the academic performance of elementary school children. *Journal of Applied Behavior Analysis, 19*, 93-98.

Pigott, H., Fantuzzo, J., Heggie, D., & Clement, P. (1984). A student administered group oriented contingency intervention: Its efficacy in a regular classroom. *Child and Family Behavior Therapy, 6*(4), 41-55.

Polloway, E., Cronin, M., & Patton, J. (1986). The efficacy of group versus one-to-one instruction: A review. *RASE, 7*(1), 22-30.

Pressley, M. (1986). The relevance of the good strategy user model to the teaching of mathematics. *Educational Psychologist, 21*(1-2), 139-161.

Pressley, M. (1988). *An overview of cognitive and metacognitive theories as they relate to special education populations and findings of pertinent intervention research.* Presentation at the ICSEMM Publishers Workshop. Washington, D.C.

Pressley, M., & Associates (1990). *Cognitive strategy instruction that really improves children's academic performance.* Cambridge, MA: Brookline Books.

Pressley, M., Goodchild, F., Fleet, J., Zajchowski, R., & Evans, E. (1989a). The challenges of classroom strategy instruction. *The Elementary School Journal, 89*, 301-342.

Pressley, M., Johnson, C., Symons, S., McGoldrick, J., & Kurita, J. (1989b). Strategies that improve children's memory and comprehension of text. *Elementary School Journal, 90*, 3-32.

Pressley, M., & Levin, J. (1987). Elaboration learning strategies for the inefficient learner. In S. Ceci (Ed.), *Handbook of cognitive, social, and neuropsychological aspects of learning disabilities* (Vol. 2, pp. 175-212). Hillsdale, NJ: Erlbaum.

Pugach, M., & Johnson, L. (1988). Peer collaboration. *Teaching Exceptional Children, 20*(3), 75-77.

Putnam, J., Rynders, J., Johnson, R., & Johnson, D. (1989). Collaborative skill instruction for promoting positive interactions between mentally handicapped and non-handicapped children. *Exceptional Children, 55*, 550-557.

Putnam, J., & Wiederhold, C. (1991). *Report from small group two.* Fourth Annual Instructional Methods Forum, Washington, DC: Information Center for Special Education Media and Materials.

Rabinowitz, M., & Chi, M. (1987). An interactive model of strategic processing. In S. Ceci (Ed.), *Handbook of cognitive, social, and neuropsychological aspects of learning disabilities* (Vol. 2, pp. 83-102). Hillsdale, NJ: Erlbaum.

Raphael, D., & Wahlstrom, M. (1989). The influence of instructional aids on mathematics achievement. *Journal for Research in Mathematics Education, 20*, 173-190.

Raphael, R. (1986). Teaching question-answer relationships, revisited. *Reading Teacher 39*, 516-23.

Raphael, T., Englert, C.S., & Kirschner, B. (1986). *The impact of text structure instruction and social context on students' comprehension and production of expository text* (Research Series No. 177). East Lansing: Michigan State University Institute for Research on Teaching.

Reese-Dukes, J., & Stokes, E. (1978). Social acceptance of elementary educable mentally retarded pupils in the regular classroom. *Education and Training of Mentally Retarded, 13*, 356-361.

Reeve, R.A., & Brown, A.L. (1985). Metacognition reconsidered: Implications for intervention research. *Journal of Abnormal Child Psychology, 13*, 343-356.

Reid M.K., & Borkowski, J. (1985). *A cognitive-motivational training program for hyperactive children.* Paper presented at the Society for

Research and Child Development, Toronto.

Resnick, L. (1987). *Education and learning to think*. Committee on Mathematics, Science, and Technology Education. Washington, D.C.: National Academy Press. (ED 289 832).

Resnick, L., & Klopper, L. (1989). Toward a thinking curriculum: An overview. In L. Resnick & L. Klopper (Eds.) *Toward the thinking curriculum: Current cognitive research*, pp. 40-58.

Resnick, L., & Omanson, S. (1986). Learning to understand arithmetic. In R. Glaser (Ed.), *Advances in instructional psychology, Vol. 3* (pp. 41-95). Hillsdale, NJ: Erlbaum.

Reynolds, C., & Salend, S. (1989). Cognitive learning in special education teacher preparation programs. *Teacher Education and Special Education, 12*(3), 91-95.

Rhodes, L., & Dudley-Marling, C. (1988). *Readers and writers with a difference*. Portsmouth, NH: Heinemann.

Rieth, H., Axelrod, S., Anderson, R., Hathaway, F., Wood, K., & Fitzgerald, C. (1974). Influence of distributed practice and daily testing on weekly spelling tests. *Journal of Educational Research, 68*, 73-77.

Riley, M. (1981). *Conceptual and procedural knowledge in development*. Unpublished doctoral thesis, University of Pittsburgh.

Riley, M., Greeno, J., & Heller, J. (1983). Development of children's problem solving ability. In H. Ginsburg (Ed.), *Development of mathematical thinking* (pp. 153-196). New York: Academic Press.

Rivera, D., & Smith, D. (1987). Influence of modeling on acquisition and generalization of computational skills: A summary of research from three sites. *Learning Disabilities Quarterly, 10*, 69-80.

Robertson, L., Graves, N., & Tuck, P. (1990). Implementing group work; Issues for teachers and administrators. In N. Davidson (Ed.), *Cooperative learning in mathematics: A handbook for teachers* (pp. 295-334). Menlo Park, CA: Addison-Wesley.

Roehler, L., & Duffy, G. (in press). Teachers' instructional actions. Chapter for inclusion in Handbook of reading research (Vol. 2).

Roehler, L., Duffy, G., Vaurus, L., Putnam, J., Wesselman, R., Sivan, E., Book, C., & Meloth, M. (1986, July). *Teacher explanation: A final report of the 1983-84 study* (Research Series No. 170). East Lansing, MI: Michigan State University, Institute for Research on Effective Teaching.

Roit, M., & McKenzie, R. (1985). Disorders of written communication: An instructional priority for LD students. *Journal of Learning Disabilities, 18*, 258-260.

Romberg, T., & Carpenter, T. (1986). Research on teaching and learning mathematics: Two disciplines of scientific inquiry. In M. Wittrock (Ed.), *Handbook of research on teaching, 3rd ed.* (pp. 850-873). New York: Macmillan.

Russell, R., & Ginsburg, H. (1984). Cognitive analysis of children's mathematical difficulties. *Cognition and Instruction, 1*, 217-244.

Ryan, E., Short, E., & Weed, K. (1986). The role of cognitive strategy training in improving the academic performance of learning disabled children. *Journal of Learning Disabilities, 19*(9), 521-529.

Rynders, J., Johnson, R., & Johnson, D. (1981). Effects of cooperative, competitive and individualistic experiences on self-esteem of handicapped and nonhandicapped students. *Journal of Psychology, 108*, 31-34.

Sabornie, E. (1985). Social mainstreaming of handicapped students: Facing an unpleasant reality. *RASE, 6*(2), 12-16.

Samuels, S.J. (1987). Information processing abilities and reading. *Journal of Learning Disabilities, 20*, 18-22.

Samuels, S.J. (1988). Decoding and automaticity: Helping poor readers become automatic at word recognition. *The Reading Teacher 41*, 756-760.

Sandeen, C. (1991). *What media and methods are effective when using cooperative learning with special education?* Unpublished Report.

Sapon-Shevin, M., & Schniedewind, N. (1989/1990). Selling cooperative learning without selling it short. *Educational Leadership, 47*(4), 63-65.

Scardamalia, M. (1981). How children cope with the cognitive demands of writing. In *Writing: The nature, development, and teaching of written communication, vol. 2, Writing: Process, development, and communication* (pp. 81-103). Hillsdale, NJ: LEA.

Scardamalia, M., & Bereiter, C. (1985). Helping students become better writers. *The School Administrator, 42*(4), 16, 26.

Scardamalia, M., & Bereiter, C. (1986). Research on Written Composition. In M.

Wittrock (Ed.), *Handbook on research in teaching* (pp. 778-803). New York: Macmillan.

Schenk, W. (1973). Pictures and the indefinite quantifier in verbal problem solving among EMR children. *American Journal of Mental Deficiency, 78*, 272-276.

Schmidt, J.L. (1984, November). The effects of four generalization conditions on learning disabled adolescents' written language performance in the regular classroom. *Dissertation Abstracts International, 45*, 1367A.

Schoenfeld, A. (1982). Some thoughts on problem solving research and mathematics education. In F. Lester & J. Garofalo (Eds.), *Mathematical problem solving—issues in research* (pp. 27-37). Philadelphia: Franklin Institute.

Schoenfeld, A. (1987). What's all this fuss about metacognition. In A. Schoenfeld (Ed.), *Cognitive science and mathematics education* (pp. 189-215). Hillsdale, NJ: Erlbaum.

Schoenfeld, A. (1988). When good teaching leads to bad results. *Educational Psychologist, 23*, 145-166.

Schultz, J. (1989/1990). Cooperative learning: Refining the process. *Educational Leadership, 47*(4), 43-45.

Schumaker, J., Deshler, D., Alley, G., Warner, M., & Denton, P. (1982). Multipass: A learning strategy for improving reading comprehension. *Learning Disability Quarterly, 15*, 295-304.

Schumaker, J., & Hazel, J. (1984). Social skills assessment and training for the learning disabled: Who's first and what's on Second? Part I. *Journal of Learning Disabilities, 17*(7), 422-431.

Schumaker, J., Sheldon-Wilgren, J., & Sherman, J. (1980). *An Observational Study of the Academic and Social Skills of Learning Disabled Adolescents in the Regular Classroom, Research Report No 22*. Lawrence, KS: University of Kansas Institute for Research on Learning Disabilities.

Schunk, D. (1981). Modeling and attributional effects on children's achievements—a self-efficacy analysis. *Journal of Educational Psychology, 73*, 93-105.

Schunk, D., & Cox, P. (1986). Strategy training and attributional feedback with learning disabled students. *Journal of Educational Psychology, 78*, 201-209.

Schwartz, S., & Shoemaker, M. (1990). *Report* from small group three. ICSEMM Third Annual Instructional Methods Forum, Washington, D.C.

Scruggs, T., & Mastropieri, M. (1992). *Teaching test-taking skills: Helping students show what they know*. Cambridge, MA: Brookline Books.

Scruggs, T., & Richter, L. (1986, Winter). Tutoring learning disabled students: A critical review. *Learning Disabled Quarterly, 9*, 2-14.

Secada, W., Fuson, K., & Hall, J. (1983). The transition from counting all to counting on in addition. *Journal for Research in Mathematics Education, 14*, 47-57.

Sedlack, R., & Cartwright, P. (1972). Written language abilities of EMR and non-retarded children with the same mental age. *American Journal of Mental Deficiency, 77*, 95-99.

Seidenberg, P. (1989). Relating text-processing research to reading and writing instruction for learning disabled students. *Learning Disabilities Focus, 5*, 4-12.

Shanahan, T. (1988). The reading-writing relationship: Seven instructional principles. *The Reading Teacher, 41*, 636-647.

Shanklin, N., & Rhodes, L. (1989). Transforming literacy instruction. *Educational Leadership, 46*, 59-63.

Sharan, S. (1990). Cooperative learning: A perspective on research and practice. In S. Sharan (Ed.), *Cooperative learning theory and research* (pp. 285-300). New York: Praeger.

Sharan, S., Hertz-Lazarowitz, R., & Ackerman, Z. (1980). Academic achievement of elementary school children in small group versus whole-class instruction. *Journal of Experimental Education, 48*, 125-129.

Sharan, S., Kussell, P., Hertz-Lazarowitz, R., Bejaran, O., Raviv, S., & Sharan, Y. (1984). *Cooperative learning in the classroom: Research in desegregated schools*. Hillsdale, NJ: Lawrence Erlbaum Associates.

Sharan, S., & Shackar, H. (1988). *Language and learning in the cooperative classroom*. New York: Springer-Verlag.

Sharan, Y., & Sharan, S. (1989/1990). Group investigation expands cooperative learning. *Educational Leadership, 47*(4), 17-21.

Share, D., Moffitt, T., & Silva, P. (1988). Factors associated with arithmetic and reading disability. *Journal of Learning Disabilities, 21*, 313-320.

Shaw, R. (1985, February). Growing support for elementary school writing instruction. *Educational Leadership, 42,* 16-18.

Sheinker, J. (1988). *Small group report group two.* Presentation at the ICSEMM Instructional Methods Forum. Washington, D.C.

Shook, S., Marrion, L., & Ollila, L. (1989). Primary children's concepts about writing. *Journal of Educational Research, 82,* 133-138.

Shufelt, G. (Ed.) (1977, December). Etcetera. *Arithmetic Teacher, 25,* p.37.

Shulman, L. (1986). Those who understand: Knowledge growth in teaching. *Educational Researcher, 15,*(2), 4-15.

Silver, E. (1985). Research in teaching mathematical problem solving: Some underrepresented themes and needed directions. In E.Silver (Ed.), *Teaching and learning mathematical problem solving: Multiple research perspectives* (pp. 247-266). Hillsdale, NJ: Erlbaum.

Silver, E. (1987). Foundations of cognitive theory and research for mathematics problem solving instruction. In A. Schoenfeld (Ed.), *Cognitive science and mathematics education* (pp. 33-60). Hillsdale, NJ: Erlbaum.

Skrtic, T. (1991). The special education paradox: Equity as the way to excellence. *Harvard Educational Review, 61,* 148-206.

Slavin, R. (1984). Students motivating students to excel: Cooperative incentives, cooperative tasks, and student achievement. *Elementary School Journal, 85,* 53-63.

Slavin, R. (1985a). An introduction to cooperative learning research. In R. Slavin, S. Sharan, S. Kagan, R. Hertz-Lazarowitz, C. Webb, & R. Schmuck (Eds.), *Learning to cooperate, cooperating to learn* (pp. 5-15). New York: Plenum Press.

Slavin, R. (1985b). Cooperative learning: Applying contact theory in desegregated schools. *Journal of Social Issues, 41*(3), 45-62.

Slavin, R. (1985c). Team-assisted individualization combining cooperative learning and individualized instruction in mathematics. In R. Slavin, S. Sharan, S. Kagan, R. Hertz-Lazarowitz, C. Webb, & R. Schmuck (Eds.), *Learning to cooperate, cooperating to learn* (pp. 177-207). New York: Plenum Press.

Slavin, R. (1989). Cooperative learning and student achievement. In R. Slavin (Ed.), *School and classroom organization* (pp. 129-156). Hillsdale, NJ: LEA.

Slavin, R. (1989/1990). Research on cooperative learning: Consensus and controversy. *Educational Leadership, 47*(4), 52-55.

Slavin, R. (1990a). Comprehensive cooperative learning models: Embedding cooperative learning in the curriculum and the school. In S. Sharan (Ed.), *Cooperative learning theory and research* (pp. 261-283). New York: Praeger.

Slavin, R. (1990b). Student team learning in mathematics. In N. Davidson (Ed.), *Cooperative learning in mathematics: A handbook for teachers* (pp. 69-102). Menlo Park, CA: Addison Wesley.

Slavin, R. (1991a). Group rewards make groupwork work. *Educational Leadership, 48*(5), 89-91.

Slavin, R. (1991b). Synthesis of research on cooperative learning. *Educational Leadership, 48*(5), 71-82.

Slavin, R. (1991c). *The role of media and materials in implementation of cooperative learning.* Presentation at the Fourth Annual Instructional Methods Forum, Washington, D.C.: Information Center for Special Education Media and Materials.

Slavin, R., & Karweit, N. (1985). Effects of whole class, ability groups, and individualized instruction on mathematics achievement. *American Educational Research Journal, 22,* 351-367.

Slavin, R., Madden, N., & Leavey, M. (1984a). Effects of cooperative learning and individualized instruction on mainstreamed students. *Exceptional Children, 50,* 434-443.

Slavin, R., Madden, N., & Leavey, M. (1984b). Effects of team assisted individualization on the mathematics achievement of academically handicapped and non handicapped students. *Journal of Educational Psychology, 76,* 813-819.

Slavin, R., Madden, N., & Stevens, R. (1989/1990). Cooperative learning models for the 3 R's. *Educational Leadership, 47*(4), 22-28.

Slavin, R., Stevens, R., & Madden, N. (1988). Accommodating student diversity in reading and writing instruction: A cooperative learning approach. *RASE, 9*(1), 60-66.

Slife, B., Weiss, J., & Bell, T. (1985). Separability of metacognition and cognition: Problem solving in learning disabled and regular students. *Journal of Educational Psychology, 77,* 437-445.

Smith, R. (1987). A teacher's views on cooperative learning. *Phi Delta Kappan, 68*(9), 663-666.

Solomon, D., Watson, M., Schaps, E., Battistich, V., & Solomon, J. (1990). Cooperative learning as part of a comprehensive classroom program designed to promote prosocial development. In S. Sharan (Ed.), *Cooperative learning theory and research* (pp. 231-160). New York: Praeger.

Spear, L., & Sternberg, R. (1987). An intervention-processing framework for understanding reading disability. In S. Ceci (Ed.), *Handbook of cognitive, social, and neuropsychological aspects of learning disabilities* (pp. 3-31). Hillsdale, NJ: Erlbaum.

Stein, N. (1986). Knowledge and process in the acquisition of writing skills. In E. Rothkoph (Ed.), *Review of Research in Education, vol. 13* (pp. 225-258). Washington, DC: AERA.

Stein, N., & Trabasso, T. (1982). What's in a story: An approach to comprehension and instruction. In R. Glaser (Ed.), *Advances in instructional psychology* (pp. 213-267). Hillsdale, NJ: LEA.

Stevens, R., Madden, N., Slavin, R., & Farnish, A.M. (1987). Cooperative integrated reading and composition: Two field experiments. *Reading Research Quarterly, 22,* 433-454.

Stevens, R., & Slavin, R. (1991a). *A cooperative learning approach to accommodating student diversity in reading and writing: Effects on handicapped and non-handicapped students.* Baltimore, MD: Johns Hopkins University.

Stevens, R., & Slavin, R. (1991b). When cooperative learning improves the achievement of students with mild disabilities: Response to Tateyama-Sniezek. *Exceptional Children, 57,* 276-280.

Stires, S. (1983). Real audiences and contexts for LD writers. *Academic Therapy, 18,* 561-567.

Stires, S. (1988). Reading and talking: Special readers show they know . In T. Newkirk, & N. Atwell (Eds.), *Understanding writing: Ways of observing, learning, and teaching* (pp. 207-215). Portsmouth, NH: Heinemann.

Stires, S. (1989). Thinking throughout the process: Self-evaluation in writing. In J. Jensen (Ed.), *Stories to grow on: Demonstrations on language learning in K-8* (pp. 71-93). Portsmouth, NH: Heinemann.

Stires, S. (1990). *Implementing a writing program for students with learning problems.* Presentation at the ICSEMM Third Annual Instructional Methods Forum, Washington, DC.

Sunstein, B. (1990). *Learning disabilities and the writing process approach.* Presentation at the ICSEMM Third Annual Instructional Methods Forum, Washington, DC.

Swing, S., Stoiber, K., & Peterson, P. (1988). Thinking skills vs. learning time: Effects of alternative classroom-based interventions on students' mathematics problem solving. *Cognition and Instruction, 5,* 123-191.

Tateyama-Sniezek, K. (1990). Cooperative learning: Does it improve the academic achievement of students with handicaps? *Exceptional Children, 56,* 426-437.

Taymans, J. (1989). Cooperative learning for learning disabled adolescents. *The Pointer, 33*(2), 28-32.

Terwel, J. (1990). Real maths in cooperative groups in secondary education. In N. Davidson (Ed.), *Cooperative learning in mathematics: A handbook for teachers* (pp. 228-264). Menlo Park, CA: Addison Wesley.

Thackwray, D., Meyers, A., Schleser, R., & Cohen, R. (1985). Achieving generalization with general versus specific self-instruction: Effects on academically deficient children. *Cognitive Therapy and Research, 9,* 297-308.

Thomas, C., Englert, C., & Gregg, S. (1987). An analysis of errors and strategies in the expository writing of learning disabled students. *RASE, 8*(1), 21-30.

Thompson, A. (1990). Thinking and writing in learning logs. In N. Atwell (Ed.), *Coming to know: Writing to learn in the intermediate grades* (pp. 35-51). Portsmouth, NH: Heinemann.

Thompson, C., & Rathmell, E. (1988, May). NCTM's standards for school mathematics, K-12. *Arithmetic Teacher, 35,* 17-19.

Thornton, C. (1978). Emphasizing thinking strategies in basic fact instruction. *Journal for Research in Mathematics Education, 9,* 213-227.

Thornton, C. (1989a). *Cognitive-based methods for enhancing the mathematical problem-solving capabilities of special education students.* Presentation at the ICSEMM Instructional Methods Forum. Washington, D.C.

Thornton, C. (1989b, April). "Look ahead" activities spark success in addition and subtraction number fact learning. *Arithmetic Teacher, 36,* 8-11.

Thornton, C., Jones, G., & Toohey, M. (1983). A multisensory approach to thinking strategies for remedial instruction in basic addition facts. *Journal for Research in Mathematics Education, 14*, 198-203.

Thornton, C., & Smith, P. (1988, April). Action research: Strategies for learning subtraction facts. *Arithmetic Teacher, 35*, 8-12.

Thornton, C., & Toohey, M. (1985). Basic math facts: Guidelines for teaching and learning. *Learning Disabilities Focus, 1*, 44-57.

Thornton, C., & Toohey, M. (1986). Subtraction facts hide-and-seek cards can help. *Teaching Exceptional Children, 19*, 10-14.

Thornton, C., Tucker, B., Dossey, J., & Bazik, E. (1983). *Teaching mathematics to children with special needs.* Menlo Park, CA: Addison-Wesley.

Thornton, C., & Wilmot, B. (1986, February). Special learners. *Arithmetic Teacher, 33*, 38-41.

Thousand, J. (1988). Addressing individual differences in the classroom. *Teacher Education and Special Education, 11*(2), 72-75.

Thousand, J., Nevin-Parta, A., & Fox, W. (1987). Inservice training to support the education of learners with severe handicaps in their local public schools. *Teacher Education and Special Education, 10*(1), 4-13.

Topping, K. (1989). Peer tutoring and paired reading: Combining two powerful techniques. *The Reading Teacher, 42*, 488-494.

Torgesen, J. (1985). Memory processes in reading disabled children. *Journal of Learning Disabilities, 18*, 350-357.

Trafton, P. (1984). Toward more effective, efficient instructions in mathematics. *Elementary School Journal, 84*, 514-528.

Turnure, J. (1986). Instruction and cognitive development: Coordinating communication and cues. *Exceptional Children, 53*, 109-117.

Valencia, S., & Pearson, P.D. (1988). Principles for classroom comprehension assessment. *RASE, 9*(1), 26-35.

Van Lehn, K. (1983). On the representation of procedures in repair theory. In H. Ginsburg (Ed.), *The development of mathematical thinking* (pp. 197-252). New York: Academic Press.

Villa, R., & Thousand, J. (1988). Enhancing success in heterogeneous classrooms and schools: The power of partnership. *Teacher Education and Special Education, 11*(4), 144-154.

Walmsley, S. (1983). Writing Disability. In P. Mosenthal, & L.W.S. Tamor (Eds.), *Research on writing: Principles and methods* (pp. 267-286). New York: Longman.

Wansart, W. (1988). The student with learning disabilities in a writing process classroom: A case study. *Reading, Writing and Learning Disabilities, 4*, 311-319.

Watson, D., & Rangel, L. (1989). Don't forget the slow learner. *The Clearinghouse, 62*, 266-268.

Webb, N. (1982). Student interaction and learning in small groups. *Review of Educational Research, 52*(3), 421-445.

Webb, N. (1985). Student interactions and learning in small groups: A research summary. In R. Slavin, S. Sharan, S. Kagan, R. Hertz-Lazarowitz, C. Webb, & R. Schmuck (Eds.), *Learning to cooperate, cooperating to learn* (pp. 147-172). New York: Plenum Press.

Webb, N., & Kinderski, C.M. (1984). Student interaction and learning in small group and whole class settings. In P. Peterson, L. Wilkinson, & M. Hallinan (Eds.), *The social context of instruction: Group organization and group processes* (pp. 153-170). Orlando, FL: Academic Press.

Weissglass, J. (1990). Cooperative learning using a small group laboratory approach. In N. Davidson (Ed.), *Cooperative learning in mathematics: A handbook for teachers* (pp. 295-334). Menlo Park, CA: Addison Wesley.

Whitman, T., & Johnston, M. (1983). Teaching addition and subtraction with regrouping to educable mentally retarded children: A group self-instructional training program. *Behavior Therapy, 14*, 127-143.

Wiens, J.W. (1983). Metacognition and the adolescent. *Journal of Learning Disabilities, 16*, 144-149.

Wilkinson, L. (1988). Grouping children for learning: Implications for kindergarten education. In E. Rothkopk (Ed.), *1988-1989 Review of research in education* (pp. 203-223). Washington, DC: American Educational Research Association.

Wolfe, J., Fantuzzo, J., & Wolfe, P. (1986). The effects of reciprocal peer management and group contingencies on the arithmetic proficiency of underachieving students. *Behavior Therapy, 17*, 253-265

Wolfe, J., Fantuzzo, J., & Wolter, C. (1984). Student-administered group-oriented contingencies: A method of combining group-oriented contingencies and self-directed behavior to increase academic productivity. *Child and Family Behavior Therapy, 6*(3), 45-60.

.Wong, B.Y.L. (1985a). Potential means of enhancing content skills acquisition in learning disabled adolescents. *Focus on Exceptional Children, 17*(5), 1-18.

Wong, B.Y.L. (1985b). Skill questioning instructional research: A review. *Review of Educational Research, 55,* 227-268.

Wong, B.Y.L. (1986a). A cognitive approach to teaching spelling. *Exceptional Children, 53,* 169-173.

Wong, B.Y.L. (1986b). Metacognition and special education: A review of a view. *The Journal of Special Education, 20,* 9-29.

Wong, B.Y.L. (1987). How do the results of metacognition research impact on the learning disabled individual? *Learning Disability Quarterly, 10,* 189-195.

Wong, B.Y.L., & Jones, W. (1982). Increasing metacomprehension in learning disabled and normally achieving students through self-questioning training. *Learning Disability Quarterly, 5,* 228-240.

Wong, B.Y.L., & Wilson, M. (1984). Investigating awareness of and teaching passage organization in learning disabled children. *Journal of Learning Disabilities, 17,* 477-482.

Yates, J. (1983). *What research says to teachers: Research implications for writing in the content areas.* Washington, D.C.: National Education Association.

Zhu, X., & Simon, H. (1987). Learning mathematics from examples by doing. *Cognition and Instruction, 4,* 137-166.

Zigler, E., Balla, D., & Hodapp, R. (1984). On definition and classification of mental retardation. *American Journal on Mental Deficiency, 89,* 215-230.

Zigmond, N., & Kerr, M. (1985). *Managing the mainstream: A contrast of behaviors of learning disabled students who pass their assigned mainstream courses and those who fail.* Paper presented at the American Educational Research Association Meeting. Chicago, IL.

Index

activities for group work, 125
  Cooperative pumpkins, 128
  Learn the States, 128
  Letter to Editor, 128
  measurement skills, 125
  "Space Travel," 125
Allardice, B., 8, 15, 83, 92
Allington, R., 34, 37
Anderson, M., 136, 137, 139
Anderson, V. , & Hidi, S., 25, 26
Andrews, j., 142, 143
Atwell, N. (1984), 55
Atwell, N. (1988) , 18, 48, 158, 159
Atwell, N. (1990) , 69, 72

Bailey, G., & Dyck, N., 110, 123
Baker, J. , 84, 166, 167
Baker, L., & Brown, A.L., 5, 11
Bandura, A., 119
Barenbaum, E. , Newcomer, p. , & Nodine,
  B. , 13
Baroody, A., 8, 9, 10, 83, 84, 87, 88, 90, 91, 92,
  95, 97, 100, 101, 103
Bereiter, C., & Scardamalia, M., 7, 8, 47, 53,
  68
Bernaqozzi, T., 122
Bley, N. & Thornton, C., 15, 16, 86, 91, 97,
  102, 103, 105
Borkowski, J.G., & Cavanaugh, J.C., 16
Borkowski, J.G., Reid, M.K., & Kurtz, B., 31
Borkowski, J.G., Weyhing, R., & Turner, L.,
  35
Bos, C., 6, 8, 20, 47, 59, 60, 63, 68
Boynton, R, 68, 78
Brady, S., & Jacobs, S., 64
Brainin, S.S., 35
Brandt, R., 179, 180
Bransford, J., 31, 33, 35, 141
Brennan, C., 50, 59, 68, 76
Brown, A.L., 2, 5, 11, 16, 17, 22, 32, 35, 36, 38,
  39, 40, 113, 141, 142, 143, 144,

Brown, C., Carpenter, T., Kouba, V., Lind-
  quist, M., Silver, E., Swafford, J., 83
Bulgren, J. & Montague, M., 9l, 97, 100, 102,
  103, 105, 106
Burns, M., 83
Busch, J., 149, 151

calculators and manipulatives, use of, 98,
  100, 106
Calkins, L., 60, 63, 64
Callahan, L., & MacMillan, D., 100, 102, 105
Campione, J., 11, 31, 33, 35, 39, 142
Carnine, D., 88, 92, 93, 102, 103, 106
Carpenter, T., 8, 9, 93, 95, 96, 161, 162, 164
Case, L., 18
Cawley, J., 13, 14, 15, 84, 88, 92, 93, 96, 97,
  100, 103, 164, 165, 166
Ceci, S., & Baker, J., 11
Charles, R., Lester, F., & O'Duffer, P., 113
Cherkes-Julkowski, M. (l985a), 15, 16, 86,
  89, 90, 98
Christenson, S., Thurlow, M., Ysseldyke, J.,
  & McVicar, R., 47
classroom media and materials, 41
  content-related, 42
classwide peer tutoring, 170, 171
  for minority, disadvantaged, and disabled
  children, 170
cognitive-based principles, 83
  content-related, 85
  instructional approaches, 84
    cognitively guided (CGI), 84
    verbal problem solving, 84
  methods-related, 85
  traditional vs. current math instruction,
  83
cognitive strategy instruction, 2, 3, 5
  emphasis of, 2
  implication for, 3
    math, end goal of, 8, 9
    reading, 4

comprehending written word, 5
word recognition, 4
writing, 3 stages, 6
Cognitive Strategy Instruction in Writing (CSIW), 155
Cognitively Guided Instruction (CGI), 161, 163, 164
classroom implementation, 163
objectives of program, 162
use of manipulatives, 162
cognitive theories of learning, 3
behaviorist point of view, 3
general characteristics of, 4
influence of, 3
instructional implications, 19
Cohen, E., 112, 113, 115, 117, 118, 122, 123, 124, 125, 129, 130, 132, 133, 134, 171, 172, 173
collaborative learning, 110
design and implementation, 115, 116
effects on mainstreamed students, 112
effects on performance, 110
on learning-problem students, 111
on regular classrooms, 110
extended to science and social studies, 137
influence on peer relationships, 111
social benefits of, 111
preparation for, 115, 116
learning methods, examples of, 169
Study Buddy program, 164
two-part curriculum, 169
Cooperative Peer Relations, 169
Reciprocal Peer Learning, 169
training program for teachers, 169
collaborative learning, motivating students to learn, 112
improvement in self-esteem, 113
collaborative learning, special counseling and training, 119
conducive classroom environment, 120
criteria for success, 130, 131
frequent evaluation, 130, 134
individual accountability, 131, 132
when to use, 123
collective learning, 110, 119
communicating through writing, 47
writing instruction, 47
cognitive strategy, 48
process writing approach, 48, 49

self-instructional strategy, 48
composition instruction, 153
comprehensive math curriculum, 90
guidance for design of, 91
conceptual understanding, 86
concept development, 86
conferences with students, 65
questions asked by teachers, 65, 66
connection between instructional procedures, 88
Conway, R., & Gow, L., 113
Cooperative Integrated Reading and Composition (CIRC), 114, 130, 136, 137, 175, 176
for use in regular classroom, 175
three components, 176
cooperative learning, 173
guidelines, 173
Johns Hopkins approach, 173, 174
Johnson & Johnson approach, 173 ff
structural approach, 179 ff
cooperative learning groups, general types, 124
ad hoc groups, 124
base groups, 124
formal groups, 124
tasks and activities, 125
measurement skills, 125
Cosden, M., & Lieber, J., 121
Crabill, C. , 125, 134

Dalton, B., 74
Danoff, B., 154, 155
Davidson, N., 114, 133, 137
Davis, B., Scriven, M., & Thomas, S., 62
De Corte, E. & Vershaffel, L., 14
Dees, R., 121, 122, 125, 127, 133
Delquadri, J., 110, 113, 115, 117, 125, 134, 170, 171
Derry, S., Hawkes, L., & Tsai, C., 9
Deshler, D., 17, 21, 32, 33, 36, 40, 86, 144, 145, 146, 147, 148
designing instruction, 121
appropriate structure, 123
objectives, 121
schedule for group activity, 123
DiPardo, A. & Freedman, S., 64
Direct Explanation Model, 21, 148, 149, 150, 151
role of teacher, 149

Dowd, M., 32, 41
DuCharme, C., Earl, J., & Poplin, M., 63, 69
Dudley-Marling, C., 4, 8, 19, 27, 29, 31, 32, 34, 35, 38, 39, 42, 43, 47, 50, 51, 59, 60, 61, 62, 64, 67, 69
Duffy, G., 5, 6, 22, 23, 35, 36, 37, 38, 40, 148, 149, 150, 151
Durkin, D., 41

educational programs, designs for, 1
cognitive strategy instruction, 1
education system, demands on, 1
Edwards, C. & Stout, J., 117, 122, 123, 125, 132
Ellis, E.L., Lenz, B.K. , & Sabornie, E.J., 21, 31, 36, 38, 40, 41, 146
Englert, C.S., 6, 7, 12, 13, 17, 36, 47, 48, 49, 53, 54, 56, 57, 60, 63, 64, 68, 156, 157

Fantuzzo, J., 111, 112
Farley, J., 12
Farnsworth, L., 72
Fear, K. & Fox, D., 59, 68, 77
Feldman, K., 38, 41
Fennema, E., Carpenter, T., & Peterson, P., 9, 84, 86, 87, 88, 92, 93, 96, 98, 161, 162, 163, 164
Ferrara, R., 31, 33, 35, 141
Fine, C., 35, 36, 42, 144
Fitzgerald, J., 8, 29, 56, 57, 67
Fitzmaurice-Hayes, A., 15, 86, 87, 89, 96, 100, 101
Fleischner, J., Garnett, K., & Preddy, D., 100
Fleischner, J., Nuzum, M., & Marzola, E., 18
Flower, L., & Hayes, J., 12
Flynn, L., 122
Fridriksson, T., & Stewart, D., 86, 92
Fuson, K., & Secada, W., 91

Garofalo, J., 96
Garofalo, J., 10, 89, 96, 100, 103
Gaskins, I., 44
Gaskins, I., Downes , M. , Anderson, R. , Cunningham, P., Gaskins, R., Schommer, M., & Teachers of Benchmark School, 24, 25
Gere, A. & Abbott, R., 63
Ghatala, E., 35
Giacobbe, M.E., 76
Ginsburg, H., 8, 15, 83, 92

Goldman, S., 14, 16, 88
Good, T., 96, 100, 106, 112
Goodstein, H., 15
Graham, S., 7, 8, 12, 13, 17, 31, 33, 35, 36, 38, 40, 43, 47, 48, 49, 50, 51, 52, 53, 54, 59, 60, 61, 62, 63, 68, 153, 154, 155
Graves, D., 51, 53, 61, 64, 62, 65, 66, 67, 68, 76, 157, 158, 159
Greenwood, C., 110, 113, 115, 117, 125, 134, 170, 171
Group Investigation, 177, 178
merging democratic with academic inquiry processes, 177
teacher training sessions, 178
Group Investigation method, 110, 111
group learning, 40
cooperative learning, 114
examples of, 114
peer tutoring, 114, 117
guidelines for constructing questions and word problems, 96, 97

handwriting, practices for teaching, 52
Harris, K., 7, 8, 12, 13, 17, 31, 33, 35, 36, 38, 40, 41, 43, 44, 47, 48, 49, 50, 51, 52, 53, 54, 59, 60, 61, 62, 63, 65, 68, 153, 154, 155
Hayes, J., & Flower, L., 6, 7, 8
Hedin, D., 123
Hidi, S., 25, 26
Hendricks, 100
Herrmann, B.A., 36, 149, 150
Hertz-Lazarowitz, R., Sharan, 5., & Steinberg, R., 177
Hiebert, J., 8, 87
hierarchies in classroom, problems of, 124
Hightower, D. & Avery, R., 169
Hillocks, G., 50, 51, 56
Hittleman, D., 69
Hittleman, D. & Moran, M., 74, 77, 78
Holmes, E., 87, 90, 96, 100
Hull, G., 7, 20, 47, 64, 65, 68

Idol, L., 42
implementing collaborative learning, 132
arrangement of classroom, 132
desired group behavior, 132
evaluation of group work, 134
monitoring group work, 133
providing ample opportunity, 133

instructional techniques, support for, 75
instruction within problem-solving framework, 92
  improving problem-solving capabilities,
93
  problem-based approaches, 96
integration of writing with other subjects,
69
Isaacson, S. 7, 12, 47, 50, 51, 53, 54, 61, 63, 68,
73, 74, 77

Jenkins, J., Heliotis, J., Haynes, M., & Beck,
K., 25
Jenkins, J., & Jenkins, L., 113, 117, 134
Johnson, D. & Johnson, R., 110, 112, 113,
114, 115, 117, 119, 120, 121, 122,
123, 124, 125, 128, 131, 132, 133,
134, 135, 173, 174
Jones, B., Palincsar, A., Ogle, D., & Carr, E.,
30, 40
Jones, B., Pierce, J., & Hunter, B., 30

Kagan, S. , 121, 122, 125, 179, 180
Kennedy, L., 100
Kilpatrick, J., 89
Kirby, D., Latta, D., & Vinz, R., 60, 69
Knudson, R., 7
Kouba, V., Brown, C., Carpenter, T., Lind-
quist, M., Silver, E., & Swafford, J.,
83

Langer, J., & Applebee, A., 53, 60, 64, 65
Lazarowitz, R. & Karsenty, G., 110, 111
  learning environment, 32
  assessment through instruction, 32
Learning Strategies Curriculum, 17, 33
Lenz, B.K., 146, 147, 148
Lester, F., 89
Lotan, R. & Benton, J., 171, 172, 173
Luftig, R., & Johnson, R., 5
Lyman, L., & Foyle, H., 125, 128

MacArthur, C., 12, 13, 17, 49, 50, 51, 52, 53,
54, 55, 56, 59, 60, 61, 63, 64, 68, 153,
154, 155
Madden, N., 96, 110, 112, 114, 130, 175, 176
Maheady, L., 110
Maheady, L., Harper, G. , & Sacca, M., 171
Maheady, L., Mallette, B., Harper, G., &
Sacca, M.K., 110

Maheady, L., Sacca, M.K., & Harper, G.,
110, 112, 113, 114, 121, 170, 171
Male, M., 112, 125
Manheimer, M., & Washington, Y., 115,
117, 118, 120, 123, 133, 134, 136, 139
manipulatives and calculators, use of, 98,
100, 106, 162
Marten, B., 103, 163
Martin, P., & Carnahan, S, 100
Marzano, R., Brandt, R., Hughes, C., Jones,
B., Presseisen, B., Rankin, S., &
Subor, C., 27, 30
Marzano, R., Paynter, D., Kendall, J., Pickering, D., & Marzano, L., 23, 24, 29,
30, 39, 51, 52, 57
Master Design, 118
Maurer, 5., 106
Mayer, R., 88
McCutcheon, D., 7
media and materials, 72
  computers, use of, 74, 78
  teacher guides to accompany materials,
139
  to support collaborative learning methods, 135
  media and materials to support problem
solving, 101
  appropriate materials, 102
  content-related recommendations, 101
  explanation of concepts, 101
  positive attitude toward math, 102
Meichenbaum, D., 32, 33, 35, 40
metacognitive capabilities, development of,
89
Meyers, C., 1, 113
modeling by teacher, 68, 77
Montague, M., 10, 13, 15, 18, 88, 89
Moran, M., 12
Morocco, C., 7, 8, 12, 13, 20, 47, 50, 51, 54, 60,
65, 69, 74, 75, 77, 78, 82
Murray, D., 65, 67
Myers, M., & Paris, 5., 6

National Council of Teachers of Mathemat-
ics (NCTM), 86, 87, 91, 100
Neuman, S., 7, 8, 12, 13, 50, 51, 54, 74
Newcomer, P., Barenbaum, E., & Nodine,
B., 13
Newcomer, P., Nodine, B., & Barenbaum,
E., 64

Nodine, B., Barenbaum, E., & Newcomer, P., 12, 13

Oka, E. & Paris, S., 11, 32

Palincsar, A., 2, 16, 17, 22, 32, 33, 35, 36, 37, 38, 39, 40, 41, 42, 44, 113, 141, 142, 143, 144,
Paris, S. & Meyers, M., 11
Paris, S. & Oka, E., 35, 36, 38
Pellegrino, J., & Goldman, S., 9, 14
Peterson, P., Fennema, E., & Carpenter, T., 84, 87, 89, 92, 93, 95, 103, 161, 162
Pigott, H., Fantuzzo, J., & Clement, P., 112
Pressley, M., 9, 10, 25, 26, 27, 28, 30, 35, 36, 38, 40, 89
process strategies in reading, 25
  activating and creating prior knowledge, 26, 34
  question answering, 28
  question generation, 27
  story grammar instruction, 28
  summarization, 25
process writing, 17, 57
  characteristics of, 158, 159
  hypotheses for development of, 157, 158
  implementation, 158
Program for Complex Instruction, 171
  for grades 2-5, 171
  importance of individual accountability, 172
  two-week teacher training, 172
Project Math, 164
purpose of education, 1
purpose of skill or strategy, 35
  modeling, use of, 36
  practice opportunities, 37
  teacher-student conferences, 38
    group meetings, 38
    prearranged meetings, 38
    roving meetings, 38
    whole-class meetings, 38
Putnam, J., Ryders, J., Johnson, R., & Johnson, D., 115
Putnam, J., & Widerhold, C., 136

Raphael, R., 28
Raphael, T., 6, 7, 12, 13, 17, 36, 47, 48, 49, 53, 54, 56, 57, 60, 63, 64, 68, 156, 157
reading and writing integrated, 31

reading as powerful tool, 51
reading conventions, meaningful teaching, 22
  process strategies, 25
reading strategically, 31
  conducive environment, 31
  motivation, 31
Reciprocal Teaching, 16, 21, 22, 40, 141, 142, 143, 144
  four stages, 141
    instructional principle, 142
    role of teacher, 143
    use of dialogues, 141
Resnick, L., & Klopper, L., 3
Resnick, L., & Omanson, S., 86
Rhodes, L., 4, 8, 19, 27, 29, 31, 32, 34, 35, 38, 39, 42, 43, 47, 50, 51, 59, 60, 61, 62, 64, 67, 69
Riley, M., 9, 15, 93, 95, 96
Riley, M., Greeno, J., & Heller, J., 9, 15, 93, 95, 96
Rivera, D., & Smith, D., 89
Robertson, L., Graves, N., & Tuck, P., 120, 122, 123, 129, 133, 134
Roe, T., 136, 139
Roehler, L., 5, 6, 22, 23, 35, 36, 37, 38, 40, 148, 149, 150, 151
Roit, M. & McKenzie, R., 47, 53
Romberg, T. & Carpenter, T., 8, 14, 92
Ryan, E., Short, E., & Wood, K., 40
Rynders, J., Johnson, R., & Johnson, D., 112
Russell, R., & Ginsburg, H., 14

Samuels, S.J., 4, 11
Sandeen, C., 136, 137
Sapon-Shevin, M., & Schniedewind, N., 113
Sawyer, R., 8, 31, 33, 35, 36, 38, 40, 48, 62, 68, 153, 154
Scardamalia, M., 7
Scardamalia, M., & Bereiter, C., 20, 48, 53, 64
Schenk, W., 15
Schmidt, J.L., 17, 41
Schoenfeld, A., 83, 88, 90, 96, 98
Schultz, J., 115, 132, 134
Schumaker, J. 16, 17, 21, 32, 33, 36, 40, 86, 144, 145, 146, 147, 148
Schwartz, S., & Shoemaker, M., 73, 74, 75, 76, 77, 78
Scruggs, T., & Richter, L., 111

Secada, W., Fuson, K., & Hall, J., 91
Sedlack, R., & Cartwright, P., 12
Self-Instructional Strategy Development (SISD), 153, 154
  basic stages of, 154
  features essential for implementation, 156, 157
  implementation, 156
    Think Sheets, 156
  prewriting, 153
Shanahan, T., 7, 31, 53, 56, 60, 69
Sharan, S., 110, 111, 112, 115, 177, 178, 179
Share, D., Moffit, T., & Silva, P., 16
Shaw, R., 76
Sheinker, J., 36, 37
Shook, S., Marrion, L., & Ollila, L., 4, 59, 68
Shulman, L., 161
Silver, E., 96
Silver, E., 9, 10, 92
skills and strategies beyond reading, 40
  regular evaluation, 41
Slavin, R., 96, 110, 112, 113, 114, 122, 130, 132, 136, 137, 139, 175, 176, 177
Slife, B., Weiss, J., & Bell, T., 16
Smith, R., 122
Social Utilization Units, 166
  built around science projects requiring math, 166
Spear, L., & Steinberg, R., 11
special education students
  difficulties 11
  problem solving, 13
  reading, 11
  writing, 12
Stein, N., 8, 56, 62
Stevens, R., 110, 111, 114, 130, 175, 176
Stires, S., 12, 17, 18, 59, 60, 61, 158, 159
strategic reading, developments 21
  reading instruction, objectives, 21
strategies for solving math problems, 88
Strategies Intervention Model, 21, 144
  Learning Strategies Curriculum, 144, 146, 147, 148
    identifying and storing information, 145
    reading oriented, 145
    report writing, 145
strategies, students control over, 39
Sunstein, B., 59, 60, 158, 159
Swing, S., Stoiber, K., & Peterson, P., 18

Tateyama-Sniezek, K., 111
teacher modeling of group skills, 117
teaching methods, support for, 103
  assessing students, 106
  manipulatives and calculators, use of, 106
  questioning of and listening to students, 106
  small-group learning, 106
  teacher modeling, 106
Team accelerated Instruction (TAI), 114, 175
  for use in regular classroom, 175
Thomas, C., Englert, C., & Gregg, S., 7, 12, 13, 53, 59, 60
Thompson, A., 72
Thornton, C., 15, 16, 88, 89, 91, 92, 96, 100,
Topping, K., 110, 115, 134
Trafton, P., 92

Valencia, S. & Pearson, P.D., 33, 34
Vandergrift, J., 92, 93, 102, 106
Van Lehn, K., 14
Verbal problem Solving for Mildly Handicapped Students project, 164, 165, 166
  program implementation 167
  role of media and materials, 165
Villa, R., & Thousand, J, 124, 133

Wansart, W., 18, 59, 64, 68, 159
Watson, D., & Rangel, L., 123, 133
Webb, N., 111
Weissglass, J., 122
Wilkinson, L., 115
Winograd & Paris, S., 23
Wolfe, J., Fantuzzo, J., & Wolfe, p., 112
Wong, B.Y.L., & Jones, W., 6, 11
writing, forms of and goals, 56
  assessment, 61
  audience for, 60
  expository, 57
  journal writing, 59
  personal involvement, 60
  supportive environment, 58
writing in groups, 63
  collaboration with peers, 63
  teacher collaboration with students, 64
writing, strategies and purposes, 53
  assessment, 76

instruction in, 54
producing draft, 55
selection of topic, 54

Yates, J., 8, 60

Zhu, X., & Simon, H., 96